The Roots of
Knowledge

The Roots of Knowledge

NATHAN STEMMER

St. Martin's Press · New York

All rights reserved. For information, write:
St. Martin's Press, Inc., 175 Fifth Avenue, New York, NY 10010
Printed in Great Britain
First published in the United States of America in 1983

ISBN 0-312-69308-7

Library of Congress Cataloging in Publication Data

Stemmer, Nathan.
  The roots of knowledge.
    1. Knowledge, Theory of. 2. Belief and doubt.
3. Cognition. 4. Similarity (Psychology) 5. Language
acquisition. I. Title.
BD161.S682   1983   121   83-8617
ISBN 0-312-69308-7

Contents

PART III The Generalization Theory of Language Acquisition GTLA

PART IV Analyticity, Similarity, and Universals

Preface

The acquisition of knowledge is one of the most interesting phenomena, and it has been studied intensively by scholars from different methodological and philosophical schools. Many valuable treatises have been written that illuminate important parts of this process. It seems, however, that there exists no study which deals systematically with the acquisition of our first knowledge, and which takes into account not only the results of psychological investigations but also the subtle aspects that have been discussed by philosophers.

This book intends to achieve these purposes. On the basis of recent psychological results, a theory is developed which accounts for the fundamental aspects of the acquisition of our first knowledge. The theory is sensitive to various subtle considerations that have attracted the attention of philosophers, but which have often been overlooked by psychologists. This has made it possible to formulate a theory that possesses a higher degree of adequacy than alternative theories, and which also allows us to solve several problems that have troubled psychologists and philosophers. This book is therefore of interest to both psychologists and philosophers. Moreover, since an important part is devoted to the acquisition of linguistic knowledge, it is also of interest to psycholinguists.

Much of this book grew out of my lectures given at Bar-Ilan University, and I am grateful to my students whose questions and comments prompted many parts of it. I am also indebted to various friends and colleagues for illuminating discussions, especially to Alex Blum, Yitshak Gorenstein, and Asa Kasher.

My thinking has been considerably influenced by my teachers Gerold Stahl and Yehoshua Bar-Hillel, and by the works of R. Carnap and W. V. Quine. I have profited greatly from conversations with Professor Quine when I was an honorary research associate at the Department of Philosophy of Harvard University, and from stimulating discussions with other members of the department. I also had many interesting conversations with the members of the Department of History and Philosophy of Science of Princeton University when I was a visiting fellow at the department. I would like to thank them for clarifying a great number of difficult issues.

I am indebted to Professor J. S. Ullian for helpful criticisms of earlier publications. They have considerably helped me to improve my thinking on many subjects. And special thanks are due to Professor R. F. Gibson Jr who made valuable comments on the present manuscript.

None of my teachers or colleagues is, of course, to be considered responsible for controversial positions I have taken. Surely, none is to blame for my mistakes or failures in insight.

This book is dedicated to the memory of my father, Salomon Stemmer, whose love for study has been a permanent inspiration for me.

Nathan Stemmer
Jerusalem

Introduction

1 The Roots of Knowledge

The acquisition of knowledge and beliefs. We possess a wealth of knowledge about the world in which we live. We know that bread nourishes our bodies and that water stills our thirst. We have discovered that fire is hot while snow is cold, that lemons are sour but sugar is sweet, that dogs bark and cats miaow. We know that the seasons of the year as well as many phenomena of the heavens succeed each other with a certain regularity, that the sun will rise tomorrow (?), that days in summer are longer than days in winter, and so forth.

Our possession of all this knowledge raises two fundamental problems. One is psychological and concerns the manner of acquiring this knowledge; specifically, how to give a correct account of the psychological processes that enables us to acquire reliable beliefs which lead to this knowledge.

The second problem is more philosophical in character. It takes its starting point from the conclusion that psychological processes do indeed enable us to acquire reliable beliefs, and we are now challenged to explain this reliability. Why are the *subjective* beliefs, acquired through psychological processes, reliable in the *objective* world? What gives these beliefs the power to become the basis of our system of knowledge?

In this book, I am concerned with both problems. I first formulate a theory which accounts for the psychological processes that enable us to acquire our first beliefs, the beliefs on which our system of knowledge is grounded. Then I propose a theory to explain why the beliefs acquired in the psychological processes do have the power to become a basis for our system of knowledge—the system that has provided us with a profusion of information about the objective world.

The theories to be proposed are scientific theories. They satisfy the usual methodological criteria which scientific theories are supposed to fulfil. Whether these theories are also true is of course another question, and no definite answer can be given.

We will see, however, that they are supported by a large amount of highly varied evidence (see especially **22** and **30**) which allows us to conclude that they possess a very high degree of confirmation.

The approach of this book agrees to a large extent with the views of empiricists such as Hume, Mill, Russell, Carnap, and Quine. In particular, close attention is paid to the experiences which we undergo and from which our knowledge derives. This does not mean, however, that the contribution of our innate faculties to the acquisition of knowledge is ignored. When I specify the experiences that give us certain knowledge, I usually discuss the faculties that enable us to process the experiences. And many of these faculties indeed turn out to be strongly determined by our genetic constitution.

Two goals. There are thus two purposes to this book: one is psychological, the other philosophical. The primary psychological goal, as stated earlier, is to advance a scientific theory that accounts for the acquisition of our first beliefs. Moreover, the intention is to formulate a theory which is sensitive to several subtle points that have frequently been overlooked by psychologists, but that have attracted the attention of philosophers. By taking these into account, the theory obtains a degree of adequacy which is higher than that of alternative theories. Although some issues may appear superfluous or uninteresting to psychologists, their investigation is fundamental to obtaining a theory which strives for a high degree of adequacy.

The most important feature of the psychological theory, to be developed in Part I and some sections of Part II, is the introduction of the notion of a *generalization class*. This gives the theory the capacity to serve as a bridge between cognitive and behaviourist approaches (see **65**). For with the help of the well-defined notion of generalization class, we are able to account for an important part of those phenomena which cognitivists have tried to explain in terms of the vague notion of a concept or in terms of other mental notions which have similar meanings. And with the help of this notion, we can also account for most of the phenomena which behaviourists have explained in terms of the highly problematic notion of similarity.[1]

The theory that will be formulated also covers the acquisition of linguistic knowledge. It explains most of the phenomena that occur during language acquisition, while adhering to the methdological principles of behaviourism. Part III will be concerned with the acquisition of this type of knowledge, but it will deal only with the most elementary aspects of the learning processes. For more advanced study, the reader is referred to other publications of the author (especially to 1973b, 1978, 1981b).

The primary philosophical goal of this book is to explain why the beliefs which we acquire in psychological processes are sufficiently reliable to serve as a basis for our system of knowledge. There are several problems that arise here, in particular, those known in the philosophical literature as Hume's problem, the Hempel and the Goodman paradoxes, and the lottery paradox. A major breakthrough in reaching the philosophical goal is achieved with the help of the "ontological" theory that will be developed in Part II. This theory, which is strongly supported by the results of the psychological theory formulated in Parts I and II and also by other types of evidence, accounts for the reliability of our early beliefs—the beliefs on which our knowledge is founded.

In addition to explaining the reliability of our first beliefs, the ontological theory makes it possible to clarify Hume's problem and perhaps even to solve it partially. Moreover, the theory also allows us to give satisfactory solutions for the paradoxes just mentioned.

Some philosophers may find it strange to use scientific theories for solving philosophical problems. This approach, however, is in agreement with a common empiricist view which Quine has eloquently expressed:

> I see philosophy not as an *a priori* propaedeutic or groundwork for science, but as continuous with science ... There is no external vantage point, no first philosophy. All scientific findings, all scientific conjectures that are at present plausible, are therefore in my view as welcome for use in philosophy as elsewhere. [1969: 126f.]

There are several advantages in using scientific theories for dealing with philosophical issues. The main advantage, however, is that even if the theories are not completely true, it is normally possible to improve them. This allows us to make real progress in philosophical issues, rather than going around in circles, as has so often been the case.

Besides clarifying and solving the above philosophical problems, the conclusions that will be obtained in this essay also throw light on various other issues with which philosophers have been concerned. For instance, the theory of language acquisition in Part III allows us to clarify the notion of meaning, which is an important topic in the philosophy of language. And three more specific philosophical topics will be studied in Part IV, in light of the results obtained in prior sections of the essay. The first concerns the relation between meanings and beliefs, and the validity of the analytic–synthetic dichotomy. The second deals with the notion of similarity. I examine the lack of explanatory and predictive power of the usual notions of similarity, and propose the replacement of this notion by the unproblematic notion of a generalization class. The final topic is the so-called problem of universals, where we arrive at a number of interesting conclusions.

A brief summary. Part I begins with a preliminary discussion of Hume's problem and of the Hempel and Goodman paradoxes. The discussion points to the need for developing a psychological theory that gives an adequate account of the inductive generalizations performed by humans and other organisms. The rest of Part I is dedicated to developing such a theory, which will be called the *generalization theory*, or *GT* for short. In GT, the generalizing behaviour of living beings is described in terms of different types of generalization classes. Some of these generalization classes derive directly from innate generalizing dispositions, while others are only indirectly connected with such dispositions.

In Part II, the evolutionary conclusion according to which innate dispositions have usually possessed survival value is applied to those generalizing dispositions that have a strong innate basis. It suggests that these dispositions have enabled those organisms possessing them to survive in their environment. Through natural selection, the dispositions adapted themselves to this environment. This result is expressed in theses T1 and T2 (see **20** and **30**), which make explicit the qualities that gave the innate generalizing dispositions their survival value. Theses T1 and T2 receive very strong support from highly varied evidence.

T1 and T2, by describing the useful features of innate generalizing dispositions, implicitly describe part of the uniformity of the world—the part to which the useful dispositions were well adapted. This gives the theory formed by the conjunction of the two theses the status of an ontological theory, a theory which partially describes the uniformity of our world.

This well-supported theory enables us to give a satisfactory explanation for the reliability of the beliefs acquired in elementary inductive generalizations. This is a direct consequence of its ontological status. Moreover, the theory also enables us to clarify

Hume's problem as well as to solve the Hempel and the Goodman paradoxes with respect to elementary inductive generalizations.

Part II continues with an examination of generalization processes that are more advanced than those studied in Part I, including generalizations regarding so-called criterial classes, feature classes, and frequencies. This investigation throws light on some further philosophical issues such as the role of trial and error in scientific inquiry, the rationality of inductive inferences, and the ontological status of features.

Part II closes with a discussion of the lottery paradox. By relying on results obtained in earlier parts of this essay, a satisfactory solution for this paradox is received.

In Part III, I investigate the processes by which we acquire linguistic knowledge. I begin with ostensive learning processes, which turn out to be instances of the generalization processes discussed in Parts I and II. Then I examine so-called contextual ostensive processes which give language its creative character, and the processes by which we learn non-ostensive terms. These, too, are generalization processes.

Thesis T3 states the basic conclusions regarding the meanings of non-ostensive expressions (see **58**). According to this thesis, the meanings of non-ostensive expressions are extensional. Yet there are various reasons for suggesting that the extensionality of these meanings has a rather modest character.

Section **61** deals with the processes that lead to the difference between terms and sentences. It also considers some aspects of the first uses of the logical quantifiers 'all' and 'some'.

The conclusions that are obtained in our study of language acquisition constitute the *generalization theory of language acquisition*, or for short, *GTLA*.

Part III concludes with an analysis of cognitive theories of language acquisition. The analysis suggests that GTLA has various important advantages over cognitive theories.

The topics of Part IV have already been mentioned. Let me only add that the discussion on similarity (see **65**) suggests that GTLA has advantages over Quine's (1973) theory of language acquisition (which makes an essential use of the notion of similarity). Since Quine's theory is probably the clearest and most adequate theory that adheres to behaviourist methodological standards, the discussion suggests that GTLA is superior not only to cognitive theories but also to the usual behaviourist theories of language acquisition.

Some remarks on notation and terminology. I generally use single quotation marks for referring to verbal expressions (e.g. the term 'dog'), but when the purpose is to clarify a verbal expression, I normally use italics (a class is said to be *regular* if and only if ...). However, italics will also be used for emphasis. Double quotation marks also have two functions. One is to refer to entities such as concepts, properties, or features (the feature "to be quadruped" is a salient feature of dogs). The other function marks the occurrence of a term which is not clearly defined (an "ontological" theory). In the latter cases, I appeal to the good will of the reader to give the term the most plausible interpretation suggested by the context. (Sometimes, the term later receives a more precise characterization. This holds in particular for the term 'similarity'. The analysis in **65** gives us important indications regarding the interpretation of informal usages of this term.)

Finally, a word on gender. I will frequently speak of persons when it is irrelevant whether they are masculine or feminine. Some writers have adopted the practice of using in these cases artificial formulations such as 'he/she' or 'his/her'. But since such cases occur very often in this essay, the artificial formulations would strongly affect the fluency of the text. I will therefore adopt here the convention of using exclusively so-called masculine forms when speaking of persons whose sex is not determined.

PART I

The Generalization Theory GT

2 Inductive Inferences: Schema S1

Schema S1. One of the most basic methods of acquiring knowledge about our world is by inductive generalizations. A child learns that lemons are sour by generalizing from a limited number of lemons he has tasted. In the same way he learns that fires are hot, that (all) water is wet, and that dogs can bark. He observes a number of entities that have a particular property, and he then arrives at the corresponding generalization, at the corresponding hypothesis.

Such generalizations have traditionally been schematized as inferences having the following form:

S1 $a_1, .., a_n$ have been observed to be C and P.
 No C has been observed that is not P.
 Therefore, all C are P.[1]

I will frequently refer to the case where $n = 1$, in which case the schema becomes:

S1′ a has been observed to be C and P.
 No C has been observed that is not P.
 Therefore, all C are P.

For example, if we have observed that a is a lemon and is sour, and we have observed no lemon that is not sour, then according to schema S1′ (or S1) we can infer that all lemons are sour.

Two problems. Two problems arise in connection with schema S1. One is a well-known problem that has been discussed for more than two hundred years. The second is more recent. It has been investigated only during the last forty or fifty years. We will see in Part II that an appropriate treatment of the second problem will be helpful for dealing with the first problem.

The first is usually called Hume's problem. It is the problem of justifying the inferences described in S1. What allows us to infer the conclusion that all C are P from the premiss that a has been observed to be C and P?[2] What justifies this inductive leap? It is clear that the justification of the inferences of S1 cannot be a logical one, since the conclusions are not logically implied by the premisses. They are wider; they state more than what is asserted in the premisses.

Hume seems to have been the first to discuss the absence of a logical connection between the premisses and conclusions of inductive inferences. For example, in the following passage of the *Enquiry* he states:

> When a man says, 'I have found, in all past instances, such sensible qualities, conjoined with such secret powers', and when he says, 'similar sensible qualities will always be conjoined with similar secret powers', he is not guilty of a tautology, nor are these propositions in any respect the same. [1748: Sec. IV, Part 2.]

Thus one cannot give a logical justification for the inferences of S1. Yet these inferences are supposed to reflect one of the most fundamental methods of acquiring knowledge about the world. Our first problem is therefore to give them a justification that is convincing without being logical.

The second problem derives from the fact that S1 does not restrict the predicates 'C' and 'P'. Any predicate which can be meaningfully applied to the observed entities $a_1, .., a_n$ is allowed by the schema. This has the consequence that a great number of the inferences described by S1 are highly counterintuitive, and many of them give rise to inconsistent predictions.

This effect of the unrestricted character of S1 is vividly illustrated by the Hempel and the Goodman paradoxes. I therefore turn now to a discussion of these paradoxes.

3   The Hempel and the Goodman Paradoxes

The Hempel paradox. The Hempel paradox is usually discussed in the context of the confirmation of hypotheses *by* certain observations rather than of the inductive inference of hypotheses *from* such observations (Hempel 1945). But this does not constitute an essential difference. I first present the paradox with respect to the confirmation of hypotheses and then point out its connection with the inductive inference of hypotheses.

According to a criterion that upon first look seems very reasonable, a hypothesis of the form 'All *C* are *P*' is confirmed by its *positive instances*, i.e. by entities that are both *C* and *P*. Following Hempel, let us call it Nicod's criterion, after Jean Nicod who gave a very explicit formulation of it (Nicod 1930).

But Hempel has shown that Nicod's criterion has counter-intuitive consequences. Consider, for example, the hypothesis:

(1) All non-blacks are non-ravens.

According to the criterion, (1) is confirmed by objects that are non-black non-ravens, e.g. by white shoes. We substitute in the criterion 'non-black' for '*C*' and 'non-raven' for '*P*'. But (1) is logically equivalent to:

(2) All ravens are black.

Since (1) and (2) make the same claim about the world—they are logically equivalent—it follows that the observation of shoes that are white confirms that all ravens are black.

There is no doubt that this result is highly counterintuitive; it is paradoxical. As Goodman expresses it:

> The prospects of being able to investigate ornithological theories without going out in the rain is so attractive that we know there must be a catch in it. [1965: 70.]

Now, the notion of a hypothesis 'All *C* are *P*' being confirmed by positive instances is very similar to, perhaps even identical with, the notion of the hypothesis being (inductively) inferred from such instances. For this reason, one can easily transform the counter-intuitive confirmations which derive from the Hempel paradox into counterintuitive inductive inferences.

To illustrate, let us use the same raven example. According to schema S1, we can infer the hypothesis (1) 'All non-blacks are non-ravens' from the observation of a white shoe. We substitute in the schema 'non-black' for '*C*' and 'non-raven' for '*P*'. Since (1) is logically equivalent to (2) 'All ravens are black', it follows that according to the schema one can also infer the latter hypothesis from such an observation; the two hypotheses make the same claim about the world. But, obviously, to infer that all ravens are black from the observation of a white shoe is not an intuitive inference.

The Goodman paradox. Goodman's paradox also shows the difficulties with Nicod's criterion (Goodman 1965: 72ff). According to the criterion, the observation of an emerald that is green confirms the hypothesis:

(3) All emeralds are green.

But now consider the predicate 'grue' which means 'green and the time is before AD 2000, or blue and the time is after AD 2000.' From the definition of 'grue' it follows that so far everything that was green was also grue, including of course all the (green) emeralds we have observed. By applying Nicod's criterion, we receive the result that the observation today of a green emerald—i.e. of a grue emerald—confirms not only (3) but also:

(4) All emeralds are grue.

But (3) and (4) make conflicting predictions about emeralds. According to the former hypothesis emeralds will be green after the year 2000, whereas according to the latter they will then be blue.

The same paradoxical results are obtained when we deal with inductive inferences of hypotheses. According to schema S1 we can infer the hypothesis (3) 'All emeralds are green' from the observation of a green emerald. But since today a green emerald also has the property of being grue, the schema also permits the inference of hypothesis (4) 'All emeralds are grue (i.e. blue after AD 2000)' from the same observation. We substitute in S1 'emeralds' for '*C*' and 'grue' for '*P*'.

Several solutions have been proposed for the Hempel and the Goodman paradoxes, and therefore for the problem deriving from the unrestricted character of schema S1. But we will see in **43** that most of them have serious shortcomings.[3]

I return to the paradoxes in **17**, **25**, **27**, and **43**. The conclusions that will be obtained in the course of our investigations will enable us to give a satisfactory solution for the paradoxes.

Intuitive inductive inferences. Schema S1 gives a general description of inductive inferences. But the paradoxes show that if we are interested in describing inductive inferences that agree with our intuitions, then S1 is too wide. It includes inferences that are clearly counterintuitive. Hence, we must restrict S1 in a proper way. In the following sections, I deal with the problem of describing inductive inferences that do agree with our intuitions.

It is important to realize, however, that in an important sense our first problem, the problem of the justification of inductive inferences (see **2**), is now easier to solve. We no longer intend to justify all the inferences of S1. Which inferences we want to justify will be examined in the next sections, and those which we are able to justify will be a major topic of Part II of this book.

4 Generalization Classes

I now turn to the problem of describing the inductive inferences that agree with our intuitions. I begin by investigating the generalizing behaviour performed by humans and higher animals. Several important conclusions will be drawn from the investigations. I then analyse these conclusions from an evolutionary point of view. The results of the analysis will allow us to make significant progress towards the clarification of the foundations of our empirical knowledge. And among these results, a satisfactory solution for the Hempel and the Goodman paradoxes will be obtained.

One of the basic dispositions of humans and many animals is their generalizing disposition (or generalizing capacity or generalizing instinct). A child who has been burnt by a fire will usually generalize from this fire to other entities; he will try to avoid coming in contact with "similar" entities.

An important characteristic of generalizing dispositions is their specificity. The generalizations normally agree with specific classes. Consider, for example, the typical learning experiment performed by Baege:

> A lighted cigarette was held near the noses of young puppies. They sniffed at it once, turned tail, and nothing would induce them to come back to the source of the smell. . . . A few days later, they reacted to the mere sight of a cigarette or even of a rolled piece of white paper, by bounding away and sneezing. [1933: 18.]

The experiment shows in the first place the generalizing dispositions of the puppies. After observing that the lighted cigarette had an unpleasant smell, the puppies generalized to other entities. They learned to avoid other lighted cigarettes, other cigarettes, rolled pieces of white paper, and probably other "similar" entities. In the second place, the experiment shows the specificity of these dispositions. A lighted cigarette is an element of many different classes, e.g. of the class of non-ravens, of non-emeralds, of the class containing cigarettes and emeralds, of the class containing the particular cigarette and all ravens living in Europe, etc. Nevertheless, the generalizing behaviour of the puppies did not agree with any of these classes. They did not learn to avoid such non-ravens as cats, water, and emeralds, or such non-emeralds as cats, water, and ravens. Rather, they generalized according to a specific class.

Since I will frequently return to the class of objects which Baege's puppies learned to avoid, I will use the letter 'K' to denote this class.

In general, experiments on generalizing behaviour, especially those on classical or Pavlovian conditioning, show the following. During a training period, an organism is stimulated m times by the entities $a_1, .., a_m$ $(1 \leq m)$, while a specific reaction R is being reinforced (positively or negatively). The m entities can be instances of the same stimulus, such as m presentations of the same cigarette, or instances of different stimuli, such as m pictures of different triangles. After the training period it is then observed that the organism generalizes (or transfers) from these m entities to the n entities $b_1, .., b_n$ $(1 \leq n)$. The n entities now elicit the reaction R. For example, when being presented n times the same cigarette, or n pictures of different geometrical figures, the organism performs the relevant reaction without being reinforced.[4]

I call the class containing the $m + n$ entities $a_1, .., a_m, b_1, .., b_n$ the organism's *generalization class* with respect to the *original* entities $a_1, .., a_m$, and I say that the organism *uses* this class in order to generalize from the original entities $a_1, .., a_m$, or that the organism's generalization from $a_1, ..., a_m$ *agrees with* this generalization class.

I use the very general term *entity* in order to describe the elements of generalization classes. The reason for choosing such a wide term is that I want it to cover all kinds of stimulations that can be used in generalizing experiments. Thus, elements of generalization classes can be three dimensional objects such as cigarettes, sounds like utterances of the word 'vase', actions such as the throwing of a stone, aspects like the being-longer-than aspect of a situation where an organism sees that stick a is longer than stick b, sensations such as headaches or feelings of cold, etc.

The generalizing dispositions of living beings are thus specific; they agree with specific generalization classes. Let me point out, however, that the specificity of the dispositions is relative to a particular time point. At some time an organism may generalize from $a_1, .., a_m$ according to class C_1 and at another time according to a different class C_2. Some of the changes in generalizing dispositions will be discussed later (see e.g. **36**).

5 Theoretical and Observational Generalization Classes

Theoretical generalization classes. The notion of generalization class that was introduced above is an observational concept. The class is supposed to contain only those entities that actually participated in a particular generalization process: the definite entities $a_1, .., a_m, b_1, .., b_n$. But I will normally use a more theoretical concept of generalization class. This concept refers to a class which contains not only the entities that actually elicited the relevant reaction, but also those that will elicit this reaction if the organism is stimulated by them. For example, the class K described by Baege is a theoretical generalization class, since it is supposed to contain all rolled pieces of white paper of a particular type and all cigarettes of a particular type, and not only those that were actually shown to the puppies.

When the difference between the theoretical and the obervational notions becomes important, I will mark it by speaking of *theoretical* generalization classes and *observational* generalization classes. This convention holds for all the different types of generalization classes that will be discussed in this book.

It will frequently be very difficult to determine the exact extension of theoretical generalization classes, and psychologists have developed several techniques that may help us to arrive at satisfactory results. But we will see in **15** that we also possess a non-conventional tool which plays a major role in allowing us to determine the extensions of such classes.

Boundary regions. Experiments on stimulus generalization (see e.g. Mostofsky 1965) suggest that many, perhaps even most, observational and theoretical generalization classes have a *boundary* region. This region contains those entities which elicit from the organism a reaction that is weaker than the reaction elicited by the original entities, or which elicit this reaction only sometimes.[5] In order to avoid complications, I will usually assume that the boundary region of a generalization class is divided in two parts: an inner and outer region. The elements of the inner region will be considered as belonging to the corresponding generalization class, while those of the outer region not. For instance, I assume that the generalization class K contains the entities that elicited from the puppies an avoidance reaction that was a little weaker, but not much weaker, than the reaction elicited by the original cigarette.

Again, we distinguish between an *observational* boundary region, which contains the entities that indeed elicited a weaker reaction, and a *theoretical* boundary region, which contains the entities that (we believe) will elicit a weaker reaction.[6]

Generalization and failure of discrimination. Some psychologists have argued that we do not really know whether organisms generalize or whether the "generalization" effects are merely a consequence of failures of discrimination. The organism fails to differentiate between the different elements of the generalization class. But we need not enter into this problem, since I use the notion of generalization for referring to what Brown calls 'a simple, concrete empirical phenomenon' and not for referring to 'some rather abstract process that underlies, mediates, and allegedly *explains* the empirical phenomenon' (1965: 7). That is, I merely describe with the term 'generalization' a particular form of behaviour, and I make no theoretical claim regarding the mechanism that causes the behaviour. Consequently, I could have used other terms as well. For example, instead of saying that an organism generalizes from $a_1, .., a_m$ to $b_1, .., b_n$, I could have said that he *transfers* the reaction from the former entities to the latter, and that the class containing these entities is the organism's (observational) *transfer* class. However, since most psychologists do use the term 'generalization' for describing these phenomena— e.g. they speak of generalization gradients rather than of transfer gradients—I will continue to use the term 'generalization'. (But if someone has very strong feelings about this issue, he can replace our notion of generalization by a more neutral notion.)

It is important to note that when I say that an organism generalizes from an entity a to an entity b, I do not require a and b to be different; a and b may be the same (identical) cigarette or the same sound of a buzzer. The term 'generalization' (or 'transfer') merely indicates that the organism generalizes (or transfers) from the perceptions of a (or the stimulations by a) which he perceived during the training period, to *new* perceptions, perhaps of the same entity or of some different entity.

6   Exposure to Pairing Situations

When describing the training period of a generalization experiment, I mentioned the entities $a_1, .., a_m$ by which the organism is stimulated, and the reaction R that is being reinforced (positively or negatively). In most generalization experiments, however, and in *all* the experiments that are supposed to reflect inductive generalizations, there are entities of a second type that stimulate the organism. They are the entities that elicit the reaction R from the organism. In Baege's experiment, for example, the puppies saw not only the cigarette, but they also perceived a particular instance of a smell. And it was the perception of this instance of the smell that gave rise to the avoidance behaviour. This is also true for the naturally occurring generalizing behaviour that corresponds to inductive generalizations. The organism observes an entity a and he notes that a has some property P, i.e. he is stimulated by a (e.g. a lemon) and also by an instance of the property P (e.g. by the sour taste).

In this book, I will be concerned exclusively with generalization experiments or with naturally occurring generalizing behaviour that reflects inductive generalizations; hence, with processes in which two types of entities—two stimuli—are involved. For simplicity, I will frequently speak only of generalization *experiments* and I will not mention explicitly the naturally occurring generalizing behaviour that is systematically investigated in generalization experiments. I will use the term *generalization processes* in order to refer to both generalization experiments and naturally occurring generalizing behaviour. All these processes are supposed to be of the type reflecting inductive generalizations: hence, processes in which two stimuli intervene.

Thus, in generalization processes there are always two types of entities involved. The instances of the first type give rise to the generalization class. They will be called the *first* stimulus or S_1. The instances of the second type elicit the reinforced reaction R and they will be called the *second* stimulus or S_2.[7] The reaction R will often be called the *typical* reaction to S_2. For example, in Baege's experiment the first stimulus was the sight of a cigarette, the second the perception of a smell, and the typical reaction to the smell was the avoidance behaviour shown by the puppies. (In the context of classical conditioning, the first stimulus is usually called the *conditioned stimulus* and the second the *unconditioned stimulus*.)

The experiences that give rise to generalizing behaviour will be described as an exposure to a *pairing situation* or to m *pairing situations*. In these situations the organism perceives two stimuli: S_1 and S_2.

Although I speak of a *pairing* situation, it is not necessary that the two stimuli be perceived at exactly the same time and location. S_2 may occur later than S_1 or at a different location, and generalizing behaviour may still occur. In exceptional cases, there may even be time differences of several hours (see e.g. Seligman and Hager 1972).

Exposure to m pairing situations is not always sufficient to give rise to generalizing behaviour. Several conditions have to be satisfied, such as that of the stimuli being sufficiently salient for the organism, the awareness of the organism, the "preparedness" of the organism with respect to the pair of stimuli S_1 and S_2, etc. I will not investigate all these conditions here, though some of them will be discussed later. The reader is referred to the relevant literature (see e.g. Seligman and Hager 1972, Mackintosh 1974, and Schwartz 1978).[8] In general, I will assume that the conditions have been satisfied, and that the exposure to the m pairing situations indeed gives rise to the corresponding generalizing behaviour. This will be assumed even if $m = 1$.

7   Neurological Traces: the First Stimulus

Individuation by effects. Let us return to Baege's experiment (see **4**). The experiment shows that after the puppies had been exposed to the pairing situation in which they saw a cigarette while perceiving an instance of a smell, they acquired the habit (or the disposition) to run away from the elements of class K. Since puppies do not normally avoid such entities, it is reasonable to attribute the acquisition of the habit to the particular experience undergone by the puppies. The experience left certain neurological traces, and one of the effects of these traces was the acquisition of the habit to avoid the elements of K.

In general, if we observe that an organism which is exposed to a pairing situation at t_1 shows generalizing behaviour at t_2 as a consequence of the exposure, then it is in agreement with widely accepted views to assume that the exposure left certain neurological traces and that the generalizing behaviour is caused by these traces.

Since the neurological traces that are left by an exposure to pairing situations play a crucial role—a causal role—in determining the specific generalizing behaviour that can be observed as a consequence of the exposure, it would of course be very convenient if we were able to account for the psychological generalization processes in neurological terms.[9] But at this stage, we cannot think of adopting such an approach. Although we do possess considerable knowledge about several types of neurological phenomena, this knowledge does not cover the *specific* traces left by the exposure to pairing situations. For instance, we are not able to describe in physical or chemical terms the difference between the neurological traces that are left when puppies observe that a white cigarette has an unpleasant smell and those left when they observe that a brown cigar has such a smell. As Quine says, we must settle for a behaviourist treatment. Nevertheless, I will formulate the behaviourist treatment of generalization processes in such a manner that it will always remind us of the neurological mechanisms that stand behind an organism's generalizations. We will see that the adoption of this approach has important advantages. It allows us to employ commonly used expressions for describing an organism's generalizations while avoiding the danger of employing uncritical mentalistic language (see **9** and **10**), and it plays a crucial role in the theory of meaning that will be developed in Part III (see especially **55**).

Our approach will be based on the conclusion that even though we cannot give a physical or chemical specification of the neurological traces left by the exposure to pairing situations, in many cases it is possible to give them an individuation that is sufficiently specific to distinguish between the traces left by the exposure to certain types of pairing situations, and those left by the exposure to other types of pairing situations. That is, we will frequently be able to decide whether two such traces are identical or whether they are different.

The individuation is possible because, with respect to the psychological phenomena with which we are concerned here, we can accept the following *principle of causality*:

PC   Differences in behavioural effects derive from differences in causes.

If we observe that certain entities produce different (behavioural) effects,[10] then PC allows us to conclude that the entities—the causes—are different. In particular, noting that the exposure of an organism to the pairing situation p_1 has different effects than the exposure to the pairing situation p_2 allows us to conclude that the neurological trace formed in p_1 is different from the one formed in p_2.[11]

Two types of effects can be distinguished in the generalizing behaviour that is caused by the exposure to a pairing situation (or to m pairing situations): those deriving from the first and those deriving from the second stimulus. Both types of effects can be used to individuate the neurological trace left by the exposure to the pairing situation.

With respect to the part of the trace that is produced by the first stimulus—to be called the *first* part (of the neurological trace)— the most important individuating instrument is the generalization class. The fact that in Baege's experiment the puppies' generalization class agreed with the class K (rather than with some other class X) enables us to use K as an individuating tool for the first part of the neurological trace left by the experience which the puppies underwent.

This becomes clearer if we consider an experiment that is identical to the one performed by Baege except for the first stimulus. The puppies perceive again the smell of a lighted cigarette, but now they are prevented from seeing the cigarette. Rather, they are shown a black triangle. The relevant literature suggests that in such an experiment the puppies will acquire a different habit. Instead of avoiding the elements of class K they will now avoid the elements of another class, say, of class L, which probably contains certain kinds of black triangles. In this case, the difference between K and L points to a difference in the neurological traces formed in the two types of experiments. The difference in effects implies a difference in the causes.

Individuation by causes. We can thus use the generalization class of a generalization process in order to individuate the part of the neurological trace that derives from the first stimulus of the pairing situation. The class reflects the effects of the part. But we also possess an additional tool for individuating this part, namely, its origin. For the specific nature of this neurological part is of course primarily determined by the specific nature of its origin: the entities that constitute the first stimulus. Had the first stimulus in Baege's experiment been a black triangle rather than a white cigarette, the trace that would have been left in the puppies' neurological system would have been different. (It would have determined a different generalization class.) We can therefore increase the precision of the individuation of the first part of the trace by using not only the generalization class which derives from the first stimulus but also the stimulus itself.

But there are two problems with this additional method. First, even if two stimuli are different, they may give rise to the same generalization classes. In this case, the conclusion that the first parts of the neurological traces are different might be insufficiently supported. The second problem is directly related to the problems exemplified by the Hempel and the Goodman paradoxes. In most cases, we can describe two different stimuli in such a way that the relevant differences disappear. For example, both a lighted cigarette and a black triangle can be described as three-dimensional objects weighing less than 20 kg, as non-ravens, as being a cigarette or a black triangle, etc. If we describe the first stimuli in such a manner, then the descriptions will often be insufficient to allow a distinction between neurological traces, even though the generalization classes show that the traces are different.

We might solve the second problem by deciding to use only descriptions that reveal the psychologically relevant features of the stimuli: those features that determine the specific nature of the trace left by exposure to the pairing situations. But of course the problem is now: how do we know which these features are? Is to be a non-raven a psychologically relevant feature of a cigarette for puppies, or is it the fact that it weighs 2.3 grams and not 2.4 grams? There probably is no general answer to this question. Yet with respect to the generalization processes we are concerned with, there is a satisfactory solution for finding the psychologically relevant features. This solution relies again on the generalization class. We have seen that the nature of this class is determined by the first part of the neurological trace formed in the pairing situation, and the nature of this part is determined by the psychologically relevant features of the first stimulus. Therefore, the nature of the generalization class gives us important information not only about the part of the trace but also about these features. Thus the fact that the generalization class of Baege's puppies contained cigarettes and rolled pieces of white paper indicates that the features that characterize the elements of this class—in particular, their colour, shape, and size—are among the features of the cigarette that were psychologically relevant for the puppies.

This analysis suggests that if we have no independent knowledge of the psychological relevant features of the first stimulus, then we should describe the stimulus in terms of the corresponding generalization class. In particular, if 'C' describes *correctly* the generalization class that originates in an entity *e* (for an organism) —that is, the description covers all and only the elements of the class—then we can describe *e* as 'a C'. In this way, we display the features of the stimulus *e* that are relevant to the particular generalization process. If we assume, for example, that the expression 'rolled piece of white paper' describes all and only the elements of the generalization class K which was used by Baege's puppies, then we can describe the lighted cigarette that was shown to the puppies as a rolled piece of white paper. The description displays the features of the cigarette that were relevant to the puppies' generalization.

If we have obtained a description of the first stimulus with the help of a correct description of the corresponding generalization class, we can then use the description in order to individuate the first part of the neurological trace. Note that this method also solves the problem mentioned earlier, since (in the absence of independent knowledge) the descriptions of two stimuli will refer us to different generalization classes only if these classes are indeed different.

We arrive, therefore, at the following conclusion. If we have independent knowledge telling us which are the psychologically relevant features of the first stimulus, then we can use this knowledge for individuating the first part of the neurological trace—the part that derives from this stimulus. But if we do not have this knowledge, then the additional method for individuating this part will be identical with the method described in the opening section. The individuation of the first neurological part will be based on the generalization class that originates in the first stimulus.

Unless otherwise indicated, I generally assume that we do not have such independent knowledge. Hence, the part of the neurological trace that is produced by the first stimulus of a pairing situation will usually be individuated with the help of the generalization class that originates in this stimulus. The class gives a very complete individuation to this neurological part, since it reflects not only its effects but also the psychologically relevant features of its origin.

I will sometimes make use of this conclusion in order to obtain an easy way to describe the first part of the neurological trace. If C is the generalization class that originates in the first stimulus of a pairing situation, then I will sometimes use [C] to describe the part of the neurological trace that is produced by this stimulus.

So far, I have left open the question of whether we should use observational or theoretical generalization classes for the individuation of a trace (see **5**). Clearly, we reduce the degree of theoreticity of our treatment if we use observational generalization classes. But this will frequently prevent us from making useful distinctions, since two stimuli that give rise to two identical observational gereralization classes may determine different theoretical generalization classes. For this reason, I will generally use the theoretical generalization class which originates in the first stimulus in order to individuate the first part of the neurological trace, the part that derives from his stimulus.

The need for a method of individuating neurological traces derives from methodological considerations. It is the first step towards giving explanatory and predictive power to our speech about such traces. And we will see in the sequel (see e.g. **9**) that the method we are discussing here does have this effect. (It is clear that these considerations also apply to mentalistic language. In the absence of an adequate individuating method for mental entities, mentalistic language is devoid of explanatory and predictive power.)

Activation processes. The generalization class which derives from the first stimulus of a pairing situation gives a good individuation to the first part of the neurological trace that is left when an organism is exposed to the situation. The elements of this class reflect the specific nature of this neurological part, since they are the entities which *activate* the trace (thus inducing the organism to give the typical reaction *R*). In other words, the nature of the trace left in the exposure is such that it is activated by certain entities,[12] while it is not activated by other entities, and the former constitute what I have called the generalization class.

This shows that the generalization class gives a very complete individuation not only to the first part of the neurological trace but also to the *activation process* of the trace. The class distinguishes between this process and activation processes that are elicited by the elements of other generalization classes.

The hypothetical character of the neurological traces. The assumption that exposure to pairing situations leaves specific neurological traces that are activated by the elements of the corresponding generalization classes is, of course, hypothetical. It is not supported by direct evidence. Rather, it is the conclusion of an inference to a good explanation (cf. Harman 1965). The assumption explains the specific generalizing behaviour that is observed after the exposure, and it harmonizes with well-established theories in adjacent and overlapping domains such as biology and neurophysiology (see also **10**).

8   Neurological Traces: the Second Stimulus

Individuation by effects. The nature of the second stimulus of a pairing situation also determines the neurological trace that is formed by an exposure to the situation. The question now arises: what can be used to individuate the *second* part of the trace, i.e. the part that derives from the second stimulus? Two main tools are available. The first makes use of the typical reaction R that is elicited from the organism by the second stimulus. The fact that after the exposure to the pairing situation, the elements of the corresponding generalization class C elicit R (or a reaction that is very similar to R)[13] rather than some different reaction X is a direct consequence of the second part of the neurological trace left by the exposure.

This becomes clearer if we imagine an experiment that is similar to Baege's but in which the second stimulus is different. In the experiment, the puppies are shown an unlighted cigarette while they are exposed to the smell of meat. In this case, we again expect the puppies to generalize according to class K or according to a class that is very close to K. However, the reaction will now be different; instead of an avoidance reaction, the elements of K will now probably elicit approaching behaviour. The difference between the reactions is, of course, an effect of the difference between the neurological traces formed in the two experiments. Hence, principle PC (see **7**) allows us to use this difference in order to distinguish between the neurological traces that derive from the different second stimuli.

Individuation by causes. The second method of individuating the second part of the neurological trace is suggested by our discussion in **7**. Since this part is primarily determined by the nature of the entities that constitute the second stimulus, we could use the stimulus itself for individuating the part. But we find here the same problem as there. One can describe two stimuli that are clearly different for an organism in such a way that the difference disappears. For example, since smells are non-ravens, we can describe both the smell of a lighted cigarette and the smell of meat as non-ravens. Or we can describe them as being the smell of meat or of a cigarette.

Hence, our problem is again to describe the stimulus in such a way that it reveals the features that are psychologically relevant for the generalization process. In the second part of **7** we solved this problem for the first stimulus of a pairing situation. We decided to employ the generalization class that originates in this stimulus to bring to light the psychologically relevant features of the stimulus. Since the nature of the generalization class is primarily determined by the nature of the stimulus, the generalization class indeed reflects the features that are relevant to the generalizing behaviour. But here the situation is different. Generalization experiments do not give us generalization classes that originate in the second stimulus. On the contrary, after the organism is exposed to the pairing situation, we try to avoid stimulating the organism with entities that we believe belong to the generalization class which the organism *would* use *were* the second stimulus to play the role of the first stimulus in a generalization process. Since such stimulations probably elicit the typical reaction, we would no longer be able to determine whether the reaction is produced by a generalization process or by the stimulation. For example, when Baege tested the puppies' generalization, he did not stimulate them with a smell like that of a lighted cigarette when showing them a rolled piece of white paper. For in this case, the puppies would have made the avoidance reaction even if the exposure to the pairing situation had not given rise to generalizing behaviour.

We see that a generalization process does not give us a generalization class that originates in the second stimulus. Nevertheless, I believe that in order to reveal the psychologically relevant features of the second stimulus we can still use a generalization class, namely, the one mentioned above: the class which the organism would use were the second stimulus to play the role of the first stimulus in a generalization process. The idea behind this proposal is that it is likely that the generalization class, which reveals the psychologically relevant features of a stimulus when it functions as a first stimulus in a generalization process, also reveals these features when it functions as the second stimulus of such a process.

Psychologists seem to agree with the view that the features of a stimulus, which are important when it plays the role of a first stimulus in a generalization process, are identical with those that are important when it plays the role of a second stimulus of such a process. There are generalization processes where a stimulus functions as a first stimulus in one stage and as a second stimulus in another stage. This occurs, for instance, in second-order conditioning and in sensory preconditioning (see e.g. Mackintosh 1974: 19ff). Now, when psychologists describe such a stimulus, they normally use the same description—e.g. 'electric shock', 'sound of a buzzer', etc.—whatever the function it is performing.

I have discussed two methods of individuating the part of the neurological trace that derives from the second stimulus in a generalization process. The first uses the reaction that is elicited in the generalization process. The second, which is implicitly assumed by most psychologists, uses the generalization class that would originate in the second stimulus (were it to play the role of a first stimulus).[14] I will generally adopt the second method. However, in those cases where we have reasons to assume that the generalization class does not correctly reflect the psychologically relevant features of the second stimulus, I will also use the first method as an additional tool.

Since generalization processes do not give us generalization classes which derive from the second stimulus, the generalization classes that reflect the psychologically relevant features of the stimulus are theoretical. Hence, the generalization classes that will be used for individuating the first as well as the second part of the neurological traces that are left in generalization processes are theoretical generalization classes.

9　Expectations, Hypotheses, and Associations

Let me summarize. It is in agreement with the views of many to attribute the generalizing behaviour which is observed after an exposure to pairing situations to certain neurological traces that are formed in the organism's neurological system as a consequence of the exposure. A theoretical distinction can be made between two parts of the trace: one determined by the first, and the other by the second stimulus of the pairing situation. The conclusions of **7** and **8** suggest that we can individuate these parts on the basis of the theoretical generalization classes which derive from the stimuli.

Let the expressions '*C*' and '*P*' describe correctly the theoretical generalization classes which derive from the first and the second stimulus of a pairing situation (for an organism at some time *t*). Then '*C*' and '*P*' together enable us to give a satisfactory individuation to the (total) neurological trace formed in the exposure to the pairing situation.[15] With their help, we can distinguish between this trace and traces formed by the exposure to other pairing situations.

But '*C*' and '*P*' allow us to do more than distinguish between different traces. Since they describe the generalization classes *C* and *P*, they also give us valuable hints about the behaviour that originates in the trace. They suggest that perceiving an element of *C* will (under certain circumstances) induce the organism to give a reaction that is usually elicited by the elements of *P*. Suppose, for example, that in Baege's experiment (see **4**) the class *K* was the theoretical generalization class that derived from the lighted cigarette, and the class *S* was the theoretical generalization class that derived from the instance *i* of the smell which the puppies perceived. Then by using '*K*' and '*S*' to individuate the neurological trace formed in the experience, we not only differentiate between this trace and other traces, but we also suggest that perceiving further elements of *K* will elicit from the puppies a reaction that is usually elicited from them by the elements of *S*.

In English, there are several ways to express such suggestions. I will use some of them when I want to individuate a neurological trace while hinting at the behaviour to which it gives origin. Thus if the exposure of an organism to the pairing of S_1 and S_2 gives rise to corresponding generalizing behaviour, and if '*C*' and '*P*' describe correctly the theoretical generalization classes that derive from S_1 and S_2, then I will say that as a consequence of the exposure the organism has *acquired the expectation* '*All* C *are* P' (or '*All* C *have* P'), or that he has *inferred* or *conjectured the hypothesis* '*All* C *are* P', or that he now *associates* C *with* P. In these formulations, the expression 'All *C* are *P*' (or 'All *C* have *P*') should be interpreted as giving an individuation to the neurological trace formed in the exposure while hinting at the behaviour to which it gives rise.

The purpose of an individuation method for non-observational entities is to confer eventually explanatory and predictive power on these entities. This goal is achieved by our method of individuating the neurological traces left by exposure to pairing situations. For we have seen that it allows us to predict, and therefore also to explain, certain types of behaviour that derive from these traces. To be sure, these are very elementary types of generalizing behaviour, and additional investigations like those described in **11** are needed to cover more complex behaviour. But since our main objective is to develop a theoretical framework, what is important for us is that the individuating method developed here is indeed able to confer explanatory and predictive power on the neurological traces, even if the power is still a modest one.

If an expression individuates a neurological trace while also hinting at the behaviour that originates in the trace, then I will often say that it (behaviourally) *describes* or *characterizes* the trace.

If an organism has acquired the expectation 'All C are P' in a pairing situation, then P will be called the *expected property*. The organism *expects* the elements of the generalization class C to have property P (or to be followed by instances of P, or to signal the appearance of such instances). And because of this expectation, he now performs the reaction R when perceiving these elements, where R is the reaction he normally performs in the presence of instances of P.

Although I speak here of properties, I am not committing myself to the existence of entities—the properties—of a special kind. By specifying an expected property P, I am merely giving a (behavioural) description to the second part of a neurological trace formed by the exposure to a pairing situation.

In **8** we decided to individuate the second part of a neurological trace with the help of a theoretical generalization class. Such an individuation is extensional, since it is based on a class. Therefore, the individuation of the corresponding expected property is also extensional; it is based on the same class. We must realize, however, that the extensionality of the individuation is a modest one. Since it is obtained with the help of a theoretical generalization class, the extensionality of the individuation is theoretical.[16]

I have thus introduced three alternative formulations for individuating the neurological trace formed in an exposure to pairing situations. I will mainly use either the first formulation, which speaks of expectations, or the second, which speaks of hypotheses. The one that speaks of associations will seldom be used. I assume, of course, that all these formulations are equivalent; they individuate the same neurological trace.

The terminology that has been introduced here will also be used in other cases where, as a consequence of certain experiences, an organism has acquired the disposition to perform a reaction P in the presence of the elements of a generalization class C. In these cases, too, I will often describe the neurological trace that gives rise to the disposition (or that reflects the disposition) as an expectation of the form 'All C are P'.

Finally, let me introduce another way of describing the neurological trace formed in the exposure to pairing situations. Instead of describing the acquired expectation (or hypothesis) as having the form 'All C are P', I will sometimes describe it as having the form 'The presence of any element of C signals the presence of an instance of P'.

This formulation may give the impression of being weaker than the earlier formulations, since it does not refer to all elements of *C*. This is not a significant difference, however, because the term '*C*' performs the same function in all these formulations. It describes the elements of a theoretical generalization class, and by doing so it individuates the part of the neurological trace that derives from the first stimulus of the pairing situations. In addition, it gives hints regarding the behaviour that originates in this part of the trace.

10   Mental Entities, Beliefs, and Contents of Beliefs

Mental entities. So far, I have spoken of the individuation of neurological traces that are formed in the exposure to pairing situations—the traces which are activated by the elements of the corresponding generalization classes. The method we have adopted does not individuate the traces in physical or chemical terms, but rather in terms that describe their causes and effects. Therefore, the method does not actually commit us to the position that what we are individuating are real neurological entities. We can in fact maintain that it actually individuates other kinds of entities. In particular, the method can also be used by those who prefer to speak of the *mental* (or *representational*) consequences of an exposure to pairing situations. Thus when saying that an organism has acquired the expectation or hypothesis 'All *C* are *P*' we can interpret this as being the individuation of a particular mental trace.

Our terminology is therefore neutral with respect to the consequences of an exposure to pairing situations. The consequences can be interpreted as neurological entities and also as mental entities. For the sake of brevity, however, I will usually speak of neurological entities. But if someone prefers to talk of mental entities, he can easily translate our discourse into this mode of speech. And such a translation does not give rise to uncritical mentalistic language, for the mental entities are individuated with the help of behavioural evidence.

The hypothetical character of the mental traces. The assumption that the exposure to pairing situations leaves specific mental traces which are activated by the elements of the corresponding generalization class is a hypothetical one. It is not supported by direct evidence. The assumption is the conclusion of an inference to a good explanation (cf. the last part of **7**). It explains the specific generalizing behaviour that is observed after the exposure.

I will not enter into the question whether generalizing behaviour is better explained by the assumption that exposure to pairing situations leaves specific neurological traces or rather by the assumption that it leaves specific mental traces.[17] With respect to the phenomena that will be studied in this book, the difference between the assumptions has no practical consequences at this stage of technical development.

Beliefs, knowledge, and contents of beliefs. We can now also introduce a notion of belief and of knowledge that is relatively close to the usual meanings of these notions. If we have direct or indirect evidence that, as a consequence of an exposure to pairing situations, an organism has acquired the expectation 'All C are P', then I will say that he has *acquired the belief* (that) 'All C are P'. If as a matter of fact all C are indeed P, then I will also say that he has acquired the *knowledge* (that) 'All C are P'. This terminology will also be used in all other cases where we have direct or indirect evidence suggesting that a neurological trace (or a mental trace) has been formed which induces the organism to make a typical P-reaction—a typical reaction to an instance of P—when perceiving an element of C.

It is important to recall that by saying that an organism has acquired the expectation 'All C are P' (or that he has acquired the belief and perhaps even the knowledge 'All C are P'), I am not really *describing* the neurological trace formed in the organism. I am merely distinguishing it from other traces, and I give hints as to the behaviour that I expect to derive from the trace. A similar assumption is made in those cases where we prefer to speak of mental traces. The expression 'All C are P' is supposed to distinguish between a particular mental trace and other mental traces, and it hints at the behaviour to which the trace may give rise. But the expression is not meant to describe the trace. In particular, it is not meant to express its *content*. Hence, even though I may speak of an organism having acquired the belief 'All C are P', where the expression is supposed to individuate a mental trace, I am not committed to the view that I am describing with this the content of a mental trace.

To give an example, suppose that a child, who at t_1 was burnt by a fire, now avoids all kinds of fires. Let F be the child's generalization class with respect to the original fire, and B the one that derives from the particular burning sensation. Further, let us assume that '*F*' and '*B*' correctly describe these classes. In this case, we can use '*F*' and '*B*' to individuate the neurological or mental trace left by the experience, or we can use any of the more familiar formulations. For example, we can say that as a consequence of the experience at t_1, the child has acquired the expectation 'All *F* are *B*'. Here, the expression 'All *F* are *B*' (or, say, 'All fires burn') does not intend to describe the content of the child's expectation. It merely individuates the mental or neurological trace, while hinting at the behaviour to which the trace may give rise.

11 Two Minor Factors

The two main factors that determine the nature of the neurological trace produced by an exposure to pairing situations are the two stimuli of the pairing situations. In addition to these, there are also a number of minor factors that determine this nature. Let me briefly discuss two types of minor factors.

The first type are factors which cause differences in the *degree of strength* of the generalizing habit that is acquired in the exposure, as measured, for example, by the degree of resistance to extinction (see e.g. Mackintosh 1974: 419ff). The main factors belonging to this type are the number of pairing situations to which the organism is exposed, the degree of salience of the stimuli, and the level of preparedness of the organism with respect to the pair of stimuli (see **6**). For example, increasing the number of pairing situations will sometimes increase the strength of the relevant reaction or will bring the organism to perform longer the reaction to the elements of the corresponding generalization class. I will not enter into a detailed analysis of these factors, except in the discussion of salience (see **13**).

When describing the neurological trace left by exposure to pairing situations in terms of the acquisition of expectations, we can also take into account these factors. This gives us a more precise description. But I will not introduce a formal terminology. Informally, we can express the effects of the factors by saying, e.g. that the organism expects *weakly*, or *strongly*, or *very strongly* that all *C* are *P*.

The second type of minor factor that determines the nature of the neurological trace is the time interval that occurs between the organism's perception of the first and of the second stimulus. Differences in the length of the interval will often be reflected by differences in the corresponding generalizing behaviour, such as differences in the time interval between the presentation of an element of the generalization class C and the production of the typical reaction R.

In order to take into account the effects of these factors, I will sometimes describe the acquired expectation (or hypothesis, etc.) by using such formulations as 'All C are *followed* by instances of the property P' or 'All C signal the *prompt* (or *delayed*, or *simultaneous*, etc.) occurrence of a P'. But normally I will use the standard formulation 'All C are P' or 'All C have the property P'. The context will generally indicate whether these formulations suggest that the organism expects a relatively long time interval between the perception of an element of C and the occurrence of an instance of P or a relatively short one.

12 Innate Generalization Classes

Species-determined generalizing behaviour. Baege's experiment suggests that the generalizing dispositions of young dogs are species-determined to a very high degree. Not only did all the puppies generalize from the lighted cigarette to other entities, but the type of generalization was very similar. All of them learned to avoid other cigarettes and rolled pieces of white paper.

Similar experiments suggest that this also holds for other species. The generalizing dispositions of the *naive* members of a species—i.e. of those individuals that have not undergone special experiences that might have influenced the particular generalizing behaviour—are species-determined to a very high degree. In particular, the experiments on stimulus generalization mentioned in **5** provide strong evidence for this conclusion. They show a very strong similarity between the generalization gradients of the naive members of a species.

(Our definition of naive members of a species is not very precise. However, a more detailed study of this notion would lead us too far away from our central topic (but see **16**). The context will usually be sufficient to make clear the sense in which the term 'naive' is being employed.)

It is very likely that the behavioural dispositions of naive organisms have a strong genetic basis, especially if the dispositions are species-determined. I will therefore call the species-determined generalizing behaviour of naive organisms *innate* generalizing behaviour, and the generalization classes with which it agrees will be called *species-determined* or *innate* generalization classes.

It is often not easy to determine whether a particular form of generalizing behaviour is innate, because we are not sure whether the organism is indeed naive with respect to the behaviour. In these cases, we may use the indirect method of comparing the behaviour with that of other normal members of the species who have had all kinds of experiences. If we note that most of these members do perform a similar generalization—that the generalization is strongly species-determined—then it is reasonable to conclude that this behaviour is strongly determined by the genetic constitution of the normal members of the species.

Interspecific validity. It is of course not surprising that the generalizing dispositions of naive members of a species—their innate generalizing dispositions—are very similar. This is a consequence of the similarity in genetic structure. What is rather remarkable, however, is that the innate generalizing dispositions of many different species are also very similar. This is especially true for well-developed species, i.e. species with highly developed capacities of discrimination, such as humans, many types of birds, many kinds of mammals, etc. Thus not only dogs, but also many other organisms, e.g. humans, cats, or pigeons, would generalize from a cigarette to the elements of class K (which, we recall, contained rolled pieces of white paper) or of a class that is very close to K, while none of them would generalize from this cigarette to the elements of "strange" classes such as of the class of non-emeralds, of the class containing cigarettes and rivers, of the class containing the particular cigarette and all kinds of symphonies, etc.

The strong similarity between the innate generalizing dispositions of well-developed species is shown especially by experiments on classical conditioning and stimulus generalization (see e.g. Mackintosh 1974, Schwartz 1978). For example, if members of such species are exposed to the pairing of a red triangle with some other stimulus, then they will usually generalize (or transfer the reaction) to "similar" geometrical figures and not to non-ravens, non-emeralds, non-rivers, etc. To be sure, in some of the species it takes longer to establish an association between two stimuli C and P—i.e. to bring the members of the species to acquire the expectation 'All C are P'—than in others, even if they are equally well-developed (see e.g. Seligman and Hager 1972). But if they do acquire such an expectation, then in most cases the generalization classes that originate in the same stimuli are indeed very similar.

In order to express this feature of the innate generalizing

dispositions of well-developed species, I will say that the dispositions show a significant *interspecific similarity*, and that their innate
generalization classes have a significant *interspecific validity*.

The interspecific similarity of the dispositions is a very surprising phenomenon, since many of the species that manifest such
similarity do not even stand in a close evolutionary relationship.
But we will see that thesis T1, to be discussed in **20**, enables us to
give a plausible explanation for this phenomenon.

Ranges of application and naturally expected properties. The innate
generalizing dispositions of many species have a further interesting
feature. Suppose we perform two generalization experiments with
naive dogs in which the first stimulus is the same but the second
stimuli are different. For example, in both experiments we use a
rolled piece of white paper as the first stimulus, while in one we
use an instance of the smell of a lighted cigarette as the second
stimulus and in the other an instance of the smell of meat. The
innate generalization classes that the puppies would then use in
order to generalize from the first stimulus would be the same or
very similar. Yet the acquired habits would be different. In one
case, the elements of the generalization class would elicit a reaction
that is typical with respect to the smell of a lighted cigarette; in the
other, they would elicit a reaction that is typical with respect to
the smell of meat.

The conclusion that in many cases, perhaps even in most cases,
the organism uses the same (or very similar) innate generalization
classes with respect to different second stimuli is confirmed by
many experiments on classical conditioning. The experiments
show that the same stimulus—e.g. the sound of a buzzer—can
be used as a conditioned stimulus (S_1) with respect to different
kinds of unconditioned stimuli (S_2), such as electric shocks, the
appearance of a sexual partner, the introduction of food, etc.

In order to express this characteristic of generalizing dispositions,
I will say that innate generalization classes have a *wide range of
application*. They apply to several types of expected properties.
(We recall that an expected property reflects the psychologically
relevant features of a second stimulus. See **8** and **9**.)

Although innate generalization classes have wide ranges of
application, the ranges have an important restriction. For they
contain only expected properties, i.e. properties that are individuated on the basis of the specific generalization classes that derive
from the second stimulus of a pairing situation. Moreover, in the
present case, the individuating classes have to be innate generaliza-

tion classes, since we are assuming that the organism is naive with respect to the generalization process. Because of this restriction, the ranges of application of innate generalization classes do not normally contain "strange" properties such as to be a non-emerald or to be the smell of this cigarette and of all rivers.

The properties that belong to the range of application of the innate generalization classes (corresponding to a species) will be called *naturally expected properties* (relative to the species).

Let me summarize. The generalizing behaviour of well-developed organisms shows the following characteristics. If the organisms are naive relative to a particular generalizing behaviour, then they normally generalize according to species-determined generalization classes: their innate generalization classes. These classes have a significant interspecific validity. Moreover, they have a wide range of application. The ranges, however, are restricted; they contain only naturally expected properties.

13   Salience

Baege's experiment (4) illustrates a further aspect of generalizing behaviour. The stimulus situation to which the puppies were exposed contained not only the cigarette and a particular instance of a smell. It also contained many other entities such as windows, tables, little spots on the floor, angles of 90 degrees (e.g. the corners of the room), tactile stimulations, noises, etc. Yet the results of the experiment indicate that the puppies did not "pay attention" to all the aspects of the stimulus situation. They did not learn to avoid angles of 90 degrees. They paid attention only to the stimuli that were *salient* for them.

I will not enter into a detailed discussion of salience. (The reader is referred to the relevant literature, e.g. Sutherland and Mackintosh 1971.) For our purposes, it is sufficient to mention the following points. First, salience is usually a matter of degree. Some aspects of a situation are more salient than others for an organism.[18] Nevertheless, in many cases the difference in salience between the various stimuli of a stimulus situation is great enough to allow us to speak of *the* salient stimulus or *the* salient stimuli.

Second, the basic conditions for salience have a strong genetic basis. For example, conditions such as focal position, brightness, and boundary contrast are strongly salient for all normal children who have reached the age in which they frequently engage in generalizing behaviour (cf. Quine 1973: 24ff). This strong species-determinacy of salience conditions gives substantial support to the conclusion that the conditions are indeed largely determined by genetic factors.[19]

Third, salience also has a significant interspecific validity. The conditions that determine whether an entity is salient for children are very similar to, frequently even identical with, the conditions that determine this for the members of many other species. In Baege's experiment, for instance, the parts of the stimulus situation which were salient for the puppies—the cigarette and the smell—satisfy most of the conditions that determine salience for children in such situations. This is also shown by many experiments on conditioning. The same types of salient stimuli—e.g. sounds of a buzzer, electric shocks, clear geometric figures—have been satisfactorily used in experiments with different species.

Just as in the case of the interspecific validity of innate generalization classes, the present interspecific validity is surprising, since it holds for many species that stand in no close evolutionary relationship. But we will see later that thesis T1 (**20**) also enables us to give a plausible explanation for this phenomenon.

It is important to realize that the notion of salience (and the related notion "to pay attention") is derived from—is secondary to—the notion of generalizing behaviour. It is *because* we observe that Baege's puppies learned to avoid cigarettes and rolled pieces of white paper (rather than, say, angles of 90 degrees) that we say that the cigarette was a salient element of the stimulus situation.

When psychologists describe generalization processes or related processes they often make no explicit mention of such salience factors. They are, however, generally presumed. Thus when psychologists speak of *the* stimulus, they usually mean the salient element of a stimulus situation.

14 Salient Features and Determining Features

Generalization experiments enable us to speak of the salient *aspect* or salient *element* of a stimulus situation. More complex generalization experiments than the usual ones often enable us to speak also of the salient *features* of this aspect or element. Suppose, for example, that Baege had also tested the puppies' reaction to rolled pieces of black paper, and that these stimuli did not elicit the avoidance reaction. In that case, the outcome of the experiment would have suggested not only that the cigarette was a salient element of the original pairing situation (for the puppies) but in addition that whiteness was a salient feature of the cigarette. (The notion of a feature will be examined in more detail in **41** and **42**.)

By performing a series of experiments of this type we can often determine most or perhaps even all the features of the salient aspect of a situation—the stimulus—which were salient for an organism during the exposure to the original pairing situation. These features will be called, somewhat misleadingly, the *determining* features of the generalization class which originates in the exposure. They determine, so to speak, the type of entities that the organism includes in the generalization class.

I have said that this terminology is somewhat misleading. This is because most experiments on generalizing behaviour show that, relative to the discriminating capacities of the organism, the features possessed by many elements of a generalization class are not exactly equal to the features of the original stimulus; they very often deviate from these features. Moreover, the deviation of some of the features may be so great that one can hardly recognize the original feature. In some of these cases we might even say that the feature is actually absent. For example, if the original stimulus was a dog with four legs, and the generalization class includes dogs with only two legs, we might say that the latter dogs *lack* the determining feature of being quadruped. We therefore leave open the possibility that some of the determining features of a generalization class are absent in some of its elements, or more exactly, that the difference between the features of the original stimulus and those possessed by some of the elements of the generalization class is so great that one would normally say that they are different features.

It should be noted, however, that if in an element of a generalization class some of the features deviate very strongly from the original features, then this strong deviation is often compensated by other features, which then show a rather small deviation. Expressing this in terms of the (absolute) presence or absence of a feature, we can say that the determining features of a generalization class form *clusters*. A minimal number of the features are always present in the elements of the class, although they may vary from case to case. (Cf. Cerella 1979: 68, 'If instances share most features in common, then exposure to a single instance may be sufficient to elicit generalization to the remainder.')

15 "Introspection" as a Legitimate Scientific Tool

Introspection is very often a dangerous tool in psychological research. But in the investigation of two types of phenomena, introspection plays not only a significant role, but perhaps the main role. These phenomena are generalizing behaviour and salience conditions.

Consider Baege's experiment with the puppies (4). He tested the generalization of the puppies by showing them rolled pieces of white paper, and the puppies indeed generalized from the original cigarette to these objects; they had learned to avoid them. But why did Baege begin with such pieces of paper? Why didn't he start by showing them, for example, other non-ravens such as cats or trees? Now, perhaps Baege had already done sufficient experiments, or had read the relevant literature, to know that dogs do not normally generalize from a cigarette to cats and trees, even though all these entities are non-ravens. But was this really necessary? Ask any person, even children, whether they would expect puppies to generalize from a cigarette to cats and trees, or rather to entities like rolled pieces of white paper. The answer will almost universally be the correct one. But on what basis do such people arrive at the answer? Most of them have not read the relevant literature. Nor have they made experiments about the generalizing dispositions of humans and even less about those of animals. What, then, enables them to make such correct guesses?

I believe the answer to be as follows. People are able to give correct answers because they base them on some kind of introspection. They ask themselves, not necessarily consciously, how would *I* generalize in such circumstances? And then they project the answer they receive to the generalizations of other people or animals. They expect them to generalize in a very similar way. Therefore, even if Baege had not possessed any previous knowledge concerning the generalizing dispositions of dogs, he could have relied on introspection as a first approximation. Only for obtaining more exact results does systematic experimentation seem to be necessary.

Notice that a large part of the interaction between children and their parents is also consciously or unconsciously based on such an introspection. Not only do parents expect their children to generalize according to the innate generalization classes of humans, rather than according to "strange" classes like those containing non-ravens, or containing one cigarette and all kinds of rivers, etc. The children, too, entertain similar hypotheses regarding the generalizations of their parents (and even of their pets).

But is our reliance on such introspection justified? Are the chances good that through introspection we will arrive at correct conclusions? The discussion in the previous sections suggests that when we deal with naive organisms that are well developed, the answer is affirmative. First, since the genetic constitution of the members of the same species is normally very similar, the generalizing dispositions of naive humans, which derive from their genetic constitution, are normally also very similar (see **12**). Hence, introspection gives us reliable clues concerning the generalizations of naive humans. Second, because of the significant interspecific validity of the generalizing dispositions of many species, especially of well-developed ones (see **12**), our introspection also gives us very good results regarding the generalizing dispositions of the naive members of such species, even if they are not humans.

These conclusions are of great importance for solving the problem left open at the end of the first part of **5**. There I raised the question of how to determine the extension of a theoretical generalization class. Our present analysis suggests the following method. We first determine by introspection the class *we* would have used in the particular circumstances for generalizing from the particular stimulus (or stimuli); that is, we determine our own theoretical generalization class. We then compare this class with the observational generalization class used by the organism in the generalizing process (if such a class is available), and we take notice of possible agreements and disagreements. In addition, we take into account our general knowledge about the organism in question. Finally, by projecting our own theoretical generalization class to the organism, while making adjustments inspired by the other data, we arrive at an estimation of the organism's theoretical generalization class.

The general knowledge about the organism which we take into account consists mainly of information about those experiences undergone by the organism that may influence his generalization, and about innate deviations from "normal" generalizing behaviour. In the following sections, I will deal extensively with the first point. Let me therefore give an example here of the second type of information we take into account.

Suppose we know that an organism's colour perceptions are like those of a normal human except for the distinction between red and green; he cannot differentiate these colours. The organism is exposed to a pairing situation in which the first stimulus is the colour red. Now, suppose the organism's observational generalization class included only red entities—by chance, or perhaps on purpose: we showed the organism only red entities after he was exposed to the pairing situation. We will nevertheless conclude that the organism's theoretical generalization class also includes green entities. Had he been stimulated by such entities, he would have made the relevant reaction.

Still, even here we determine the organism's basic generalization trend with the help of introspection. We do not expect the organism to generalize, say, according to the class containing stimuli that are redack, i.e. red today and black tomorrow.

Let me point out that the introspection I have mentioned here is a normal instance of generalizing behaviour, although sometimes a very complex one. Consider a dog who has observed that his master, when walking with him in the forest, sometimes picks up a stick and throws it (and the dog is happy to bring it back). After a number of such experiences, the dog now expects that in other walks in the forest, his master will take "similar" sticks and repeat the action. *We* know that the similarity in question is the one perceived by the master, more exactly, the generalization is determined by the master's generalizing dispositions. But the dog "determines" the master's generalizing dispositions by using his own dispositions. The sticks he expects to be thrown are those that belong to his—the dog's—generalization class. And the high degree of correct matching is a consequence of the significant similarity between human and canine generalizing dispositions.[20]

Similar conclusions hold for the determination of salience conditions. Most people who are told about an experiment like the one performed by Baege will expect a lighted cigarette as well as its smell to be much more salient for the puppies than the small spots on the floor, the colour of the paintings, the fact that the legs of the table were 90 cm long and not 90.5 cm, etc. And the frequent correctness of these intuitions—based again on some kind of introspection—is explained by the genetic basis of the salience conditions of naive humans, and by the significant interspecific validity of these conditions for many species.[21]

16   Intuitive Inductive Inferences: Schema S2

We are now ready to return to schema S1 (**2**), which represents inductive generalizations in a general way. We have seen in **3** that although some of the instances of S1 agree with our intuitions, many of them do not. For example, the inference of 'All non-blacks are non-ravens'—i.e. of 'All ravens are black'—from the observation of a white shoe, is counterintuitive, although it is an instance of S1.

In order to obtain a schema that indeed reflects our intuitions, we must introduce restrictions in S1. Now, the conclusions we have formulated so far enable us to describe in a very precise manner the generalizations that derive from the generalizing dispositions of naive humans. Since it is reasonable to assume that these generalizations agree very strongly with the intuitions of naive humans about such generalizations—they reflect our innate generalizing feelings—we can formulate the following schema which introduces appropriate restrictions in S1.

S2   If C is an innate generalization class for humans and P a naturally expected property for humans, then the inductive inference of the hypothesis 'All C are P' from the observation of a salient element of C that is P is intuitively valid for naive humans.

S2 gives only a sufficient condition for an inductive inference to be intuitively valid for naive humans. I have preferred to state this weaker schema rather than one that also establishes a necessary condition. This is because our present knowledge seems to be insufficient to justify the claim that these are the only inductive inferences that are intuitively valid for naive humans.

In schema S2, I use the notion of naive humans. We recall the characterization of a naive organism (relative to a generalizing behaviour) as an organism that has not undergone experiences that might have influenced the particular generalizing behaviour. I would like to state here a more specific claim concerning these experiences. In the present case, I assume that the naive person has not gone through experiences that give him knowledge of (or belief in) the existence of evidence suggesting that 'All C are P' is false. In particular, I assume that the person has not observed *negative* or *falsifying* instances of the hypothesis; that is, he has not observed elements of C that are not P.

According to S2, the observed entity must be a salient element of C. This is actually a shortened formulation. The intention is that both the element of C as well as the particular instance of P be salient for the relevant people.

17　S2 and the Paradoxes

S2 is not affected by the Hempel paradox discussed in **3**. S2 requires C to be an innate generalization class for humans and P a naturally expected property, also for humans. But neither is the class of non-blacks such a class nor the property "to be a non-raven" such a property. It follows that S2 does not claim that the inference of the hypothesis 'All non-blacks are non-ravens' from the observation of non-black non-ravens—e.g. of white shoes—is intuitively valid. Consequently, S2 does not claim that the counterintuitive inference of 'All ravens are black' from such observations is intuitively valid. Hence, the Hempel paradox does not pose a difficulty for S2.

There are two ways of showing that S2 is not affected by the Goodman paradox (see **3**). The first, which I believe to be the most important one, is to show that grue is not a naturally expected property. But since naturally expected properties can be individuated with the help of appropriate innate generalization classes (see **9** and **12**), and since it is easier to deal with classes than with properties, I will try to show rather that the class of grue entities—i.e. objects that are green until AD 2000, or blue after this year—is not a (theoretical) innate generalization class for humans. To this effect, I will have to show that a naive human who observes today a green entity does not generalize from this entity to objects that are blue after AD 2000. Clearly, this cannot be shown on the basis of observational generalization classes only. We would have to wait until the year 2000. But we can apply here the method discussed in **15** for determining the extensions of theoretical generalization classes, namely, introspection.

Applying this method, I first ask myself how I would generalize from a grue object, i.e. an object that today is green, to other objects. Introspection tells me that I would not generalize to other grue objects, i.e. objects that are blue after the year 2000, but rather to objects that remain green after this year. I then project the result of my introspection to other people, arriving at the conclusion that for other (normal) persons as well the class of grue entities is not an innate generalization class. It does not agree with their innate generalizing feelings. Finally, I conclude from this that grue is not a naturally expected property for humans. Hence, S2 does not allow the inference of 'All emeralds are grue' from the observation of an emerald that today is grue.

Nevertheless, it is possible that the projection is incorrect. Even though such generalizing feelings are usually species-determined, perhaps my feelings are abnormal, and the innate generalization class of normal humans with respect to a green object is the class of grue entities. In this case, S2 still remains valid, since then the inference of 'All emeralds are grue' from the observation of a green emerald is intuitively correct for normal humans. It agrees with *their* innate generalizing feelings; for the property to be grue, i.e. the property *P* of the schema, is in this case a naturally expected property for naive humans.

The second way of showing that S2 is not affected by the Goodman paradox is related to the last argument. The paradox arises because we assume that today the inference of 'All emeralds are grue' from the observation of a green (i.e. grue) emerald is counterintuitive. We do not normally expect objects that are now grue (i.e. green) to be grue (i.e. blue) after the year 2000. But if this is so, then grue is not an intuitively expected property. Hence, in this case, schema S2 does not include this counterintuitive inference.

But suppose we are mistaken, and the inference of 'All emeralds are grue' from the observation of a grue emerald is not counterintuitive for normal humans. Rather, the inference of 'All emeralds are green' from such an observation opposes our intuitions. S2 then remains valid because, as noted above, in this case the former inference and not the latter is intuitively valid for normal humans.

Although the second method is basically correct, it gives the impression of being trivial. For this reason, I have said that the first method is probably the most important one. And the fact that the first method makes a crucial use of introspection is no defect. For we have seen in **15** that introspection is a legitimate and heavily used tool in the investigation of generalizing behaviour.

18 The Generalization Theory GT

We have now arrived at a series of conclusions regarding the most basic learning processes of humans and other organisms, and we have developed a conceptual framework that describes these processes and their results in a simple and intuitive way. Since the notion of a generalization class plays a central role in the framework, I call it the *generalization theory*; for short, *GT*.

According to GT, the beliefs which organisms acquire in these learning processes derive from two sources that are equally important: innate predispositions and specific experiences. This approach is usually identified with empiricist views. We can therefore conclude that GT is basically an empiricist theory.

There exist other theories that try to account for these learning processes, among them theories that also agree with empiricist views. But the discussion in **63** and **65** will suggest that GT is simpler and more intuitive than two of the most important alternative theories that have been proposed for this purpose.

GT contains the conclusions that have been obtained so far, including schema S2. The theory will be expanded later by including in it the conclusions about more advanced learning processes that will be obtained in Part II and Part III. But I will not always explicitly mention the addition of these conclusions to GT.

PART II

The Justification of Inductive Inferences

19   The Survival Value of Generalizing Dispositions

In **16**, I formulated schema S2 which describes a class of inductive inferences that are intuitively valid for naive persons. Since a significant part of our beliefs about the world have been acquired by drawing such inductive inferences, the question arises: is it possible to justify the inferences? It is clear that one cannot give a logical justification for them (cf. **2**). The inferred hypotheses state more than what is given by the evidence. We must, therefore, try to find another kind of justification. In the following sections, I will argue that for an important subclass of the inferences of S2, a satisfactory justification can indeed be given. The inferences are described in the schemata S3 and S5 (see **23, 30**). (Schema S4 of **28** also describes justified inductive inferences, but their justification has a somewhat problematic character.)

According to our theory GT, humans and many animals are born with very definite generalizing dispositions (see **4, 12**, and **13**). They induce these organisms to generalize according to innate generalization classes that are specific, that have a significant interspecific validity and a wide range of application, and that originate in stimuli that are salient (for the species and frequently for many other species as well). This raises two questions:

(1) Why do these organisms have generalizing dispositions?
(2) Why do these dispositions have the described features?

Evolutionary theory apparently gives an answer to the first question. To generalize is to learn from experience. The child who has been burnt by a fire and now avoids other fires has learnt from experience. Since learning from experience has usually had survival value, the possession of the generalizing capacity by living beings can be attributed to its survival value. Natural selection has favoured those organisms which have generalizing dispositions.

But this answer is incomplete. Learning from experience has not always had survival value. If what was learned was largely *incorrect*, then of course the disposition to generalize—to learn from experience—was normally not useful. Let us assume that in general the following happened. Whenever an organism acquired an expectation 'All C are P' by observing some C that were P, most of the elements of C were not P.[1] In this case, the disposition to generalize would not only have been useless, but generally detrimental. Thus suppose that when children were burnt by a fire they usually learned to avoid the elements of F, but most of these elements were not hot. Rather, they possessed properties that were useful for children. For instance, F contained all kinds of edible things besides a couple of fires. Then learning to avoid the elements of F after being burnt by a fire would not only have been a waste of energy, but it would have deprived the children of useful things.

This shows that when I said earlier that learning from experience has had survival value, I actually meant the learning to be *correct* learning, at least in many cases. Hence, in order to explain the possession of generalizing dispositions by living beings as a consequence of their selectional value, we must rely on the assumption that at least in many cases these dispositions have enabled the organisms to learn correctly from their experience. But how was this achieved? What has ensured the frequent correctness of the acquired expectation?

The most plausible answer is that this was ensured by the specific characteristics of the generalizing dispositions. Because of these characteristics, the generalizing dispositions have enabled the organism to acquire expectations that were frequently reliable.

We now have also arrived at a plausible answer to the second question. The generalizing dispositions of living beings have the described characteristics because this gave them the power to ensure the frequent reliability of the acquired expectations, the conjectured hypotheses.

Since this is a very important conclusion, I will spell out in more detail the argument. Evolutionary processes did not normally produce useless or detrimental dispositions. And even if, by accident, such dispositions became a part of the genetic constitution of a particular species, they were usually eliminated by natural selection. This selectional mechanism did not affect the generalizing dispositions that are at present possessed by well-developed species. Biological theory tells us that the dispositions have been in existence for a long time. Hence, they were not eliminated by natural selection. Moreover, the dispositions are possessed by many species that have no close evolutionary relationship. This strongly supports the conclusion that, at least until now, generalizing dispositions have been useful for most of the species that possess them; they increased their fitness.[2]

Now, if generalizing dispositions have been useful for most of these species, then what does this imply for these dispositions? It implies that by relying on these dispositions the members of the species were often able to learn correctly from their experience. In other words, if an organism had acquired with the help of his generalizing dispositions the expectation 'All *C* are *P*', then very often the expectation was reliable. Many *C* indeed possessed property *P* (or were followed by instances of *P*, or signalled the presence of such instances, etc.).

Looking at this conclusion from another point of view, we can say that natural selection, by favouring organisms that generalized according to reliable expectations, has shaped the generalizing dispositions of living beings in such a way that the dispositions enabled them to acquire expectations that were often reliable in their environment. That is to say, through evolutionary processes, the (useful) generalizing dispositions of living beings came to reflect part of the uniformity of our world.

20   The Regularity of Innate Generalization Classes: Thesis T1

Highly regular classes. We have arrived at the conclusion that the generalizing dispositions of living beings, by having certain characteristics, have enabled these beings to make generalizations that were frequently successful in the environment in which they lived. They reflected part of the uniformity of our world. This brings us to the rather surprising result that we can acquire information about our world merely by investigating the characteristics of these generalizing dispositions. Since the dispositions came to reflect part of the environment in which they evolved, this part of the environment was therefore reflected in the dispositions. In this section, I pursue this line of thought. Our conclusions will enable us to formulate thesis T1, which will play a central role in the rest of Part II.

The most interesting aspect of the generalizing dispositions of naive organisms, especially of those belonging to well-developed species, is their agreeing with specific innate generalization classes. These classes have a significant interspecific validity and also a wide range of application with respect to naturally expected properties. Let us now apply to these classes the evolutionary conclusion according to which natural selection has shaped the generalizing dispositions of living organisms in such a way that they enabled them to perform generalizations that were frequently successful. We can then conclude that the innate generalization classes of these organisms must have possessed a particular quality—say, quality Q—that made possible these successful generalizations. It is this quality that thesis T1 will make explicit.

But before we turn to the formulation of T1, let me point out that it is not necessary for the quality Q to have been possessed by the innate generalization classes themselves. It is sufficient that it was possessed by some of their subclasses. The reason is that (theoretical) innate generalization classes contain not only entities that came in contact with living beings but also other kinds of entities, e.g. objects from Venus or the Moon. But most of these entities played no role, or only a very insignificant role in shaping the generalizing dispositions of (terrestrial) organisms. Hence, evolutionary theory allows us to attribute the quality Q only to those subclasses of innate generalization classes that contained the entities that indeed came in contact with living beings.

These subclasses of innate generalization classes will be called *terrestrial* innate generalization classes.

In order to describe in more detail the quality Q, let me introduce a few technical expressions.

D1 Class S is a *wide* subclass of class C iff (if and only if) S is a subclass of C, and S contains a large proportion of C, i.e. iff S is a subclass of C, and S contains many elements of C (C is finite).

D2 Class S is *completely regular* with respect to property P iff all elements of S are P (or have P, or signal the appearance of an instance of P, etc.).

D3 Class C is *highly regular* with respect to property P iff C has a wide subclass S that is completely regular with respect to P, i.e. iff a large proportion of C are P.

D4 Class C is *highly regular* with respect to the properties $P_1, .., P_n$ iff for every P_i there is a class S_j which is a wide subclass of C, and S_j is completely regular with respect to P_i ($j = 1 .. m$, $i = 1 .. n$, $1 \leq m \leq n$).

D5 Property P is *represented* in class C iff at least one element of C is P (or has P, or signals the appearance of P, etc.).

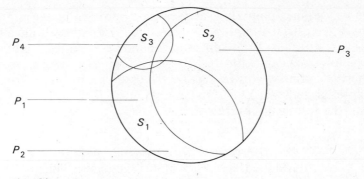

Figure 1   Class *C*

Class *C* of figure 1 is highly regular with respect to the properties $P_1, .., P_3$ (which are represented in *C*). For each of these properties, there exists a wide subclass of *C* that is completely regular with respect to the property, i.e. all the elements of the subclass have the property. The subclasses are: S_1 for P_1 and P_2, and S_2 for P_3. *C* also contains a subclass that is completely regular with respect to the represented property P_4, namely subclass S_3. But *C* is not *highly* regular with respect to P_4, since the size of S_3 indicates that it is not a *wide* subclass of *C*.

To give a concrete example, suppose class *C* in figure 1 is the class of dogs, and $P_1, .., P_4$ the properties "to eat", "to swim", "to bark", and "to have rabies". These properties are represented in *C*, since each is possessed by at least one dog. Now, *C* is highly regular with respect to $P_1, .., P_3$ since many dogs can eat, swim, and bark. That is, *C* has wide subclasses that are completely regular with respect to $P_1, .., P_3$. But *C* is not highly regular with respect to P_4, since only few dogs have rabies.

Thesis T1. The following thesis, to be called the *thesis of the regularity of innate generalization classes,* describes the quality *Q* of terrestrial innate generalization classes that gave them the power to frequently ensure successful generalizations. For reasons that will be discussed later, the thesis deals only with the terrestrial innate generalization classes of well-developed species.

T1   Many terrestrial innate generalization classes of well-developed species, that originated in entities that were salient for these species, were highly regular with respect to many of the properties that were represented in the classes and which were naturally expected properties for these species.

If we assume that in figure 1, the only naturally expected properties that are represented in *C* are $P_1, .., P_4$ then (neglecting some of the finer points) C satisfies the condition given in T1 for being a terrestrial innate generalization class of well-developed species. C contains wide subclasses, namely S_1 and S_2, that are completely regular with respect to many of the represented properties, namely with respect to $P_1, .., P_3$.

Expressing thesis T1 by using the notion of probability, we obtain the following formulation:

> T1′ If C was a terrestrial innate generalization class for well-developed species that originated in entities that were salient for the species, and if P was a naturally expected property for the species and represented in C (i.e. at least one element of C had property P), then there is a significantly high degree of probability that C had a wide subclass S which was completely regular with respect to P, i.e. it is significantly probable that many elements of C possessed P.

The degree of probability which is mentioned in T1′ depends on two factors that are expressed in T1 by the term 'many': the number of terrestrial innate generalization classes that were highly regular and the number of the represented properties with respect to which the classes were highly regular. Although we cannot say anything definite about this degree, we are allowed to conclude that it is sufficiently high to have ensured the survival value of the generalizing dispositions that agreed with these generalization classes.

Let me give an example that illustrates T1′. Suppose D is the class which naive children use when generalizing from a normal dog to other entities. It is likely that D contains most normal dogs, as well as other entities that are sufficiently "similar" to the original dog. Now, the (naturally expected) property "to be able to swim" was represented in D, since at least some elements of D were able to swim. According to T1′, it is therefore significantly probable that many terrestrial elements of D were able to swim.

T1 (and therefore T1′ also) reflect our conclusions about the survival value of the generalizing dispositions of well-developed species. The regularity which it ascribes to the terrestrial innate generalization classes of these species ensured that their generalizing dispositions often enabled them to learn correctly from their experience. The generalizations that agreed with these classes were frequently highly reliable.

An ontological thesis. T1 describes a regularity that was possessed by certain innate generalization classes. Since the regularity of these classes was a regularity *in our world*, the thesis also specifies a particular *structure* or *uniformity* of the world, a uniformity that conferred this regularity upon the classes. Hence, T1 tells us not only something about these generalization classes but also about the world. To express this feature of T1, I will say that besides being a regularity thesis, T1 is also an *ontological* thesis.

21 Special Features of Thesis T1

T1 is weak in several senses. It asserts that many rather than all terrestrial innate generalization classes of well-developed species were highly rather than completely regular with respect to many rather than all the naturally expected properties that were represented in them. These qualifying aspects derive from the evolutionary conclusion according to which innate dispositions may have possessed survival value even if they did not always lead to successful behaviour. Frequent success may have been enough. It was therefore sufficient that the generalizing dispositions of well-developed species led them to generalizations that were frequently reliable. And, of course, this is also the reason why we cannot replace in T1 the vague terms 'many' and 'highly' by more definite ones. We can only say that the values of these terms must have been sufficiently high to have ensured the frequent reliability of the generalizations.

Another weak point of T1 is the following lack of completeness. T1 does not claim that the only classes that had the described regularity were the (terrestrial) innate generalization classes (of well-developed species).[3] It leaves open the possibility that other kinds of classes may also have possessed this regularity. The reason is clear. Although evolutionary theory claims that, in general, innate dispositions were useful, it does not maintain that every disposition that might have been useful has actually found its way into the genes of living beings. It is therefore possible that other classes also had the regularity described in T1.

That this is indeed the case is confirmed by all those scientific discoveries which show that many classes that were not innate generalization classes, such as the class of metals or of mammals, had the regularity described in T1. It is important to realize, however, that in order to discover such kinds of regular classes it is not sufficient to investigate the generalizing dispositions of living beings and to draw some conclusions from evolutionary theory. They must be discovered by normal scientific procedures. (See also **39**.)

Related to the second weakening point is the condition that the generalization classes originate in entities that were salient for well-developed species. Again, T1 does not assert that only such classes had the described regularity. Classes that derived from other entities may also have possessed the regularity. But such classes, too, must be discovered by usual scientific methods.

A third characteristic of T1 is the use of the past tense. It states that the classes *were* highly regular with respect to the properties. The reason is again clear. Evolutionary theory only tells us that innate dispositions *have had* survival value. It does not affirm that in the future these dispositions will continue to have such survival value. (I return to this topic in **26**.)

T1 also restricts the innate generalization classes and the naturally expected properties to those of well-developed species, the species which have good capacities of discrimination. This restriction is actually unnecessary, since evolutionary theory tells us that it is likely that the innate dispositions of all species, well-developed or not so well-developed, had survival value. I have introduced this limitation for two reasons. The purpose of thesis T1 is to justify the intuitive inferences of S2. Since these inferences are intuitive for naive humans, it will be easier to apply our conclusions to these inferences. (We recall that the human species is a typical well-developed species.)

The second reason is inspired by the desire to obtain an increase in generality. In order to make this clear, we must state in more detail the usefulness of generalizing behaviour. Generalizing behaviour consists of making the reaction R, which is normally elicited by the second stimulus S_2—the property P—without perceiving an instance of S_2. Perceiving an element of the generalization class C is sufficient to elicit the reaction (e.g. Baege's puppies learned to perform a reaction, that is normally elicited from them by the smell of a cigarette, without perceiving the smell—observing an element of K was sufficient to elicit the reaction). Normally, such generalizing behaviour was useful only if the element of C indeed signalled the presence of an instance of P, at least in many cases. For in these cases, the organism could perform the reaction R on the right occasion. It was therefore very important that, with respect to P, the class C had the high regularity specified in T1, since this made it likely that when the reaction was performed an instance of P was present; many elements of C had the property P (or signalled its presence, etc.). However, it is clear that the high regularity of C with respect to P was useful for the organism only if P normally elicited a reaction R from the organism. If P did not elicit such reaction, then it did not matter for the organism whether C was highly regular with respect to P or highly *ir*regular, i.e. whether only very few elements of C had P.

This conclusion would actually compel us to deal separately with the innate generalization classes of each species and to assert their high regularity only with respect to those properties that normally elicited reactions from the members of the species. But we can avoid this. Since the innate generalization classes of well-developed species have a significant interspecific validity—the classes are very often extremely similar (see **12**)—we can pool the properties. If C_1 was highly regular with respect to P_1, and C_2 was highly regular with respect to P_2, and if C_1 was almost identical with C_2, then the definitions in **20** suggest that usually C_1 and C_2 were highly regular with respect to both properties: P_1 and P_2. Many of their elements had P_1 and also P_2.

Hence, by restricting T1 to the generalization classes of well-developed species we actually gain in generality, even though we probably exclude certain generalization classes that were also highly regular with respect to certain properties—some of the generalization classes of less-developed species. For the significant interspecific validity of the former classes allows T1 to speak in general of naturally expected properties of well-developed species, without having to distinguish between those of individual species.

22 The Plausibility of T1

The specific generalizing dispositions. One cannot prove the truth of T1. The thesis has the status of a theoretical hypothesis that is supported by the facts it explains. We will now see that T1 is supported by a very great number of facts. Moreover, and this increases substantially the degree of support of T1, the facts are of two types; they come from two different domains.

To the first type belong all the observations showing that many species, especially well-developed ones, are born with the generalizing dispositions described in **12**. Thesis T1, together with other well-supported scientific conclusions and theories, explains why the organisms possess the dispositions and why these dispositions have certain specific characteristics. To repeat very briefly the reasoning of **19** and **20**: the organisms have the dispositions because they enabled them to learn from experience, and the dispositions had the characteristics because in this way they ensured the frequent correctness of this learning. Their generalizations agreed with classes which, according to thesis T1, often had the appropriate regularity. Therefore, evolutionary processes selected the species that possessed such generalizing dispositions.

Note the crucial role which T1 plays in this explanation. It is because the generalization classes had the regularity described in T1 that we can apply the evolutionary argument. To state this point with more acuity, let us make the assumption that T1 is false, in the sense that most of the terrestrial innate generalization classes of well-developed species were highly *irregular* with respect to most of the naturally expected properties that were represented in them. In this case, living beings would have lost their generalizing dispositions; they would have been not only useless but often very detrimental. Hence, whereas T1 accounts for the great number of observations showing the possession of specific generalizing dispositions by many species, the "negation" of T1 would imply radically different observations.

It is also important to note that thesis T1 accounts for the surprising interspecific validity of the innate generalization classes of many species, even of species that are not closely related. The generalizing behaviour that agreed with classes having the regularity described in T1 was useful for *any* species. It enabled the members to make generalizations that were often reliable. Therefore, in those cases where the similarity between the innate generalization classes of different species cannot be attributed to a common origin, the evolutionary phenomenon known as *convergence* explains this similarity. Unrelated animals often evolved in a similar manner, if the manner was useful in the environment in which they lived.

A similar argument shows that T1 also explains the significant interspecific validity of the salience conditions of many species. According to T1, the classes that derived from entities which were salient for well-developed species had the described regularity. Hence, it was useful for these species to have such perceptions of salience. But, then, the possession of similar salience perceptions was also useful for other species.

We have seen that T1 explains the great number of observations concerning the possession of specific generalizing dispositions by living beings. Moreover, T1 seems to be the most intuitive as well as the simplest proposition that explains these observations.

Furthermore, T1 harmonizes with many other well-confirmed propositions, especially with those of evolutionary theory. All this suggests that the conjecture of T1, on the basis of these observations, has the status of an *inference to the best explanation* (cf. Harman 1965). Consequently, we are allowed to conclude that the many observations—the large evidence—confer a high degree of plausibility to T1.

The reliability of inductive inferences. But T1 is also supported by another type of data. They are the observations which show the remarkable reliability of a very large number of the inductive inferences made by humans and many animals on the basis of a few positive instances. From the perception of very few instances, people have inferred that dogs can swim, that fires are hot, that snow is cold, that lemons are sour, that horses can eat, etc. Although these inferences were not always correct, they were frequently very close to correct. Most dogs indeed can swim, most fires are hot, etc. The high reliability of these inductive inferences is the more remarkable, if we consider that many of them were inferred by ordinary people, even by children, and were based on the observation of few instances, sometimes even of a single instance. Since T1 accounts for the high reliability of many of these inductive inferences, it explains the data which show the reliability. Consequently, we are now allowed to assign a still higher degree of plausibility to T1; it has an even stronger explanatory power.

We note that T1 explains two kinds of facts belonging to very different domains. One contains psychological facts: the data showing the possession of specific generalizing dispositions by many species. The other contains, so to speak, sociological or biological facts: the data showing the high reliability of many of the inductive generalizations made by humans and animals. Hence, T1 is supported by two very different types of phenomenon; the evidence is highly varied. We have here, what Whewhell calls a *consilience of induction* (1847: 65). This gives us still more reason for assigning to T1 a high degree of plausibility.[4]

23   The Justification of Inductive Inferences: Schema S3

Ignoring some minor points, we can derive the following conclusion regarding the high probability of certain hypotheses from the plausible thesis T1, or perhaps more easily, from the alternative formulation T1' (20):

> CH   Let *C* be a terrestrial innate generalization class for humans and *P* a naturally expected property for humans, then the observation of a salient (for humans) element of *C* that is *P* gives a significantly high probability to the hypothesis 'Many *C* were *P*'.

As explained in the discussion of T1', the degree of probability of the hypothesis depends on two factors that are expressed in T1 by the two uses of 'many': once in connection with the generalization classes and once with the expected properties. (The term 'many' that appears in the hypothesis 'Many *C* were *P*' derives from the assignment of a high rather than of a complete regularity to the innate generalization classes of T1. See definition D3 in **20** and the last phrase of T1'. See also figure 1.)

According to CH, which derives from the plausible thesis T1, there is a significantly high probability that in the circumstances described in CH the inferred hypothesis is indeed true. It seems, therefore, a proper use of the term 'to justify' to conclude that in these circumstances we are *justified* in inferring the hypothesis. We so arrive at the following schema which describes a basic type of justified inductive inferences:

> S3   If *C* is a terrestrial innate generalization class for humans and *P* a naturally expected property for humans, then the inference of the hypothesis 'Many *C* were *P*' from the observation of a salient (for humans) element of *C* that is *P* is a *justified inductive inference*, provided there is no evidence available suggesting the falsity of the hypothesis.

S3 makes a more stringent demand than conclusion CH by requiring the absence of evidence suggesting the hypothesis to be false. The reason for this requirement is that even if all the other conditions of S3 are satisfied, we might have independent observational or theoretical reasons which suggest that only very few elements of *C* were *P*. In this case, it would no longer be a proper use of the term 'to justify' to say that the inference of the hypothesis is a justified one.

S3 allows us to justify certain inductive inferences. Behind S3 stands conclusion CH and therefore ultimately T1. Now, I advanced T1 in order to explain the psychological, biological, and sociological data described in **22**. Clearly, the inference of T1 from these data is not a logical one. T1 states much more than what they affirm. The conjecture of T1 from the data is rather of the type of the inductive inferences of S3; it is ampliative.

Does this mean that we are involved here in a circle? On the one hand, T1 intends to justify certain ampliative inferences: the elementary inductive inferences of S3. On the other hand, T1 itself is conjectured with the help of an ampliative inference. The answer is that this circle is one which we must accept. In order to acquire knowledge that goes beyond the observed, we must make ampliative inferences. The only thing we can demand is that the inferences satisfy the criteria that are at present accepted by the scientific community. And so far as I can see, the ampliative inference of T1 from the described data—the inference to the best explanation—indeed satisfies these criteria.

The methodological legitimacy of this circle has been expressed very clearly by Quine in the passage already quoted in **1**:

> I see philosophy not as an *a priori* propaedeutic or groundwork for science, but as continuous with science ... There is no external vantage point, no first philosophy. All scientific findings, all scientific conjectures that are at present plausible, are therefore in my view as welcome for use in philosophy as elsewhere. [1969: 126f.]

Of course, one cannot *prove* that this is the correct approach for dealing with philosophical problems. But its plausibility becomes apparent once it is realized that even scepticism about scientific knowledge presupposes the validity of scientific knowledge itself. In Quine's words: 'Doubt prompts the theory of knowledge, yes; but knowledge, also, was what prompted the doubt. Scepticism is an offshoot of science' (1975b: 67). The main basis for scepticism is the awareness of illusion, the discovery that we must not always believe our eyes. This, however, presumes a distinction between reality and illusion; yet, it is science which tells us that such a distinction exists. Since even the sceptic's arguments are based on scientific conclusions, it is not surprising that a theory about the origin of knowledge also has to appeal to such conclusions. (See also Quine 1973: 2-4, for a further discussion on the sceptic's reliance on scientific knowledge.)

Moreover, as I already said in **1**, the use of scientific results normally allows us to make real progress in philosophical issues rather than going around in circles. And our well-supported empirical conclusions T1 and CH suggest that this also holds for our topic (see also in **30** the empirical thesis T2).

24   The Schemata S2 and S3

By comparing the intuitive inferences of S2 (see **16**) with the justified inferences of S3 we note two main differences. The hypotheses of S3 are formulated in the past tense, while those of S2 are in the (neutral) present tense. And this present tense is usually meant to cover not only the present but also the future, at least the near future (besides the past). The reason for this difference between S2 and S3 has been explained above. Since evolutionary theory tells us only that innate dispositions *have had* survival value, T1 only states that the innate generalization classes *were* highly regular (with respect to the described properties). Therefore, T1 can only justify inferences of hypotheses concerning the past. The inferences of S2, on the other hand, reflect the expectations acquired in generalization processes. It is reasonable to interpret such expectations as also referring to the future. The child who has been burnt by a fire expects not only that all fires were hot but also that they will be hot in the future.[5]

The second difference between S2 and S3 is that the hypotheses of S2 say that all C have P while those of S3 only state that many C have this property. We have seen that this difference also derives from evolutionary conclusions. Generalizing dispositions may have possessed survival value even if they led to generalizations that were only frequently reliable. In addition, the difference derives from direct evidence which tells us that in many cases indeed the inferred hypotheses were only partially correct.

The requirement of S3 that no evidence should be available suggesting the inferred hypothesis to be false, does not constitute a significant difference. The inferences of S2 are intuitively correct for *naive* humans. And one of the characteristics of a person who is naive with respect to an inference of S2 is his ignorance of the existence of evidence falsifying the inferred hypothesis (see **16**).

In spite of these differences, the inferences of S3 are also intuitively valid. For the only effect of the differences is to make the hypotheses of S3 weaker than those of S2, and also to make it more difficult to infer such hypotheses. And if the inference of the strong hypothesis 'All C are P' is intuitively valid, then it is reasonable to conclude that the inference of the weaker hypothesis 'Many C were P' is also intuitively valid, especially in the absence of evidence suggesting that the hypothesis is false.

25   S3, The Paradoxes, and Hume's Problem

S3 and the Hempel and Goodman paradoxes. Since the Hempel and Goodman paradoxes are concerned with the inference of hypotheses of the form 'All *C* are *P*', we cannot immediately examine the effects of the paradoxes on the inferences of S3. We therefore have to use some modified version of the paradoxes. However, we do not have to spend much time on this, since it is easy to see that the modified versions of the paradoxes will not affect the inferences of S3. With respect to the Hempel paradox it is sufficient to note that the class of non-black objects is not an innate generalization class for humans. Hence, we cannot substitute 'non-black' for '*C*' in S3. It follows that S3 does not justify the inference of 'Many non-blacks were non-ravens' from the observation of non-black non-ravens, such as white shoes. Consequently, the first step that leads to the Hempel paradox is already blocked.[6]

The immunity of the inferences of S3 with respect to the Goodman paradox is even stronger; in fact, it is absolute. The reason is that the inferred hypotheses of S3 are concerned with the past. Yet, the use of Goodmanian properties or classes have paradoxical effects only when we are concerned with the future. It does not matter whether we infer today the hypothesis 'All emeralds were green' or 'All emeralds were grue' from the observation of a green—i.e. a grue—emerald. The two hypotheses make the same claim concerning the way emeralds looked in the past.

A partial solution to Hume's problem. We are now ready to return to Hume's important insight that one cannot give a logical justification to inductive inferences. This is indeed true. Hume's problem, as the problem of giving such a justification is usually called, cannot be solved. Nevertheless, our conclusions do shed light on this problem, since we have seen that T1 indeed justifies certain inductive inferences, namely, those of S3. To be sure, T1 itself cannot be logically justified. In Hume's terms, there is no demonstrative argument showing the truth of T1. Therefore, we cannot consider it as a complete solution to Hume's problem, which is as it should be. But we are allowed to call it a partial solution, since we have seen that from a scientific point of view there are many reasons for assigning to T1 a very high degree of plausibility. Therefore, although T1 does not give a logically valid justification to the inferences of S3, it gives them a scientifically valid justification. And this justifies our conclusion that, with respect to the inferences of S3, we have obtained a partial solution to Hume's problem (see also **28**).

T1 justifies only certain types of inductive inferences: those of S3. I will later investigate other types of inductive inference that can also be justified with the help of plausible theses. We will see that in these justifications, T1 continues to play a central role.

26 Hypotheses about the Future: Schema S3f and Postulate CP

The inferences of S3 (**23**) are weak in two senses. The inferred hypotheses are about the past, and they state that many rather than all C have the property P. Is it possible to justify the inferences of hypotheses that do not have these limitations? In the present section, I will deal with the justification of inferences that are stronger than those of S3, since the inferred hypotheses do refer to the future.

As mentioned previously, evolutionary theory cannot justify the inference of hypotheses that concern the future. Such justification requires additional means. We will see that by assuming the validity of a modest postulate, it will be possible to justify those inferences that are obtained from S3 by replacing the hypothesis 'Many C were P' by the hypothesis 'Many C will be P'.

More concretely, let schema S3f be like S3 except that the inferred hypothesis has the form 'Many C will be P'. Then, by adding to thesis T1 a modest postulate, it will be possible to justify the inferences about the future of S3f.

Notice that the inferences of S3f are intuitively valid. They are probably even more similar to the intuitively valid inferences of S2 (**16**) than S3's inferences about the past. For the hypotheses of S2, which reflect our acquired expectations, are normally supposed to refer also to the future, and perhaps preferentially to the future.[7]

In order to arrive at a justification for the inferences of S3f let us return briefly to the ontological aspect of T1 (see **20**). Thesis T1, by describing a regularity that was possessed by certain innate generalization classes, also specifies a particular uniformity of the world. This uniformity ensured the frequent reliability of the generalizations that agreed with these classes, among them the generalizations that correspond to the inductive inferences of schema S3. Since these are intuitive inductive inferences, I will say that the uniformity described by T1 is an *intuitive* uniformity.

Thesis T1 tells us that the world possessed an intuitive uniformity. But what about the future? Will the world continue to be intuitively uniform? It is clear that no conclusive answer can be given. We do not know (in an absolute sense) what will happen tomorrow. I will therefore merely postulate that the answer is positive. More formally, I introduce the following *continuity postulate*:

CP   The world will continue to be intuitively uniform.

By accepting CP we can justify the inferences about the future of S3f. The uniformity that has so far ensured the frequent reliability of the intuitive inferences about the past of S3 will continue to ensure the frequent reliability of the intuitive inferences about the future of S3f.

27   The Partial Support for Postulate CP; Rationality

The support for CP. CP is supported by the fact that in the past, at least in the recent past, the world has been intuitively uniform to a high degree. It ensured, in general, the frequent reliability of the intuitive inferences of S3 and it did not, in general, ensure the frequent reliability of certain non-intuitive inferences such as those about non-ravens or about the property *gruex* (i.e. green and the time is before AD 1900, or blue and the time is after AD 1900). Yet the support is only partial. In the first place, the uniformity of the world has so far also ensured the frequent reliability of some non-intuitive inferences, such as those about *emerubies* (i.e. emeralds and the time is before AD 2000, or rubies and the time is after AD 2000) or about the property *grue* (see 3).[8] In the second place, the evidence that supports CP belongs in its totality to the past, while CP refers to the future.

The first factor that weakens the support for CP is that the uniformity of the world has so far also ensured the frequent reliability of certain non-intuitive inferences such as those about emerubies and grue. One might think of reducing the importance of this factor by noting that not only are these inferences non-intuitive, but the classes and properties with which they are concerned have a particular temporal character. For example, Niiniluoto and Tuomela (1973: 190) observe that:

> ... of any objective criteria [for the application of primitive descriptive predicates] we (or any normal human being) can conceive of, 'green' will need only one criterion (or one set of criteria) whereas 'grue' requires two (first that used for 'green' and then another one after AD 2000).

Now, so would the argument go, this temporal character is also possessed by another type of non-intuitive inference, namely, by those dealing with classes like *emerubiex* (i.e. emeralds and the time is before AD 1900, or rubies and the time is after AD 1900) or properties like gruex. Yet, these inferences were *not* frequently reliable. This suggests that similar inferences—i.e. inferences that are likewise non-intuitive and which deal with classes and properties having such a temporal character—also lack frequent reliability. We only have to wait for the appropriate time to arrive, and we will verify this. Just as in the year AD 1900 we observed that inferences about emerubiex, which until then were as reliable as those about emeralds, actually did not possess a frequent reliability, in the year AD 2000 we will realize that inferences about emerubies likewise did not possess a frequent reliability. In this case, the fact that so far inferences like those about emerubies and grue were indeed frequently reliable would no longer constitute negative evidence for postulate CP.

But this argument is of little help, because the temporal character of classes and properties like emerubies and grue is relative to the perceptual mechanisms of humans and other species.[9] To be sure, characteristics which derive from human perceptual mechanisms have been important characteristics so far; in particular, they had survival value. But we do not know whether the characteristics will continue to be sufficiently important to base on them a *similarity inference* as the one just mentioned. In order to use such characteristics in similarity inferences we need a postulate stating that such characteristics will continue to be important; for example, they will continue to have survival value. But there is no significant difference between a postulate stating that human perceptual mechanisms will continue to be important for inductive generalizations and CP. Hence, this argument increases very little the support for CP.

The second factor that weakens the support for CP is that the evidence supporting CP belongs to the past while CP refers to the future. One of its consequences is that unlike thesis T1, postulate CP is not the conclusion of an inference to the best explanation. There are so far no facts to explain. Hence, with respect to explanatory power, CP does not differ from alternative postulates which make different claims about the uniformity that will govern the world in the future.

With the help of the partially supported postulate CP (and of the plausible thesis T1) we can thus justify the inferences of S3f. Of course, people do not justify these inferences because they consciously accept CP. They justify the inferences because they agree with their innate generalizing dispositions. Nevertheless, we see that the reliability of the hypotheses about the future that are derived in the inferences of S3f, and probably of many other hypotheses about the future, does depend on the validity of CP or of a similar postulate.

Rationality and instincts. Our analysis suggests an important conclusion regarding the notion of rationality as applied to inductive inferences. When we qualify as *rational* or *reasonable* certain elementary inductive inferences, such as the inference of 'All emeralds are (and will be) green' from the observation of a green emerald, we actually do not refer to some kind of transcendental or logical property which we have discovered in these inferences. We merely express by this that the inferences agree with our innate generalizing feelings—the feelings which we share with the members of many species. In other words, the sensations of rationality we feel with respect to these inferences have their origin in our innate generalizing feelings. And these sensations are being reinforced continuously by our observations showing that (so far) the inferences were indeed frequently reliable.

Similar conclusions hold for *irrational* or *unreasonable*. When we say that it is irrational or unreasonable to infer, e.g. that all emerubies are green from the observation of green emeralds, we are merely saying that the inference disagrees strongly with our innate generalizing feelings.

With respect to elementary inductive inferences, rationality is therefore basically instinctive. And until now, we had no reasons to restrain the prominent role played by our instincts in our judgements of rationality, because the instincts, by being well adapted to the world, were so far highly successful. They induced us to infer hypotheses that were indeed highly reliable. Moreover, we will soon see that even in those cases where the inferred hypothesis was unreliable, our instincts—i.e. our innate behaviour mechanisms—had further qualities that often allowed us to replace unreliable hypotheses by more reliable ones.

The close connection between rationality and innate generalizing feelings is shown not only by the role of the continuity postulate CP in the justification of certain inductive inferences. It is already shown by the role of thesis T1 (**20**) in this justification. But at least T1 is well supported by a wide range of data; it is the conclusion of a methodologically correct inference to the best explanation. Postulate CP, on the other hand, has very little support, in spite of the fact that its validity is presumed in most of our inferences about the future. It therefore shows in a sharper way the role performed by our instincts in our judgements about rationality.

28   The General Schema S4 and the "Principle of Induction"

The inferences of S3 (**23**) deal with hypotheses about the past, while those of S3f with hypotheses about the future. By joining these schemata we obtain a schema of inferences dealing with hypotheses about the past as well as about the future:

S4   If C is a terrestrial innate generalization class for humans and P a naturally expected property for humans, then the inference of the hypothesis 'Many C were and will be P' from the observation of a salient (for humans) element of C that is P is a justified inductive inference, provided there is no evidence available suggesting the falsity of the hypothesis.

Our previous analysis shows that the inferences of S4 can be justified by assuming the validity of two propositions. One is thesis T1 which allows us to infer general hypotheses of the form 'Many C were P' from the observation of a number of positive instances. The second is postulate CP which allows us to transfer these hypotheses to the future.

Most philosophers who have been concerned with the justification of inductive inferences mention only one proposition or one assumption which stands behind the justification. Mill, for example, discusses the *principle of the uniformity of the course of nature* which he formulates informally as:

> ... there are such things in nature as parallel cases; that what happens once, will, under a sufficient degree of similarity of circumstances, happen again, and not only again, but as often as the same circumstances recur. [1895: Book III, Chapter III, Sec. 1.]

Russell proposes the following *principle of induction*:

> The greater the number of cases in which a thing of the sort A
> has been found associated with a thing of the sort B, the more
> probable it is (if no failure of association are known) that A is
> always associated with B. [1912: 104.]

One assumption is sufficient for these philosophers because they
normally interpret the assumption to be sufficiently wide for
justifying the inference of hypotheses about the past as well as
about the future.[10] Thus, Mill states in the same section:

> ... we infer ... from the known to the unknown; from facts
> observed to facts unobserved ... In this last predicament is the
> whole region of the future; but also the vastly greater portion
> of the present and of the past.

In the treatment I have adopted here, the justification of
inductive inferences presupposes the validity of two assumptions:
T1 and CP. We will see that in this way we obtain a stronger
justification than in the approach where the validity of a single
assumption is presumed.

Consider the evidence which supports the single assumption.
Generally speaking, it is the fact that, so far, a great number of
inferences that are justified by the assumption were successful. For
instance, Black describes the evidence by stating that 'the use of
inductive rules has often led to true conclusions about matters of
fact' (1958: 718). But this evidence also supports our two
assumptions. In **22** we have seen that T1 is supported by the
high reliability of a very large number of the inferences made by
humans and animals, and in **27** we have seen that this evidence
also supports CP. (Of course, the reasons that make this only a
partial support for CP also hold for the single assumption.)
Hence, with respect to this type of evidence, the single assumption
and our two assumptions are equally well supported. However,
and this is crucial, T1 is also supported by a second type of
evidence, namely, by the psychological data which show that
living beings are born with specific generalizing dispositions
(see again **22**). This additional evidence, which is taken from an
entirely different domain, increases very largely the degree of
plausibility of T1. It confers upon T1 a very high degree of
consilience.[11]

But the additional evidence—the psychological observations—
does not contribute to the support of the single assumption.
In the first place, the people who have proposed the assumption

did not require the classes and properties that occur in the inferences to reflect innate generalizing dispositions. Hence, the evolutionary argument, which transforms the observations in supporting evidence for T1, cannot be applied to the single assumption. But even if they had required the classes and properties to fulfil the conditions of S4, their single assumption would not have been supported by this evidence. Since the evolutionary argument holds only for the past, the psychological data can become supporting evidence only for propositions that make claims about the past. Yet, by definition, the single assumption also makes claims about the future.

We have seen that one of the two assumptions which in our treatment justify the inferences of S4, namely T1, is supported not only by the "usual" evidence—the frequent success of the inferences in the past—but also by psychological evidence. But our second assumption, postulate CP, has no additional support. With respect to this postulate, therefore, our approach gives us no additional benefit. It is important to realize, however, that CP plays only a minor role in the justification of the inferences of S4; it does not intend to justify the inference of generalities from particulars. This justification is provided by the well-supported thesis T1, which attributes to the world a uniformity that justifies certain inferences of past generalities from particulars. CP is only a transfer postulate; it merely transfers past generalities to the future.

Hence, by basing the justification of the inferences of S4 on our two assumptions we achieve the following advantage over the approach that relies on a single assumption, on a single "rule of induction". The first of our assumptions, thesis T1, which plays the most important role in the justification, is much better supported than the single rule of induction. Its degree of consilience is much higher. The second assumption, which plays only a subsidiary role in the justification, has the same support as the single assumption. Therefore, the total support for the justification of the inferences is much greater in our approach than in the one relying only on the single assumption.

It is interesting to note that Hume already distinguished between two assumptions that are very close to our assumptions. For example, in the *Enquiry* he states:

> ... all inferences from experience suppose, as their foundation, that the future will resemble the past and that similar powers will be conjoined with similar sensible qualities. [1748: Sec. IV, Part II.]

Hume's second assumption, that similar powers will be conjoined with similar sensible qualities, justifies the inference of a general hypothesis of the form 'All *C* are *P*' from the observation of a *C* that is *P*. This assumption corresponds to the somewhat weaker thesis T1 which also justifies the observation of a general hypothesis from such an observation, namely, of the hypothesis 'Many *C* were *P*'. The analogy between the two assumptions holds even though Hume specifies the relation between the observed *C* and *P* and the other elements or instances of *C* and *P* in terms of similarity, while T1 specifies this relation in terms of being an element of an innate generalization class or of being an instance of a naturally expected property, for this is largely a terminological difference. When Hume speaks of similarity, he has in mind a psychological similarity which corresponds very closely to the relations expressed in T1 in terms of innate generalization classes and naturally expected properties. (See my conclusions in **65** on the informal notion of similarity.)

Hume's first assumption is that the future will resemble the past. We see that this assumption is almost identical with our continuity postulate CP which says that the uniformity of the world will continue to be an intuitive uniformity.

It is somewhat surprising that most philosophers who have dealt with the problem of induction have paid little attention, or no attention at all, to Hume's distinction between the two assumptions. This is perhaps the reason why so far not much progress has been made in solving or clarifying the problem.

Let me also point out that Hume came very close to the evolutionary conclusion of **19**. He realizes that our inductive inferences derive from innate dispositions and that the dispositions reflect—we would say, came to reflect—the course of nature:

> Here, then, is a kind of pre-established harmony between the course of nature and the succession of our ideas ... this operation of the mind by which we infer like effects from like causes ... As nature has taught us the use of our limbs without giving us the knowledge of the muscles and nerves by which they are actuated, so has she implanted in us an instinct which carries forward the thought in a corresponding course to that which she has established among external objects ... [1748: Sec. V, Part II.]

If we interpret Hume's term 'implanted' in an evolutionary sense—which is probably not the interpretation Hume had in mind—there remain only minor differences between Hume's conclusion and the conclusions that led us to thesis T1.

29   Restricted Expectations

The inferences of S4 are stronger than those of S3 (23) since the hypotheses inferred in the former also concern the future while those inferred in the latter—which have the form 'Many C were P'—refer only to the past. I will now examine inferences that are stronger than those of S3 in another way. In these inferences, the proportion of the elements of the generalization class C, which according to the inferred hypothesis had the property P, is greater than in the inferences of S3.

Let C be an innate generalization class (for well-developed species) and P a naturally expected property (also for well-developed species) that was represented in C by an entity e (which was salient for such species).[12] According to thesis T1, or perhaps more perspicuously according to the alternative formulation T1', there are good chances that C had a wide subclass which was completely regular with respect to P, i.e. all its elements were P (20, see also figure 1). Suppose this was indeed the case, and that this subclass was S. Now, T1 implies that using C as a generalization class had frequent survival value. It often enabled the organism to perform his reaction to a property P on the right occasion (without having to perceive an instance of the property). It is clear, however, that with respect to the property P the use of the subclass S was much more useful. Since all its elements were P, it always enabled the organism to perform his reaction to P on the right occasion.

But even the use of a proper subclass of C which contained S was more useful than using C itself. The proportion of the elements of this subclass that were P was greater than the proportion of the elements of C that were P. Hence, using such a class instead of C increased the chances of the generalizing organism to perform his reaction on the right occasion. It was now more likely that when the organism perceived an element of the class, an instance of P was present. This raises the question: are living beings able to exploit the advantage of replacing the innate generalization class C by such subclasses (when performing their reaction to P)?

Experiments on discriminating behaviour suggest that natural selection has indeed provided many well-developed species with the capacity to improve accordingly their generalizing behaviour. Suppose that in a first stage a child eats some grapes and notices that they are sweet. Such an experience—the exposure to a pairing situation in which the child sees a grape while experiencing afterwards a sweet taste—will normally bring the child to acquire the expectation 'All G are sweet', where G is the child's innate generalization class with respect to the original grapes and "to be sweet" the naturally expected property corresponding to the second stimulus.

But now suppose that in a second stage the child observes a falsifying or negative instance of the expectation: he eats a sour grape. If the child also notes that the falsifying instance lacks a discriminating feature F which he had observed in the positive instances—say, the sweet grapes were red while the sour one does not have this feature; it is green—then such falsifying experience will usually induce the child to restrict his expectation. Instead of expecting all G's to be sweet, he will now expect only the elements of GF to be sweet, where GF is the subclass of G that contains only those G's that have feature F. Assuming that F is indeed the colour red and that G contains only grapes, the child will now expect only red grapes to be sweet.

In general, experiments on discrimination show the following (see, e.g. Mackintosh 1974, Schwartz 1978). Suppose that at t_1 a naive organism acquires the expectation 'All C are P' as a consequence of an exposure to an appropriate pairing situation. That is, after t_1 the elements of C elicit from the organism his normal reaction R to P, where C is the organism's innate generalization class with respect to the original entities. At t_2, the organism observes a falsifying or negative instance of the expectation; he observes an element of C that is not P. Moreover, he notes on this occasion that the falsifying instance lacks a feature F which he observed in the positive instances. Then, as a consequence of this experience, the organism will usually restrict his expectation. Instead of expecting that all C are P, he will now expect the property to be possessed only by the elements of CF, where CF is the subclass of C that contains only entities that have feature F. That is, after t_2 the reaction R will be elicited only by the elements of CF and no longer by all the elements of C.[13]

If after going through such experiences the reaction R is now elicited only by the elements of CF, where CF is a subclass of the original innate generalization class C, then I say that the organism has *replaced* the original expectation (or hypothesis, or belief, etc.) 'All C are P' by the *restricted* expectation (or hypothesis, etc.) 'All CF are P'. With this terminology, I intend again to individuate the neurological (or mental) trace that is formed in such experiences, while hinting at the behaviour that derives from the trace (see **9** and **10**).

Classes like *CF* will be called *restricted generalization classes*; for short, *restricted classes*. These classes are still generalization classes, because they contain more entities than were observed by the organism. The behaviour in which an organism replaces an innate generalization class *C* by the restricted subclass *CF* will be called *restricting* behaviour.

Since restricted classes are generalization classes, the distinction discussed in **5** between observational and theoretical generalization classes also applies to restricted classes. This also holds for the boundary regions of (observational and theoretical) generalization classes that were studied in **5**. Hence, restricted classes usually also have boundary regions.

When describing a restricted expectation as 'All *CF* are *P*', I assume, as usual, that '*CF*' correctly describes the theoretical restricted class *CF*. That is, I assume that the expression '*CF*' covers all and only the elements of class *CF*.

Although I have used '*CF*' for describing a restricted subclass of an innate generalization class *C*, the '*F*' that occurs in this expression does not necessarily refer to the discriminating feature of the original element that makes possible the restriction. '*CF*' is supposed to be a single term that describes a particular subclass of *C*, just as the term 'poodles' describes a subclass of the class of dogs. Still, the letter '*F*' that appears in '*CF*' comes to suggest that if we are able to describe the simple or complex discriminating feature that differentiates between the elements of *C* and those of *CF*, then we might use '*F*' as an abbreviation of this description. In this case, '*CF*' indeed refers to the *C* that have feature *F*. For instance, instead of using 'poodles' to describe poodles, we might use 'the dogs that are *F*', where '*F*' is supposed to describe the complex of features that separate poodles from other dogs. And when speaking earlier of the class of red grapes, I followed this practice. Whereas 'grapes' is supposed to describe the innate generalization class used by the child, 'red grapes' is meant to describe the restricted subclass of this class: the grapes that are red.

It is important to realize that all kinds of stimuli can become discriminating features. For example, an organism which has acquired the expectation that the water of a lake is lukewarm may later notice that only when the sun is near the zenith is the water lukewarm. The discriminating feature is here "when the sun is near the zenith".

30   Thesis T2 and Schema S5

Restricting behaviour derives from innate behaviour mechanisms. Evolutionary theory, therefore, suggests that it had survival value. This prompts the question: what was the survival value of restricting behaviour? Now, the conclusions formulated at the beginning of the preceding section immediately suggest an answer. They suggest the validity of the following thesis:

> T2   If an organism, by undergoing appropriate falsifying experiences, replaced his original expectation 'All C are P' by the restricted expectation 'All CF are P', then in many cases the latter expectation was more reliable than the former. In other words, if S was the subclass of C which, according to thesis T1 (20), was completely regular with respect to P, then the restricted class CF was very often closer to S than C.[14]

Thesis T2 implies that in the described circumstances, it is likely that the restricted subclass CF of the original innate generalization class C was *more regular* with respect to the particular property P than the class C, i.e. the proportion of CF that were P was greater than the proportion of C that were P.

We cannot prove the truth of thesis T2. Like T1, it is supported by the facts it is able to explain. But there is sufficient evidence to conclude that T2 is indeed extremely well supported. Again, the evidence consists of data from two domains. In the first place, T2 is supported by a very great number of observations which show that many species have discriminating or restricting dispositions. T2, together with the well-supported thesis T1, makes it possible to explain why the organisms possessed the dispositions. They enabled them to improve their generalizing behaviour—in many cases, the new expectation was more reliable. Hence, T2 enables us to explain why the restricting dispositions were selected by evolutionary processes. They had considerable survival value.

In the second place, T2 is supported by direct evidence. Our general knowledge tells us that many, perhaps even most, restricted expectations that were acquired by animals, children, and ordinary people (after observing falsifying instances lacking a discriminating feature) were much more reliable than the original unrestricted expectations. The proportion of CF's that were P was indeed much greater than the proportion of C's that were P.

T1 and T2 together constitute a theory that is extremely well supported. They explain not only (i) the possession by many species of specific generalizing dispositions, and (ii) the high reliability of many of the inductive inferences made by naive organisms (see **22**), but also (iii) the possession by many species of restricting dispositions and (iv) the still higher reliability of many of the restricted hypotheses that were adopted by the members of the species who underwent appropriate falsifying experiences.

T2 is a very modest postulate, since it is not really a regularity thesis. It does not affirm the existence of classes that were regular with respect to certain properties. Our regularity thesis is T1. This thesis claims that innate generalization classes usually had many wide subclasses that were completely regular with respect to certain naturally expected properties. T2 only adds that by restricting an innate generalization class (after going through appropriate falsifying experiences) the organism very often came closer to these subclasses.

This conclusion points to the central role of T1 in giving the theory T1-T2 the status of a well-supported theory. T2 alone cannot explain the data behind (iii) and (iv). The main contributor to the considerable explanatory power of the theory T1-T2 is thesis T1. This further increases the high degree of plausibility of T1.

The theory T1-T2 justifies the following schema which covers inductive inferences that are stronger than those of S3 (**23**):

S5   If *CF* is a restricted subclass of the innate generalization class *C*, that has been restricted as a consequence of observations of positive and negative instances such as those described in **29**, then the inference of the hypothesis 'A very great number of *CF* were *P*' from these observations is a justified inference (provided there is no evidence available suggesting the hypothesis to be false).

The hypotheses of S3 have the form 'Many *C* were *P*' while those of S5 have the form 'A very great number of *CF* were *P*'. This terminological difference—the difference between 'many' and 'a very great number of'—intends to express the likelihood that *CF* was more regular with respect to *P* than *C*, i.e. that the proportion of *CF* that were *P* was greater than the proportion of *C* that were *P*.

31 Conjunctive Expected Properties

Before continuing with our study of restricting behaviour, I will briefly examine the inferences of expectations that concern more than one expected property. Suppose that at t_1 a child sees a dog who is running. As a consequence he acquires the expectation 'All C can run', where C is the child's innate generalization class with respect to the dog, and "can run" the expected property relative to the particular running instance. At t_2 the child observes the dog while he is eating, and at t_3 while he is barking. Assuming that in the meantime nothing has happened that has changed the child's generalizing dispositions with respect to the dog, then the further experiences will induce the child to acquire the expectations 'All C can eat' and 'All C can bark'. (Again, I assume that the expressions 'can eat' and 'can bark' describe the expected properties.)

By forming the conjunction of the expectations, we can now say that the child has acquired the *conjunctive* expectation 'All C can run, eat, and bark', or in short 'All C are P', where P is the property to be able to run, eat, and bark.

It is not always necessary for the child to go through three different experiences for acquiring the conjunctive expectation 'All C are P'. For example, at t_1 the child might have observed the dog while he is running and barking at the same time. In this case, the child could have acquired the expectation 'All C can run and bark' at t_1 already.

In general, by being exposed to pairing situations, perhaps only to one, an organism may acquire a conjunctive expectation of the form 'All C are P_1, and P_2, ..., and P_n'.

If P is the conjunction of the expected properties $P_1, .., P_n$, then I will say that P is a *conjunctive* expected property. But I will frequently omit the term 'conjunctive', since in many cases there is no need to distinguish strictly between conjunctive expected properties and (normal) expected properties.

An experience that falsifies a conjunctive expectation can affect all the constituents of the conjunctive expected property or only some of them. Let us assume, for example, that the innate generalization class C, which the child used when generalizing from the dog, contained not only dogs but all kinds of medium-sized quadrupeds such as cats and foxes. After the child had acquired the expectation 'All C can run, eat, and bark', he observes a cat and he notices that it does not bark; it miaows.

If the child notices that the cat lacks a discriminating feature F which was possessed by the dog—say, the typical shape of the dog's head—then he may now restrict his expectation with respect to barking, i.e. with respect to only one of the constituents of the conjunctive expected property. After the falsifying experience he may expect that only the C that have F can bark, but he may still expect that all C, including those that lack F, can run and eat.

32   Further Restrictions, Individuals, and Alternative Restrictions

If a restricted hypothesis 'All CF are P' is not completely reliable, i.e. if not all CF are P, then in a third stage the organism may find falsifying instances even of the restricted expectation. Now, certain experiments on discrimination indicate that if the organism notices that these falsifying instances lack a further discriminating feature G which he noticed in the positive instances of the restricted hypothesis 'All CF are P', then in many cases he will further restrict the expectation (see e.g. the discussion on discrimination learning with compound relevant stimuli in Mackintosh 1974: 573ff). Instead of expecting that all CF are P, he will now expect that only the elements of CFG are P, where CFG contains those CF's that also have the discriminating feature G. In more observational terms, only the elements of CFG will now elicit the organism's reaction to P.

Suppose, for example, that in a first stage a child acquires the expectation 'All (medium-sized) quadrupeds can bark' by observing a black dog which is barking. In a second stage, he observes a white cat that does not bark. This induces him to replace the original expectation by the restricted expectation 'All black quadrupeds can bark'. In a third stage, he sees a black cat that does not bark. As a consequence, he replaces the restricted expectation by the still further restricted expectation 'All black quadrupeds with a typical dog's head (i.e. all black dogs) can bark'.

The process can go further and in certain cases the subclass of the innate generalization class C may be so restricted that it contains what we would call only one object or one individual. For example, a child may learn that only his own dog Fido has a series of expected properties $P_1, .., P_n$. That is, he acquires the expectation that the elements of the subclass of quadrupeds which have the features $F_1, .., F_m$, that discriminate between Fido and all other quadrupeds, have these expected properties. Note that, psychologically speaking, this subclass is still a generalization class. For it contains all the appearances of Fido, and perhaps even of Fido's identical twin brother.[15] (I return to this in **66**.)

But observing additional falsifying instances will not always induce the organism further to restrict the expectation. In certain cases, such an experience will bring him to change the trend of the restriction. He will restrict the original expectation in a different way. Instead of adding the second discriminating feature G to the first discriminating feature F—which produces the restricted class CFG—he will now use G instead of F—which produces the restricted class CG.

In our example, the child may in the third stage replace the restricted expectation 'All black quadrupeds can bark' by the expectation 'All quadrupeds with a typical dog's head can bark', which is restricted in a different manner. He now uses the feature "to have a typical dog's head" as a discriminating feature instead of the feature "to be black".

Speaking somewhat anthropomorphically we can perhaps describe this behaviour as the organism's search for the *cause* of the falsification. The organism first believes that, because of the absence of F, his original expectation turned out to be mistaken, and he then conjectures that perhaps it was mistaken because of the absence of G. In a positive formulation, he first believes that, because the original element of the innate generalization class C possessed the feature F, the element had property P, and he then conjectures that it was because it possessed the feature G.

There are several types of discrimination experiments that study this kind of behaviour, especially those showing what has been called *hypothesis behaviour* (see e.g. Sutherland and Mackintosh 1971: 88ff). They suggest a form of systematic trial-and-error behaviour which consists in replacing certain restricted expectations by others. In Krechevsky's terms (1932: 525): 'What we have here is a series of systematic attempts at solution'.

Since several well-developed species show hypothesis behaviour, it is very likely that it had survival value. Now, the theses T1 and T2 suggest that the usefulness of the behaviour was the following. Suppose the innate generalization class C had two subclasses S_1 and S_2. S_2 was completely regular, while S_1 was only partially regular with respect to an expected property P.[16] Further, suppose that in a first stage an organism had acquired the expectation 'All C are P', but in a second stage, after going through falsifying experiences, he replaced it by the restricted expectation 'All CF are P', where CF is close to S_1. Then hypothesis behaviour gave the organism the opportunity to shift his restrictions towards a "better" class, in particular, towards S_2 which was completely regular with respect to P.

33 Trial and Error and our Innate Predispositions

It is important to realize the strong dependence of restricted hypotheses on psychological predispositions. A restricted generalization class CF is determined by two boundaries. One is the innate generalization class C of which CF is a subclass. The other is the discriminating feature F. C is of course strongly determined by psychological predispositions, since it is the innate generalization class of a naive organism. But F, too, is strongly determined by such predispositions. Just as the expected property P is a naturally expected property, the feature F is a *naturally* discriminating feature (for a naive organism). For example, a child who eats sweet red grapes and sour green grapes *could* use features such as "to be redeen" (i.e. red and the time is before AD 1980, or green and the time is after AD 1980) in order to distinguish between the sweet and sour grapes. Yet discriminating experiences indicate that children do not normally base their discriminations on such "artificial" features.

Our conclusions show the crucial role which our well-adapted psychological predispositions play in the acquisition of knowledge. Were it not for our tendency to use only certain classes, properties, and features in our inductive inferences, these inferences would probably never have enabled us to arrive at many of the reliable hypotheses which people have indeed obtained. Without such tendencies, the observation of a red sweet grape might induce us to infer 'All non-ravens are sweet' while the subsequent observation of a green sour grape might lead to the "improved" hypothesis 'All non-green non-ravens are sweet' or 'All non-ravens that are not exactly 1.14 cm long are sweet' (assuming that this was the length of the sour grape), and so forth. Notice that if the sweet grape had induced us to conjecture 'All non-ravens are non-bitter', then the sour grape would not even have been a falsifying instance of this expectation. It would have been a normal additional positive instance.

These conclusions have to be taken into account when assessing the method of trial and error. This method has been viewed by several scholars as a major tool in the acquisition of knowledge.

For example, Popper states:

> The method by which a solution is approached is usually the same; it is the method of *trial and error*. ... It is clear that the success of this method depends very largely on the number and variety of the trials: the more we try, the more likely it is that one of our attempts will be successful. [1968: 312.]

We see that if the method of trial and error is formulated in this way, then we are ignoring the most fundamental factor: our innate generalizing predispositions.[17] Mere trial and error, even if the number and variety of the trials is very high, leads to nothing, if it is not aided by useful innate predispositions. If we were not guided by such predispositions, there would be no reason why even the observation of thousands of grapes and non-grapes, sweet and non-sweet, redeen or non-redeen, would ever have led us to an even halfway reliable hypothesis.

34   The Limited Usefulness of Restricted Generalization Classes

According to T2 (**30**), if the observation of falsifying instances of an expectation 'All C are P' brings an organism to conjecture the restricted expectation 'All CF are P', then CF was often more regular than C with respect to P. That is, CF was closer to the subclass S of C which was completely regular with respect to P. Restricting dispositions were therefore normally useful, for they increased the organism's chances to perform his reaction to P on the right occasion.

But T2 does not imply that it was useful to permanently replace the innate generalization class C by the restricted class CF. T2 only implies that, with respect to the property P which occurred in the falsified expectation, it was normally useful to replace C by CF. It does not follow, however, that with respect to other properties that were represented in CF, it was also more beneficial to use CF than C. Since CF contained fewer entities than C, using CF rather than C might have prevented the organism from acquiring useful expectations about those elements of C that were not in CF (see figure 1 in **20**). For example, with respect to the properties "to grow on vines" or "to have seeds", the class of grapes was a more useful generalization class than the restricted class of red grapes. It has been more beneficial to expect that all grapes grow on vines or that all grapes have seeds than to expect that only red grapes have these properties.

This suggests that in many cases, perhaps even in most cases, it has been more useful for an organism to continue to generalize according to his innate generalization classes rather than according to the restricted subclasses he had the opportunity to use (with respect to certain expected properties). It seems that the generalizing dispositions of many species are indeed built accordingly. Very often, undergoing a few falsifying experiences does not introduce major changes in an organism's generalizing dispositions.[18] For example, it is probable that a child who sees a red grape growing on a vine will acquire the expectation that all grapes (red and green) grow on vines, even if he has previously acquired the restricted expectation that only red grapes are sweet.

35 The Double Effect of Falsifying Experiences

I have examined so far only one effect of falsifying experiences. They usually have a second effect also. Consider again the naive child who at t_1 eats a sweet grape, and consequently acquires the expectation 'All grapes are sweet'. (I am assuming here that the class of grapes is indeed the child's innate generalization class relative to the original grape.) At t_2 he observes a falsifying instance of the expectation; he eats a sour grape. Moreover, he remembers that the positive instance was red, while the negative instance is green. He therefore replaces the falsified expectation by the restricted expectation 'All red grapes are sweet'.

But the green sour grape is not only a falsifying instance (of the original expectation). It can also serve as a positive instance of a suitable expectation, for instance, of 'All grapes are sour' or 'All green grapes are sour'. And it is very likely that the child will indeed acquire an expectation with respect to which the green grape is a positive instance.[19]

In general, if a falsifying instance of an expectation 'All C are P' lacks a feature F that is possessed by the positive instances, then the falsifying instance has a discriminating feature G that is not possessed by the positive instances. (For example, the sour grape does not have the feature "to be red" (F), while it possesses the feature "to be green" (G). And the latter feature was not possessed by the positive instance of 'All grapes are sweet' that was observed by the child.) Moreover, if the positive instances have the expected property P, then the negative instances have an expected property Q. This property is different from P, which is the reason why the instance is a negative instance of the original expectation. (Q may simply be the absence of P, such as the absence of any taste in a grape made of plastic material.) Therefore, the observation of a negative instance of an expectation 'All C are P', which lacks a discriminating feature F—and therefore possesses some different discriminating feature G (which may be simply the absence of F)—normally gives origin to two different expectations. One is 'All CF are P' and the other is (probably) 'All CG are Q'. CG is the restricted subclass of C whose elements have the feature G, and Q is the expected property that is possessed by the negative instance instead of P. In our example, the child, after observing the negative instance of 'All grapes are sweet', i.e. the green sour grape, replaces this expectation by the restricted one 'All red grapes are sweet'. In addition he acquires the restricted expectation 'All green grapes are sour'.

36 Discriminating Features; Changes in Salience Conditions

In **14**, I discussed certain experiments that may enable us to specify the determining features of a generalization class. These experiments may also reveal the determining features of a restricted (generalization) class. One of these features is of course the discriminating feature itself which even has a "preferred" status. Whereas most, perhaps even all of the other determining features are optional—the features form clusters—the discriminating feature is obligatory. All the elements of the restricted class must have this feature. Expressed more cautiously, whereas the other discriminating features have sometimes a very wide range of deviation, the discriminating feature always has a narrow range of deviation. Consider the restricted class of red grapes mentioned in **35**. After observing a negative instance of the original expectation 'All grapes are sweet' (namely, a green sour grape), the child replaced this expectation by the restricted expectation 'All red grapes are sweet'. Now, the restricted class of red grapes probably contains entities that differ considerably from the original grape, say, in hardness. The original grape was rather soft, while some of the elements of the restricted class are quite hard. But with respect to colour the deviation will be minimal, since the difference between the positive and the negative instance was precisely a difference in colour. The positive grape was red while the negative was green.

Instead of speaking of the *determining* features of a generalization class, we can also speak of the features of the original stimulus that are *salient* for the child during the exposure to the pairing situation that gives rise to the generalizing behaviour

(see the first part of **14**). This terminology can also be applied
to restricted classes. Certain features of the entities that give rise
to a restricted class are much more salient for the organism than
other features. Again, the discriminating feature has a special
status. Whereas before the falsifying experience this feature had
a low degree of salience, as a consequence of the experience it
acquired a high degree of salience.

In general, falsifying experiences often modify the conditions of
salience of an organism. While searching for the "cause of a
falsification" (see **32**), the organism comes to pay attention to
features which he had previously neglected. Sometimes, the
organism will even pay preferent attention to a particular
discriminating feature that proved to be successful in a previous
restricting behaviour, and therefore neglect features which he would
have normally taken into account. If he has noted, for example,
that the colour of an object determines the presence or absence
of a particular property P, he may tend to pay attention almost
exclusively to the colour of a stimulus and neglect the geometrical
form of the objects. (See e.g. the discussion of intradimensional
and extradimensional shifts in Mackintosh 1974: 597f.)

In **13**, I pointed out that our basic notion is the notion of
generalization class and that the notions of salience (and the
derived notions "to pay attention" and "to be a determining
feature") derive from—are secondary to—this basic notion. This
also holds for our present conclusions. It is *because* we observe
that the child now expects only red grapes to be sweet—the
restricted class contains only red grapes—that we say that the
colour of the grapes has now become salient for the child.

37   Disjunctive Expected Properties

In the previous sections, I discussed cases where an organism
observes falsifying instances of an expectation, while noticing a
feature F that discriminates between the positive and negative
instances. I will now examine cases where the organism does not
notice discriminating features.

Suppose a child, who has acquired the expectation 'All G are
sweet' upon eating some sweet grapes, observes a negative instance
of the expectation; he eats a sour grape. However, he notices no
difference between the sweet grapes and the sour one (except,

of course, the difference in taste). He therefore cannot restrict the class G. In this case, the falsifying experience will usually have consequences that can be described as the replacement of the original expectation by the *disjunctive* expectation 'All G are sweet or sour (but not bitter, tasteless, etc.)'.

In general, certain experiments on probability learning show the following (see e.g. Mackintosh 1974: 190ff). At t_1, a naive organism acquires the expectation 'All C are P' as a consequence of an exposure to an appropriate pairing situation. That is, after t_1, the elements of C elicit from this organism his normal reaction to P. At t_2, the organism observes a falsifying instance of the expectation. He observes an element of C that is Q, where Q is different from P for the organism; it elicits a different reaction. Apart from noting that the positive instances were P while the negative instances are Q, the organism notices no further difference between the instances (perhaps because there are no differences, or perhaps because the organism does not pay attention to them). In this case, the experiments show that after t_2, perceiving an element of C will often elicit the reactions to P and Q in some alternative manner (see also **44**).

This effect can be described as the replacement of the falsified expectation 'All C are P' by the *disjunctive* expectation 'All C are P or Q'. Properties like "P or Q" will be called *disjunctive* (expected) properties.

Whether it was useful to replace an original falsified expectation 'All C are P', by a disjunctive expectation 'All C are P or Q', is difficult to say. It probably depended on several factors such as the type of reactions elicited by P and Q. But it is very likely that, in general, it was much more useful to find the cause of the falsification, that is, to find discriminating features that would enable the organism to replace the falsified expectation by two restricted expectations. This would spare the organism the need for choosing between two different reactions, of which one might be inappropriate.

Natural selection has exploited this usefulness. It has given to many species the disposition to engage in "hypothesis behaviour" (see **32**). For these dispositions induce the organism, which is going through a series of falsifying experiences, to look for and continuously try out different discriminating features, until he finds a feature F (perhaps a very subtle feature) that enables him to replace a disjunctive expectation 'All C are P or Q' by two restricted ones: 'All CF are P' and 'All C that are not F (or are G) are Q'.

38   Criterial Classes I

I have so far dealt only with a few types of generalization process that enable organisms to arrive at relatively reliable hypotheses. In spite of ignoring several important points, there are so many issues to consider that my treatment is already very complex. Yet, I am still concerned with the inferences of hypotheses having a very elementary character. Their predicates refer to simple classes such as cigarettes, grapes, red grapes, or simple properties such as signalling the presence of a smell, being sweet, etc. Nothing has so far been said about the processes that enable one to arrive at reliable hypotheses whose predicates refer to entities such as mammals, metals, gravitation, atoms, ideas, numbers, etc.

It is clear that an exhaustive study of these processes would be so complex and would have to consider so many details that at the present stage it is worthless even to begin to think about such a project. Yet, there are two types of process that are somewhat less complicated, and which can be investigated with the help of the framework developed so far. One will be studied in the following sections (**38–41**) and the other in **44**.

Consider the class of mammals. Clearly, the class is not an innate generalization class for humans. Children do not normally generalize from a bat to a horse and a human. And, of course, it is not a restricted subclass of an innate generalization class. Rather, the class is wider than any innate generalization class for humans that derives from a single instance.

Now, on the basis of certain observations, people, perhaps primarily scientists, have arrived at hypotheses concerning mammals such as 'All mammals have kidneys'. Moreover, many of these hypotheses have been highly reliable. This suggests two questions:

(1)   What kinds of psychological process enabled these persons to arrive at hypotheses about mammals?
(2)   Why were many of the hypotheses highly reliable?

In order to arrive at an answer to the first question, let us examine more closely the class of mammals. (The second question will be considered in **39**.) Roughly speaking, the class of mammals consists of animals such as dogs, horses, and bats who possess a series of criterial properties $P_1, .., P_n$ such as being able to eat, to breathe, to have milk glands, etc. In other words, the class of mammals consists of the union M of classes like the class of dogs, of horses, of bats, etc., and it is believed that the elements of the classes share a number of criterial properties.

The classes that make up the union M of mammals are familiar to us. They are identical with, or very similar to, the innate or restricted generalization classes of humans that originate in appropriate entities. (For instance, children who generalize from a horse to other entities will normally use a generalization class that is very close to the class we call 'horse'.) Therefore, people can acquire hypotheses about the elements of the classes that make up M by exposure to a few appropriate pairing situations and by going, when necessary, through suitable falsifying experiences. And, indeed, people have acquired hypotheses such as 'All horses can eat' by observing a few positive instances (and perhaps some falsifying instances, if the original hypothesis was too wide, e.g. if the generalization class included statues of horses).

More formally, let $C_1, .., C_n$ be the innate or restricted generalization classes that make up the union M of mammals, and let P be the conjunction of a number of naturally expected properties, such as to be able to eat, to breathe, to have milk glands, etc. Then, people can acquire the hypotheses 'All C_1 are P', ..., 'All C_n are P' by exposure to appropriate pairing situations and by going, if necessary, through appropriate falsifying experiences.

By forming the conjunction of these hypotheses, we obtain the hypothesis 'All M are P', i.e.

(3) All mammals are P,

since M is the union of the classes $C_1, .., C_n$.

Thus, by undergoing the described experiences people can acquire hypotheses about mammals. But people have also acquired hypotheses about mammals by a shorter procedure. After they had acquired the conjunctive hypothesis (3), they acquired new hypotheses about M—say, the hypothesis 'All M are Q'—by observing positive instances that belonged only to *some* of the classes $C_1, .., C_n$. It was no longer necessary for them to observe elements of each of these classes having the property Q.

Suppose a person acquired the hypothesis 'All M are Q' by observing a number of elements of M having Q, but he did not observe elements of each of the classes $C_1, .., C_n$ having Q—which means that he did not acquire the hypothesis 'All M are Q' because he formed a series of hypotheses 'All C_1 are Q', ..., 'All C_n are Q'. Then the person used M as a generalization class. He generalized from the observed elements to all the elements of M.

To make this analysis more concrete, let us assume that at some stage of scientific development, people had already acquired the hypotheses that all elements of C_1, .., C_n can breathe, eat, and have milk glands, by observing positive instances of each of the classes C_1, .., C_n. However, they had not yet made a systematic investigation concerning their having kidneys. In this case, observing elements of some of the classes C_1, .., C_n, and noting that they have kidneys, may have been sufficient for them to acquire the hypothesis that all mammals have kidneys. If this occurred, then the class of mammals functioned as a generalization class for them. Observing that some of its elements have property Q—but not necessarily elements of each of the classes C_1, .., C_n—made people acquire the hypothesis that all mammals have this property.

These generalization processes are different from those we have studied so far, since the class of mammals is wider than any of the innate generalization classes that originate in a mammal (for humans). The question now arises, what kind of generalization process is this? In particular, do such processes also occur in other species? I will now discuss two types of experiments suggesting that certain organisms can indeed learn to generalize according to classes that are, like M, unions of innate and/or restricted generalization classes, provided the organisms undergo certain experiences. These experiences are similar to those that brought humans to believe (3), if we assume that the observations leading to (3) were made by a single person.

Consider the following experiment described by Pavlov (1927: 55f). A dog was exposed to three types of pairing situations in which the sound of a buzzer, the sound of a metronome, and a tactile stimulus were paired with food. This had two consequences. The first was the acquisition by the dog of three expectations 'All B signal (the appearance of) food', 'All M signal food', and 'All T signal food', where B, M, and T are the dog's innate generalization classes with respect to the sound of the buzzer, the sound of the metronome, and (the particular instance of) the tactile stimulus. The acquisition of these expectations was confirmed by the fact that, after the exposure, the elements of the three classes elicited from the dog food reactions such as salivation.

Let N be the union of the classes B, M, and T. We can then say that as a result of the exposure to the three kinds of pairing situations the dog acquired the expectation:

(4)   All N signal the appearance of food.

The second consequence of these exposures was the transformation of N into a generalization class for the dog. This was
shown in the second part of the experiment in which the food
reactions were inhibited with respect to the sound of the
metronome. It was then observed that the inhibition generalized
to the other two stimuli: the sound of the buzzer and the tactile
stimulus. Since dogs do not normally generalize from the sound
of a metronome to the sound of a buzzer and a tactile stimulus,
the class N is not an innate generalization class for dogs. However,
for this dog it had become a generalization class as a consequence
of the exposure to the three kinds of pairing situation with a
constant second stimulus: the presentation of food. This suggests
that the union U of a number of innate generalization classes
$C_1, .., C_n$ can become a generalization class for dogs, if they are
exposed to such pairing situations, that is, if they had the
experiences that enable them to acquire expectations of the form
'All C_1 are P', ..., 'All C_n are P'.

Similar conclusions are suggested by some of the experiments
on semantic generalization (see e.g. Razran 1939). Consider the
class containing sounds of 'vase'. The class is probably an innate
or restricted generalization class for humans or very close to such
a class. Normal people, even if they do not know English, usually
generalize from one sound of 'vase' to another. The same holds
for sounds of 'urn'. But now consider the class containing both
sounds of 'vase' and of 'urn'. This class is not an innate generalization class for humans, since there are many people who do not
generalize from the sound of 'vase' to the sound of 'urn'. However,
experiments on semantic generalization show that the class has
become a generalization class for people who speak English,
i.e. people who underwent the experiences that enabled them to
learn the meanings of the terms. These persons indeed acquired
the disposition to generalize from sounds of 'vase' to sounds of
'urn'. Now, different speakers of English have probably learned
these meanings in different ways. But it is very likely that many
of them, especially children, have learned the meanings by exposure
to pairing situations. They heard utterances of 'vase' (perhaps
within some verbal context) while observing a vase and they heard
utterances of 'urn' while observing an urn (see **49**). Moreover, the
vase and the urn shared a salient property P, namely, to have a
vase-like shape. These experiences transformed the union of the
two innate generalization classes—sounds of 'vase' and sounds of
'urn'—into a generalization class. This therefore confirms that for

people, who are exposed to pairing situations in which the elements of an innate generalization class C_1 are paired with an instance of property P, and the elements of another innate generalization class C_2 are paired with instances of the same property, the union U of the two classes can become a generalization class.

There probably are differences between these processes and those that took place when people learned to generalize according to the class of mammals. But there is also a clear similarity between the processes. Let us assume that a single person has made the observations about mammals that enabled him to acquire the hypotheses 'All C_1 are P', ..., 'All C_n are P', by observing instances of C_1, .., C_n having P. In this case, the person has been exposed to a series of pairing situations in which the first stimuli were elements of the innate or restricted generalization classes C_1, .., C_n while the second stimulus consisted of instances of an expected property P, say, the conjunctive property of being able to eat, to breathe, and to have milk glands. Just as in the processes described above, here too one of the consequences of these experiences is the transformation of the union M of these classes into a generalization class. Observing that some of its elements have a property Q—e.g. they have kidneys—enables him to acquire the hypothesis that all M have Q.

If by having such experiences the union U of a number of innate or restricted generalization classes has become a generalization class for an organism, then I say that U is an *expanded* generalization class (for the organism). I also call it a *criterial* (generalization) class, stressing by this that U has become a generalization class because the organism has observed that its elements share a number of criterial properties. (In Pavlov's experiment, the criterial property is "to signal the appearance of food" while in the semantic generalization experiment regarding 'vase' and 'urn' it is something like "to signal the possible appearance of objects that have a vase-like shape".)

39   Inductive Inferences about Criterial Classes

With the help of evolutionary conclusions we were able to justify the inductive inferences of S3 and S5 (**23**, **30**). Can we also give a general justification for the inferences in which the generalization class is a criterial generalization class? The answer seems to be negative. To be sure, the disposition that enables an organism to acquire a criterial class as a generalization class derives from his genetic constitution, which suggests that it had survival value. However, the particular class U that has become a generalization class is not innately determined. It is determined by the particular experiences through which the organism has gone.

It seems therefore that evolutionary theory cannot justify for criterial generalization classes a general regularity thesis such as thesis T1 **(20)**. If we want to justify inferences about such classes we will have to appeal to other arguments, e.g. that a well-confirmed theory supports the regularity of these classes with respect to certain properties. This was already suggested by Ullian in the following passage:

> . . . treatment of the highly sophisticated, multiply nested inferences of mature science or mature common sense may call for rather different techniques from treatment of simpler cases. [1961a: 738.]

It is of course important to find the reasons that stand behind our justification for inferences such as those about mammals. But an investigation of this problem lies beyond the scope of the present essay. Consequently, I will not try to give a general answer to the second question I raised at the beginning of **38**, namely, why many hypotheses about criterial classes were highly reliable.

Although the justification for inductive inferences about criterial generalization classes cannot be derived (in a general way) from evolutionary theory, there is a crucial factor behind this justification that is essentially dependent upon evolutionary conclusions. This is the reliability of the hypotheses 'All C_1 are P', . . . , 'All C_n are P' which transform the class U into a generalization class. In so far as P is a salient naturally expected property (or a conjunction of such properties), the hypotheses are justified by theses T1 and T2. T1 and T2 **(20, 30)** ensure the reliability of the hypotheses. (I am ignoring here some differences between the hypotheses justified by T1 and T2 and the present hypotheses such as the use of the past tense there versus the present tense here.) For example, the hypothesis that all horses can eat, whose reliability is of course a fundamental reason for including horses among the mammals—were they not able to eat, we would not include them— is justified by the theses. This shows that even in our inferences about (all) mammals, the fact that our generalizing dispositions are well adapted plays a crucial role.

40　Criterial Classes II

There are some points regarding criterial classes that should be discussed in more detail.

I said previously that the class of mammals is the union of a number of innate or restricted generalization classes such as the classes of dogs, horses, and bats. It is possible, however, that some of these classes are themselves criterial classes. Consider, for example, a tiny poodle and a big St. Bernard. It is possible that children do not normally generalize from one of these dogs to the other. In this case, the class of dogs is probably a criterial class; it is the union of a number of innate or restricted generalization classes that share certain criterial properties such as being able to eat, to run, and to bark.

It is thus possible that among the classes that make up the class of mammals there are, besides innate or restricted generalization classes, also (lower level) criterial classes. In this case, the class of mammals can be considered as a criterial class of a higher order.

Many of the classes with which scientists are concerned can be classified as criterial classes of different orders. For example, if one looks at the class of vertebrates as being composed, among others, of the class of mammals, then it would have a higher order than the class of mammals.

To give one further example, consider the class containing objects of copper. This class, which is wider than any innate generalization class (for humans), is probably a criterial class. Its elements share a number of criterial properties. If this is so, then the class of metals can be classified as a criterial class of a higher order. It is the union of a number of classes, some of which (or perhaps all of them) are themselves criterial classes.

The second point I would like to examine is the fact that in the psychological processes we studied in **38**, the organism acquired a criterial class U after he himself had made the observations leading to the expectations 'All C_1 are P', ..., 'All C_n are P'. With respect to criterial classes like mammals or metals, however, the history of science suggests that the observations were made by different persons. Therefore, most of these observations, and the hypotheses that were inferred from them, became known to them not by direct observation but by verbal (or written) communication. It is important to keep this difference in mind, although one might entertain the hypothesis that the effects of such verbal communication are very similar to the effects of direct observations (cf. **61**).

Finally, let me point out that from the classes $C_1, .., C_n$ one can form not only the union U which comprises all these classes but also smaller unions that comprise only some of them. Let $C_1, .., C_m, C_n$ be the classes that make up the class M of mammals, where C_n is the class of whales. Let L be the union of the classes $C_1, .., C_m$. The class L is then also a criterial class, since the elements of the classes that form L share a number of criterial properties, namely, the usual criterial properties of mammals.

It is likely that the historical development of the notion of "mammal" involved the addition of certain classes to a previously formed union, producing in this way a wider criterial class. At a certain stage, scientists discovered that the elements of the classes $C_1, .., C_m$ had the mammalian criterial properties. This had the consequence that they treated the union L of these classes as a criterial generalization class, perhaps even using the term 'mammal' to refer to them. In a later stage, they discovered that the elements of C_n also had the criterial properties. This transformed the union M of the classes $C_1, .., C_m, C_n$ into a criterial generalization class.

41   Feature Classes

A criterial (generalization) class is the union of a number of innate and restricted generalization classes $C_1, .., C_n$ with respect to which the organism has acquired the expectation that their elements have an expected property P: the criterial property. The organism has acquired this expectation by exposure to several pairing situations in which elements of the classes $C_1, .., C_n$ were paired with instances of P. A slightly different type of generalization class is that in which the property P is a perceptual part of the elements; it is one of their features.

Suppose the class R contains everything that is red. The red grape a is therefore one of its elements. Let G be the innate generalization class (for humans) that originates in grape a, and let us assume that G contains not only red objects but also objects having another colour, say, green grapes. In this case, G has a restricted subclass D_1 which contains only red G's, i.e. elements of G having the discriminating feature "to be red". Clearly, D_1 is a subclass of class R since D_1 contains only *red* entities.

By considering other elements of R we obtain further subclasses of R that are at the same time restricted subclasses of certain innate generalization classes. Suppose b is a red table. Of course, b is an element of R, which contains everything that is red. Let T be the innate generalization class that originates in b. Then T has a restricted subclass D_2 which contains those T's that are red, and D_2 is again a subclass of R. By considering still further elements of R, e.g. ripe tomatoes, red sunsets, rubies, blood, etc., we obtain additional restricted subclasses of the corresponding innate generalization classes, until we arrive at a point where the union U of these classes, say, of the classes $D_1, .., D_n$ make up the whole class R.

We see that class R is the union of a series of classes $D_1, .., D_n$ whose elements share the discriminating feature "to be red". The classes $D_1, .., D_n$ are restricted subclasses of innate generalization classes which originate in some of the elements of R. (With respect to certain special elements of R, however, the corresponding restricted class D_i may be a limiting case, in the sense that D_i completely or almost completely coincides with the corresponding innate generalization class. For example, if the original element is a large red board, then it is possible that the innate generalization class which originates in the board contains only red things and nothing having a different colour.)

Experiments on discrimination with a constant (possibly single-dimension) discriminating feature (see e.g. Schwartz 1978: 195ff) show that an organism can learn to use the class R as a generalization class with respect to an expected property P by having the following experiences. The organism is exposed to a series of pairing situations in which different elements of R are paired with a property P. For instance, he sees a red grape while receiving an electric shock, he sees a red table while receiving such a shock, a sample of blood while ..., etc. As a consequence, the organism acquires a series of expectations 'All C_1 are P', ..., 'All C_k are P', where $C_1, ..., C_k$ are the organism's innate generalization classes that originate in these entities. Moreover, with respect to each expectation 'All C_i are P' $(i = 1 .. k)$, the organism also has falsifying experiences. He sees an element of C_i and he receives no shock, and all these falsifying instances are not red, i.e. they lack the discriminating feature "to be red".[20] As a consequence, he replaces the falsified expectation by the restricted expectation 'All D_i are P', where D_i is the restricted subclass of C_i which contains only entities possessing the discriminating feature "to be red".[21] Once this process finishes,

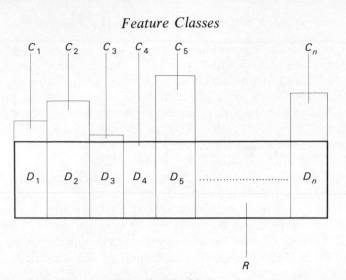

Figure 2   Class *R* containing all red objects

Figure 2 shows the class *R* of red objects, which is the union of the classes $D_1, .., D_n$. Each of these classes is a restricted subclass of one of the innate generalization classes $C_1, .., C_n$ that originate in a red entity, and the discriminating feature that distinguishes between the elements of the latter classes and those of $D_1, .., D_n$ is "to be red". (Class D_4 illustrates the limiting case where the restricted class coincides with the corresponding innate generalization class.)

the organism will possess the expectations 'All D_1 are P', ..., 'All D_k are P'.

But such experiences will often have an additional consequence. The organism will now expect that not only the elements of $D_1, .., D_k$ signal (the occurrence of) an electric shock but also the elements of the classes $D_k, .., D_n$, which are the other classes that make up the class *R*. All the elements of *R*—i.e. all kinds of red object—will now elicit the particular reaction. Hence, *R* has now become a generalization class for the organism with respect to the property of signalling an electric shock. In more common terminology, the organism now associates the colour red (possessed by all and only the elements of *R*) with electric shocks.

(Psychologists often speak in this case of a property or stimulus coming to control a behaviour. For example, Schwartz (1978: 199) describes such a process in the following terms:

... discrimination training effectively eliminates control of responding by incidental stimuli [background aspects of the environment]. No longer is the controlling stimulus a compound which includes colour; now, the controlling stimulus is effectively colour alone.)

If R has become a generalization class with respect to a property P for an organism, I will say that R is a *feature* generalization class for the organism. In general, if by going through experiences like those described here, the union U of the restricted classes $D_1, .., D_n$ has become a generalization class with respect to a property P, I will say that U is a *feature generalization class*; for short, a *feature class*.

Let 'F' describe correctly the feature class U in the sense that it describes all and only the elements of U. Then I say that F is the *determining* feature of U. For example, if the English expression 'to be red' indeed describes all and only the elements of R, then the determining feature of R is *to be red*.

If U is a feature class for an organism and F is the determining feature of U, then the elements of each of the classes $D_1, .., D_n$ that make up U have the feature F. For example, the elements of the classes $D_1, .., D_n$ that make up the class R have the feature of being red.

Let me point out that the classes $D_1, .., D_n$ that make up a feature class U are usually not the only restricted subclasses of the original innate generalization classes $C_1, .., C_n$. (For instance, the class G of grapes has many other restricted subclasses besides the class of red grapes D_1, e.g. the class of green grapes, of soft grapes, of grapes having an eliptic form, etc.) But apparently only some of these subclasses can become a basis for the formation of a relatively wide feature class U. For example, the organism which has learned that red grapes, square tables, and soft beds signal the reception of an electric shock will usually not generalize from the instances of the three classes to other kinds of entities. He will find no common feature which, he believes, "causes" the electric shock. Note, in particular, that the class of gruez entities, which contains those entities that were green until AD 1980 but red afterwards, is not a feature generalization class for normal humans. People did not generalize from objects that were gruez to objects that are gruez, even if they had the experiences described earlier.

Most feature classes include feature classes as their subclasses. These subclasses are more specific feature classes than the classes in which they are included. For example, the feature class RF which contains red fruits is a subclass of the feature class R which contains red objects. We see that the number of the restricted classes $D_1, .., D_m$ that make up the union RF is less than of those that make up R. They are the D_j $(j = 1 .. m)$ that contain only red fruits. Now, it will often happen that an organism will learn to use a more specific feature class (rather than a wide one) as a generalization class with respect to a property *P*. Suppose that instead of seeing red grapes, red tables, and blood when receiving a shock, the organism in our example had seen red grapes, red tomatoes, and red apples. It is then possible that the organism would have generalized from these instances to the class of red fruits rather than to the class of red objects. Instead of acquiring the expectation 'All red objects signal an electric shock' he might have acquired the expectation 'All red fruits signal such shocks'. In this case, the feature class containing red fruits (which is a subclass of the feature class containing red objects) would have become the organism's generalization class with respect to the property of signalling the reception of an electric shock.

The most specific instance of a feature class is obtained when there is no additional generalization at all. In this case, the restricted generalization class *D* is identical with the feature generalization class *U*. The union *U* contains only the single class *D*.

Thus, organisms can learn to generalize according to feature classes with respect to some property *P*. Do evolutionary conclusions justify these generalizations? It seems that the answer depends on the degree of specificity of the feature classes. In those cases where the feature class *U* coincides with a restricted class *D*, the evolutionary theses T1 and T2 provide a quite general justification (see **30**). With respect to feature classes that are somewhat more general, such as the class of objects that are red, round, soft, and grow on trees, the evolutionary justification is less general, since only organisms which go through a series of appropriate experiences learn to generalize according to such classes. But they still receive a significant degree of justification, because a relatively high number of organisms indeed undergo such experiences, and the feature classes which they learn to use are significantly similar. This suggests that several of the generalizations that agreed with such classes were frequently reliable. Finally, generalizations that agree with very general feature classes, such as the class containing all red objects, or all square objects, seem to receive little justification from evolutionary considerations. Only certain organisms, which go through certain very specialized experiences, learn to generalize according to such classes. Therefore, we cannot formulate strong conclusions about the survival value of these generalizations.

42   The Elimination of Features

When dealing with restricted classes I have often made use of
the notion of a discriminating feature. For instance, the restricted
subclass of an innate generalization class has frequently been
described as the class containing those elements of the innate
generalization class that have a discriminating feature F. But the
conclusions obtained in the previous section show that instead
of speaking of discriminating features, we can speak of discriminating (feature) classes. Instead of saying that D is the
restricted subclass of the innate generalization class C whose
elements have the discriminating feature F, we can say that D is
formed by the intersection between C and an appropriate feature
class U. In these cases, the feature class U will be called the
discriminating (feature) class which separates the elements of the
restricted class D from the other elements of C. I have spoken,
for example, of the class of grapes that have the discriminating
feature of being red. But I can also specify this class as being
the intersection between the class of grapes and the discriminating
(feature) class R which contains all and only red objects.

There are thus two ways of specifying restricted classes. The
first employs the notion of a generalization class and it specifies
the restricted class D as the intersection between an innate
generalization class C and an appropriate feature generalization
class U. The second uses the notion of a generalization class
and in addition the notion of a feature, since it specifies a restricted
class D as the class containing those elements of the generalization class C that have the feature F. But if there are two such
alternatives, then considerations of simplicity—or perhaps more
properly Occam's razor, which recommends not multiplying
entities beyond necessity—suggest that the additional entities do
not really exist. There actually are no discriminating features;
there exist only discriminating (feature) classes.

But I will not enter into the problem of whether we should
indeed conclude that discriminating features do not really exist.
What is important is that the notion of a discriminating feature
can be replaced by the notion of a discriminating class. This
allows us to eliminate the notion of a discriminating feature.

In addition to the notion of a discriminating feature, I also
introduced the notion of a salient feature of a stimulus (see **14**
and **36**). For example, I imagined that Baege had also tested the
puppies' reaction to rolled pieces of black paper, and that these

stimuli did not elicit the avoidance reaction. This result would have suggested that although the original cigarette possessed not only the feature of being white but also the feature of being white or black, for the puppies the former (and not the latter) was a salient feature of the stimulus. And this would then explain why the generalization class K contained (let us assume) only white cigarettes and white pieces of paper; whiteness was one of the determining features of K.

This (imaginary) result can also be described by using only the notion of a generalization class. Thus we can say that although the cigarette was not only an element of the feature class W of white entities but also of the feature class WB containing white and black entities, for the puppies the class W (and not the class WB) was one of the determining feature classes of the ensuing generalization. And this explains why the generalization class K was (let us assume) a subclass of the feature class W while none of the K's belonged to the feature class B of black entities. Hence, the notion of a salient feature (of a stimulus) is also dispensable.[22]

The notion of a determining feature class can also be used when we want to specify a generalization class C in terms of the features possessed by its elements. Suppose that all the elements of the generalization class C have feature F (e.g. all are red). Moreover, suppose that the feature class U corresponds to the feature F in the sense that 'F' describes all and only the elements of U (cf. **41**). Instead of saying that the elements of C have feature F, we can then say that C is a subclass of the feature class U, or that U is one of the determining features classes of C.

Let me illustrate this with an example. Suppose F is the feature to be red and that 'to be red' describes correctly the elements of the feature class R depicted in figure 2 (**41**). Let C be the class of red grapes. Then, instead of saying that the elements of C have the feature to be red, we can say that C is a subclass of the class R of red objects, or that R is one of the determining feature classes of C.

Our analysis shows that in order to account for the elementary learning processes we have discussed so far, we have no need of the notion of a feature. We can account for the processes in terms of certain generalization classes. Hence, we need not assume the existence of entities such as features.

The notion of a feature is widely used by both philosophers and psychologists. Very few, however, have given a satisfactory definition of it. The results obtained here are therefore of great importance, for they allow us to define it with the help of the clear notion of a feature generalization class.

43   The Solution to the Hempel and Goodman Paradoxes

Projectible predicates. We have now examined several types of predicates—classes and properties—that play a role in enabling us to infer hypotheses that were reliable.[23] These roles are often different. For example, in the inferences of S3 (**23**) the innate generalization class C is the antecedent predicate of the inferred hypothesis, while the naturally expected property P is the consequent predicate of this hypothesis. Alternatively, consider restricted classes. Their main usefulness—as antecedent predicates—can be asserted only with respect to the property P that was absent in the falsifying experiences (see **34**). Similarly, disjunctive expected properties, criterial classes, and feature classes also help us to infer reliable hypotheses, but each in their specific manner (**37**, **38**, **41**).

Following Goodman (1965), let us say that predicates which play positive roles in enabling us to infer reliable hypotheses are *projectible*. They allow us to project from the observation of particular instances to other instances. Hence, the predicates we have investigated here are projectible.

Our conclusions suggest a number of fundamental distinctions in the notion of projectibility. One is the distinction between intuitive and objective projectibility. A predicate is *intuitively* projectible, if its use in inductive inferences is intuitively valid; it is *objectively* projectible, if this use enables us to infer hypotheses that are reliable in the objective world. Another distinction is between objective projectibility in the past and objective projectibility in the future. A predicate *was* objectively projectible if it enables us (or enabled us) to infer reliable hypotheses about the past, and it *will be* objectively projectible, if it enables us to infer reliable hypotheses about the future.

The predicates we have investigated so far are intuitively projectible, although in different ways. Innate generalization classes, for example, are intuitively projectible for all members of a species, while criterial classes are intuitively projectible only for those who have undergone the experiences described in **38**, or who have acquired similar information in some other way. As to objective projectibility, theses T1 and T2 (**20**, **30**) suggest that a great number of the predicates we have dealt with here were indeed objectively projectible. And if we accept the continuity postulate CP (**26**), then these predicates will continue to be objectively projectible.

Besides the predicates examined here, there are many other predicates that are intuitively and probably also objectively projectible. Some of them can perhaps be derived relatively easily from the predicates examined here, for example, by forming disjunctions or conjunctions of the predicates. Others seem to have no obvious connection with these predicates, such as 'gravitation', 'momentum', 'phlogiston', 'evolution', 'electron', 'Oedipus complex', etc. But since such predicates are used in relatively advanced stages of the acquisition of knowledge, and since this book is concerned only with the most basic aspects of the acquisition of knowledge, I will not examine here the problems regarding the projectibility of these predicates.

The solution to the paradoxes. Let us now return to schema S1 which reflects Nicod's criterion of confirmation (see **2** and **3**). S1 allows us to infer the hypothesis 'All C are P' from the observation of n elements of C that are P, provided no elements of C have been observed that are not P. But we have seen that because of the unrestricted character of the predicates 'C' and 'P', S1 is affected by the Hempel and Goodman paradoxes. It permits, for example, the inference of 'All ravens are black' from the observation of a white shoe, and of 'All emerubies are green' from the observation of a green emerald. (We recall that emerubies are emeralds when the time is prior to AD 2000, or rubies when the time is not prior to AD 2000.)

In order to avoid the paradoxes, different types of restriction to S1 have been proposed. It has been suggested, for example, that the predicates (or the corresponding classes and properties) should be qualitative (Carnap 1947), well entrenched in language (Goodman 1965), sortals (Ackerman 1969), or simple, (Friedman 1973). But most of these proposals have at least one of the following two shortcomings:

(1) No clear definition is provided for the relevant terms.

For example, it is not clear whether the property of being an emeruby, which is possessed by all emerubies, is or is not qualitative or simple (see also n. 9).

(2) The restricted schemata still allow counterintuitive inferences.

Since 'emeruby', for example, is a sortal predicate which applies to emerubies, the counterintuitive inference of 'All emerubies are green' from a green emerald is not avoided. See also Blum (1971).

Moreover, and this is crucial, all the proposals suffer from this shortcoming:

(3) No satisfactory explanation is given for the high reliability in the past of the inductive inferences that are supposed to agree with the restricted schemata.

Thus, no independent reason has been given why there should be a connection between reliability on the one hand, and qualitativeness, entrenchment in language, sortalness, or simplicity, on the other hand. Why, for example, should the qualitativeness of 'emerald' be relevant to the reliability of the inductive inferences that agree with this predicate? Why not non-qualitativeness? Of course, if we postulate that the world is qualitative, then the reliability might be explained. But this would not be an independent reason.

Yet there is one feature, which apparently is a virtue, that is shared by the proposals:

(4) They are based on a single criterion, and most of them are supposed to apply to all or to most inductive inferences.

I have also introduced restrictions in schema S1 in order to avoid the paradoxes. But no single criterion has emerged. Rather, we found several different types of predicates that are relevant to the intuitiveness and reliability of inductive inferences, and the intuitive and objective projectibility of the predicates varies from case to case. Moreover, the predicates we have examined apply only to relatively simple inductive inferences: the inferences described in schemata S2, S3, S4 and S5 (**16**, **23**, **28**, **30**) and those about disjunctive, criterial, and feature properties or classes (**37**, **38**, **41**). Our solution of the paradoxes is therefore more complex and has a narrower domain of application than the alternative solutions.

But our solution possesses three features which are clearly virtues. First, the different types of predicate have been clearly defined on the basis of well-known psychological phenomena. Second, the inductive inferences that agree with the predicates are intuitively valid (provided the inferences satisfy the specified conditions that ensure the intuitive projectibility of the predicates). Finally, and this is the most important feature, theses T1 and T2 (**20, 30**), which are supported by two different (independent) types of evidence (see **22, 30**), give a satisfactory explanation for the high reliability of the inferences about the past described in S3 and S5. Hence, our solution is not affected by the shortcomings of the alternative solutions.[24]

Our solution is thus more complex than the alternative solutions. But is this really a defect? Only if we have reasons to believe that a simple solution indeed exists. Yet it is unlikely that a single criterion will account satisfactorily for different types of inductive inference. Consider the predicates 'poodle' and 'dog'. Both are probably qualitative, well entrenched in language, sortals, and simple. Nevertheless, there is a clear difference between them with respect to projectibility. We can infer, for example, 'All poodles have kidneys' and 'All dogs have kidneys' from the observation that poodle *a* has kidneys. The latter hypothesis, however, is much more useful. (In our approach, the difference between 'poodle' and 'dog' corresponds approximately to the difference between innate generalization classes and their restricted subclasses, and the difference between their projectibility is discussed in **34**.) Therefore, the fact that our solution is not based on a single criterion may be more of a virtue than of a vice.

Our solution has also a narrower field of application. But, first, the solution is not incompatible with a correct account of more sophisticated inductive inferences. On the contrary, the conclusions we have obtained suggest that further progress will be made if our psychological and evolutionary framework is taken as a basis for additional investigations. Second, what good does it do to have a comprehensive solution if it has the above mentioned shortcomings?

Our solution to the Hempel and Goodman paradoxes does not have these shortcomings. This suggests that it is more adequate than the alternative solutions that have been mentioned here, and than those solutions that are likewise affected by the shortcomings (see e.g. Ullian 1961b, Goodman 1972: 357ff, and Stemmer 1971a, 1975, for criticism of some other solutions). The fact that our solution is more complex and less comprehensive than the alternative solutions is more than compensated for by the absence of the shortcomings (1)–(3).[25]

44   Inductive Inferences about Frequencies

In **37**, I investigated the processes by which an organism acquires
a disjunctive hypothesis. In the first stage, the organism infers the
hypothesis 'All *C* are *P*' by observing an element of *C* that is *P*.
In the second stage, he observes another element of *C* and he
notices that it is not *P*; it is *Q*. Moreover, the organism perceives
no difference between the two elements of *C* (except the one
between *P* and *Q*). As is shown by several experiments, especially
those on probability learning, this will often bring the organism
to replace the original hypothesis by the disjunctive hypothesis
'All *C* are *P* or *Q*'.

But various species show more sophisticated behaviour. They
seem to take into account the number of the elements of *C* which
(they observed) were *P* and of those which were *Q*. (See e.g. the
study on matching behaviour in fish and maximizing behaviour
in rats in Mackintosh 1969.) In the following, I will investigate
disjunctive inferences, i.e. inductive inferences of disjunctive
hypotheses, in which the inferred hypothesis indeed reflects such
frequencies. The inferences will be called *frequency inferences* and
the inferred hypotheses (or expectations, beliefs, etc.) will be called
frequency hypotheses. But I will no longer try to relate these
inferences to the behaviour of animals. Rather, I will examine only
frequency inferences made by humans, and the account will be
based on our general knowledge of such inferences. Moreover, I
will restrict myself to the study of very elementary types of
frequency inference.

Suppose some (not too young) children eat ten green grapes
and they note that eight are sweet while two are sour. Moreover,
they do not perceive any difference between the sweet and the
sour grapes (except the difference in taste). Assuming that the
class of green grapes is the children's generalization class with
respect to the ten grapes and "sweet" and "sour" the expected
properties, then such an experience will probably bring the children
to acquire (at least) the disjunctive hypothesis:

(1)   All green grapes are either sweet or sour (but not,
      e.g. bitter, or tasteless, etc.).

But depending on the age and (perhaps) the intelligence of the
children, the experience may also bring them to expect something
about the relative frequency of the expected properties among

green grapes. Thus when asked what they believe about another class of ten green grapes, some children might answer that they expect most of them to be sweet, and perhaps there will be a few genuises who will say that they expect eight of them to be sweet and two to be sour. That is, they acquire the frequency hypothesis:

(2)   In any class of ten green grapes there are eight sweet and two sour grapes.

Note that the inference of the frequency hypothesis (2) is a generalization process. The children have observed a frequency in a particular class of ten grapes, and they now expect such frequency in other classes of ten grapes.

Instead of asking the children's opinion about other classes of ten green grapes, we might have asked them about classes of other sizes, e.g. classes of five green grapes, of a hundred green grapes, and perhaps even about the whole population, i.e. about all the elements of the corresponding generalization class. But I prefer to stay with this example in order to make as few as possible changes between the inferred hypothesis and the sample, i.e. the observed evidence.

Now it does not matter whether there really are children who acquire hypotheses such as (2) upon having the described experience. The purpose of the present discussion is to advance a plausible conjecture about the way adults have come to make frequency inferences. According to the conjecture, one of the most primitive forms of frequency inference is the sophisticated disjunctive inference we have been imagining here.

The inference of the frequency hypothesis (2) has a number of characteristics. First, it is assumed that the person perceives no difference between the elements of the sample that are sweet and those that are sour. Second, the classes to which (2) refers are of the same size as the sample. Finally, the frequency of the properties which (2) attributes to the other classes is identical with the frequency (of the properties) observed in the sample.

Frequency inferences that have these characteristics will be called *primitive* frequency inferences.

Primitive frequency inferences are a special type of disjunctive inference. The main difference between them is the occurrence of the concepts of class and number in the former. Whereas (1) speaks of green grapes that are sweet or sour, (2) speaks in addition about classes of green grapes that have ten elements and it asserts that eight of the elements are sweet and two are sour.

Moreover, the person must pay attention to the frequency of the properties in the sample, and he must have the disposition (or the will) to generalize from the frequency of the sample class to other classes. But except for these differences, the inference of (2) does not seem to require new generalizing abilities. In particular, and this is a very important point, there is no need for changes in projectibility intuitions. The hypothesis (2) contains the same intuitively projectible predicates 'green grapes', 'sour' and 'sweet' as (1).

People, or perhaps only experts, introduced improvements in the primitive frequency inferences. Among the earliest changes, the following seem to have been the most important: to expect the other classes to have a frequency that is only close to (rather than identical with) the frequency of the sample, to try to increase the size of the sample, and to increase the size of the other classes with respect to which the frequency is expected.

Experience showed that many of the improved inferences were usually more reliable than the corresponding primitive inferences. It must be noted, however, that this increase in reliability did not require changes in projectibility considerations. There was no need to replace the intuitively projectible predicates that occurred in the primitive frequency inferences (and in the disjunctive inferences that stood behind these inferences). On the contrary, replacing e.g. the predicates of (1) and (2) by predicates that are not intuitively projectible such as 'non-raven' or 'grapes or oceans or salt' would have produced frequency hypotheses that would have been very often highly unreliable. Even if a person observed a hundred non-ravens and noticed that eighty were sweet while twenty were sour, and even if he did not observe any difference between the hundred non-ravens—e.g. they were all green grapes— the frequency of these properties in other classes of a hundred or more non-ravens was in most cases very different from the observed frequency.

One of the conditions of a primitive frequency inference is that the person has not observed any feature that enables him to distinguish between the elements of the sample that have the different expected properties. Now, there exists a particular type of event which almost always satisfies this condition. These events concern objects that are perceptually symmetric with respect to certain properties, such as symmetric dice, roulette wheels, regular coins, etc. For example, a person usually perceives no difference between throwing an ace and throwing a six with a perceptually symmetric die (except the difference in outcome).

Now, with respect to such events it has been observed—or perhaps people arrived at the conclusion by some kind of reasoning—that in many large classes of such events, the frequency of the expected properties reflected very closely the particular symmetry of the corresponding objects. For instance, the symmetry of a die is related to the number six, since a die has six faces. And it was indeed observed that the relative frequency of each of the expected properties—to obtain an ace, a two, etc.—was very often very close to 1/6. (Again, these results usually failed to occur, if the events were described by using non-intuitively projectible predicates such as 'to obtain an ace or a raven'.)

Many other discoveries have been made regarding frequency inferences. Let me mention one of them. It was observed that even if the elements of a sample possessed features that distinguished between those that had different expected properties—e.g. the sweet grapes were big while the sour ones were small—we could still obtain reliable frequency hypotheses, if the sample and the projected classes were chosen in a "random" way. Although the investigation of the conditions that ensured a random selection is of the greatest importance, I will not enter into this topic. It goes beyond the scope of the present essay.

45 Two Kinds of Probabilities

Suppose we have reasons to believe that only m elements of class C, which contains n elements, have property P ($m < n$). Moreover, we do not know of any feature that distinguishes between the elements of C that have P and those that do not have P (besides the difference between having and not having P). In this case, it is in agreement with one of the usual meanings of the term 'probability' to say that the probability that the element e of the class C has property P is equal to m/n. In order to make such a probability statement it usually does not matter whether our belief that m elements of C have P is based on direct observation or whether it is obtained in some other way, say, as a consequence of a frequency inference. For example, with respect to the situation described in **44** which led to the inference of hypothesis (2), we would assign the probability of 8/10 to the green grape e being sweet in the case where e is an element of the sample, and also in the case where e is an element of one of the "projected" classes mentioned in (2).

But the term 'probability' is also used in cases that are significantly different. Consider the statement:

(1)   The sun will rise tomorrow.

Although we believe very strongly that the sun will indeed rise tomorrow, we cannot be absolutely sure of this. Prediction (1) presupposes the truth not only of thesis T1, T2, and of the continuity postulate CP, but probably of many other hypotheses as well. To be sure, these hypotheses are well confirmed. But this does not guarantee their truth. Now in order to express this state of affairs, we again use the notion of probability. We say that it is highly probable, or extremely probable that (1) is true. Yet there is an important difference between this use of the term 'probability' and the former one. There the evidence enabled us to assign a definite numerical value to the probability, namely, m/n. In the present case, however, the evidence contains no information that allows us to assign a definite number to the probability.

In many cases, this difference between the two kinds of probabilities does not matter. Sometimes, however, it may become critical. In particular, the problem commonly known as the lottery paradox is related to this difference. In the following section, I will examine the paradox and propose a solution. The solution will be based on the distinction between the two probabilities and on a related distinction between two kinds of uncertainty (see also Stemmer 1982).

46   The Lottery Paradox

Two principles. The lottery paradox, formulated by Kyburg (1961: 197), seems to show that our intuitions regarding the belief or the acceptance of hypotheses is inconsistent. Kyburg considers two principles that appear to be intuitively valid. The first is the *conjunction principle*:

CONJ   If it is rational to believe p, and if it is also rational to believe q, then it is rational to believe p and q.

The second principle is:

KYB   It is rational to believe a hypothesis that is highly probable relative to what is already believed.[26]

Since KYB has been defended by Kyburg, let us call it the Kyburg principle.

But if KYB is interpreted in the manner suggested by Kyburg, then the two principles together may produce contradictory results. Suppose that with respect to a fair lottery with one million tickets we consider the hypothesis:

(1) Ticket number 1 will not win.

According to Kyburg, it is rational to believe (1), because it satisfies KYB. Thus, he says:

> Since there is only one chance in a million that this hypothesis ['ticket number 7 will not win'] is false ... this is reason enough to accept the hypothesis. [1970a: 56.]

and:

> Surely, if a sheer probability is ever sufficient to warrant the acceptance of a hypothesis, this [a probability of 0.999999] is a case. [1970b: 176.]

Now if it is rational to believe (1), it is also rational to believe that ticket number 2 will not win, that ticket number 3 will not win, etc. By applying the conjunction principle CONJ, we should therefore believe:

(2) No ticket will win.

But this contradicts our premiss that the lottery is fair, which means that one ticket will win.

Kyburg concludes from this result that the conjunction principle should be rejected. But since this principle appears to many persons as highly intuitive, it is worthwhile to examine whether perhaps some of the other presuppositions, including Kyburg's principle KYB, are the causes of the paradoxical results.

An unwarranted assumption. It is easy to see that one of Kyburg's assumptions is clearly unjustified. A probability of 0.999999 is not sufficient for accepting a hypothesis. No rational person will advise me to accept a bet of £100,000 against one penny that (1) will indeed occur. Hence, even if the probability that hypothesis h is true is 0.999999, this is not yet sufficient to believe or to accept h.[27]

To make this point clearer, suppose we have two urns, urn A

and urn *B*. At t_1 we put in urn *A* one million green balls, and in urn *B* we put 999999 green balls and one blue ball. At t_2 the urns are well mixed and we now consider the following hypotheses:

(3)   The first ball randomly drawn from urn *A* is green.
(4)   The first ball randomly drawn from urn *B* is green.

The acceptance of (3) is normally considered to be a rational one. Since we usually assign to (3) a probability of 1, we cannot propose a bet which shows that it should not be accepted. Thus it is indeed rational to accept a bet of £100,000 or even of a million pounds against one penny that (3) will occur. But (4) is clearly different. Just as in the case of (1), the probability of (4) is normally considered to be only 0.999999. We can therefore propose a bet which shows that it is not rational to accept (4). For example, one should not accept a bet of £100,000 against one penny that (4) will indeed occur. Hence, we cannot say that it is rational to accept or to believe (4).

We thus see that a probability of 0.999999 is too low to make it rational to believe a hypothesis *h*. One can propose a bet which indicates that it is not rational to accept *h*. But then any probability whose value is a definite rational number less than one is too low. One can always propose a bet concerning the truth of *h* whose acceptance would not be rational.

If this analysis is correct, then it sheds doubts on principle KYB itself. Perhaps no hypothesis whose probability is less than one ought to be believed.

Humean and evidential uncertainty. What are Kyburg's reasons for proposing principle KYB? His discussion suggests that it is the fact that most, perhaps even all, of our empirical beliefs are affected by Humean uncertainty. Let me quote:

> ... one should take experience as one's guide. But how are we to do this? The fact that something has happened once provides no logical warrant that it will happen again. If we have observed that *A* has followed *B* once, or *n* times, we are still free to suppose, without contradicting ourselves, that *A* will not follow *B* the next time *B* occurs. This thesis was cogently argued by Hume, and is periodically reasserted in the philosophical periodicals. But while we may readily admit that no amount of evidence will in itself logically entail that a given statement about the future will be true, it is nevertheless easy to say that when we have enough evidence this predictive statement becomes overwhelmingly probable ...

[Hence] to base one's expectations on past experience is to take probability as one's guide in life. [1961: 2f.]

There is no doubt that Kyburg's conclusion is correct. Many of the beliefs that people consider rational are affected by Humean uncertainty. But is the uncertainty that occurs in the lottery paradox the Humean uncertainty? A closer look at the paradox shows that this is not the case. Consider again hypothesis (3) concerning the ball of urn A. We have assigned to (3) a probability of one. But clearly our evidence does not *imply* that (3) is true, because, as Kyburg says, no amount of evidence will in itself logically entail that a given statement about the future will be true. Perhaps the continuity postulate CP is false, and the world will not continue to be intuitively uniform. In this case, it is possible that objects which at t_1 were *gruet* (i.e. green and the time is before t_2, or blue and the time is after t_2) will continue to be gruet, or that the balls in urn A have become ravens (hence, black) or blood (hence, red). On any of these possibilities, (3) will turn out to be false.

Hypothesis (3) is thus affected by Humean uncertainty (see also **28**). Consequently, it is only probably true. It must therefore be assigned a probability that is less than one. But this implies that the probability we assign to (4) must be different from 0.999999. For besides considering the evidence that one of the balls of urn B is blue—more exactly, that at t_1 one of the balls was blue—we also have to consider Humean uncertainty. Perhaps the balls are now black, or red, or colourless. This shows that (4) is affected by two types of uncertainty. One is *evidential* uncertainty, i.e. the uncertainty which has its origin in the evidence according to which we put only 999999 green balls in urn B. This evidence stands behind the definite numerical value of 0.999999 which one normally assigns to the probability of (4). The other is the *Humean* uncertainty which modifies this probability.

The same holds for hypothesis (1). This hypothesis about the future is affected by two types of uncertainty. One is the evidential uncertainty which gives the probability of 0.999999 to the hypothesis that ticket number 1 will not win. The other is the Humean uncertainty which modifies this probability. But the paradoxical situation that arises in connection with hypothesis (1) derives from its evidential rather than from its Humean uncertainty. It is because the evidence tells us that one ticket will win—the lottery is fair—that we do not believe (2).

One can perhaps define a lottery in such a way that, unlike hypothesis (4) which refers to the balls in box B, hypothesis (1) will not be affected by Humean uncertainty, e.g. if we decide that "miraculous" or "gruelike" changes in the numbers of the roulette wheel (which, say, is the instrument used for determining the winner in the lottery) will not be taken into account. That is, we eliminate by convention those cases where Humean uncertainty manifests its effects. But since this move does not block the paradox, it shows again that the paradox derives from the evidential uncertainty which affects (1) and not from its Humean uncertainty.

Note also that the possibility of proposing a bet showing the non-rationality of accepting (1) and (4) derives from evidential rather than from Humean uncertainty. For it is evidential uncertainty that enables us to assign to these hypotheses the definite value of 0.999999. Humean uncertainty tells us nothing about this value, just as it does not give us a definite probability value with respect to hypothesis (3).

Humean and evidential probability. The two kinds of probabilities discussed in **45** correspond to the two kinds of uncertainty I have just analysed. The extremely high probability we assign to the prediction that the sun will rise tomorrow reflects the very low Humean uncertainty that affects this prediction. On the other hand, the probability of 0.8 that we assign to the prediction that the green grape *e* is sweet (see **45**) reflects evidential uncertainty. It is because our evidence tells us that only eight grapes of the sample were sweet that we infer the hypothesis (2) of **44**. And this hypothesis (or perhaps a hypothesis that is weakened in accordance with the improvements discussed in **44**) suggests the assignment of the probability of 0.8 to the prediction. (If *e* is an element of the sample rather than of one of the projected classes, then the probability of 0.8 derives directly from the evidence.)

Let us call the probability that expresses Humean uncertainty *Humean probability* and the one expressing evidential uncertainty *evidential probability*. Then our discussion suggests that perhaps the following modified version of Kyburg's principle avoids the paradoxical results:

KYB′   It is rational to believe a hypothesis which, relative to what is already believed, has an evidential probability of one and a very high degree of Humean probability.

Before examining whether KYB′ indeed avoids the paradox, we must clarify somewhat more the concepts that occur in it. The principle presupposes a distinction between Humean and evidential uncertainty. Now I am not sure whether one can define this distinction with respect to all kinds of hypothesis. However, it is not difficult to find paradigm cases that are sufficiently clear to allow us to rely on this distinction at least with respect to *simple hypotheses*, i.e. hypotheses of the form 'All *C* are *P*' and their positive instances such as 'This *C* is *P*'. Consider again the two urns mentioned earlier. Urn *A*, we recall, contains one million green balls. Here, the available evidence supports the general hypothesis

(5) All balls of urn *A* are green.

and there is no evidence available suggesting that (5) is false. Therefore, the general hypothesis and all its positive instances such as hypothesis (3) are affected only by Humean uncertainty, in particular, by the uncertainty regarding the truth of the continuity postulate CP.

Urn *B* contains 999999 green balls and one blue ball. Here, too, there is evidence (actually a great deal of evidence) that supports the general hypothesis:

(6) All balls of urn *B* are green.

But in the present case we also have evidence which falsifies this hypothesis, since our evidence tells us that one of the balls is blue (and there is no evidence suggesting that this is not true). Therefore, the general hypothesis (6) and its instances are affected by both Humean and evidential uncertainty.

This suggests that with respect to simple hypotheses we can use the following criterion for distinguishing between Humean and evidential uncertainty. If our evidence supports the general hypothesis

(7) All *C* are *P*

and there is no evidence available suggesting that there are some *C* that are not *P*, then the hypothesis and its positive instances are affected only by Humean uncertainty. But if there is not only supporting but also falsifying evidence, then the hypothesis and its instances are affected by both Humean and evidential uncertainty.

The second concept that has to be clarified is that of a hypothesis having a very high (degree of) Humean probability.

Now, it is unlikely that one can state precisely the conditions that have to be satisfied by a hypothesis in order to be assigned a very high Humean probability, even if we restrict ourselves to simple hypotheses of the form 'All C are P'. To be sure, with respect to certain types of simple hypothesis our earlier conclusions, especially theses T1-T2 (**20, 30**), postulate CP (**26**), and the schemata S3-S5 (**23, 30**), throw some light on this topic. But even this is insufficient for giving a precise criterion. I will therefore say only a few generalities about degrees of Humean probability.

One must distinguish between two types of simple hypothesis. The first contains the hypotheses that are supported exclusively by the observation of positive instances. As suggested by S3-S5, the degree of Humean probability of these hypotheses seems to depend basically on three factors: the existence of positive instances (not necessarily many), the absence of evidence suggesting the existence of negative instances, and the degree of objective projectibility of the predicates that occur in the hypotheses.

To the second type belong the hypotheses that are part of, or derived from, theoretical frameworks. Their degree of Humean probability seems to depend mainly on the degree of "goodness" of the theory,[28] on the absence of evidence suggesting the existence of negative instances, and, to a certain extent, on the existence of positive instances and the degree of objective projectibility of the predicates that occur in the hypotheses.

If a hypothesis of the form 'All C are P' has a very high degree of Humean probability, then its instances—the statements 'Element e_1 of C is P', ..., 'Element e_n of C is P'—also have a very high degree of Humean probability.

The modified principle KYB′. Let us now examine whether principle KYB' avoids the paradox. First we note that if hypothesis h satisfies its conditions, then h has a very high Humean probability. From our clarification of the latter notion, it follows that in this case there is no evidence available suggesting the existence of instances that falsify h. Hence, the evidence does not give us data that enable us to determine a definite rational number which expresses its degree of Humean probability. We are therefore unable to propose a concrete bet that would show that it is not rational to believe hypothesis h.

Moreover, the principle appears to be compatible with the conjunction principle. If we have reasons to attribute to a number of hypotheses a very high degree of Humean probability—e.g. if they satisfy to a high degree the conditions mentioned above—

then the degree of Humean probability of their conjunction seems to remain sufficiently high to make it rational to believe the conjunction. To illustrate, let me use an example that is given by Peirce in order to make a related point:

> Here is a stone. Now I place that stone where there will be no obstacle between it and the floor, and I will predict with confidence that as soon as I let go my hold upon the stone it will fall to the floor ... and if anyone present has any doubt on the subject, I should be happy to try the experiment, and I will bet him a hundred to one on the result. [1934: 64.]

It is not only rational to bet a hundred to one but even a million to one that the stone will fall.[29] Moreover, it would be rational to propose such a bet not only with respect to one stone but also with respect to thousands of (carefully examined, heavy) stones, with respect to thousands of iron balls, of gold bars, etc.; hence, with respect to the conjunction of a very large number of hypotheses. Now hypotheses such as 'This stone will fall when dropped', 'That iron ball will fall when dropped', have a very high Humean probability. They satisfy to a high degree the conditions discussed above. This therefore supports the conclusion that if the Humean probability of a hypothesis is very high, then we believe not only the hypothesis itself, but also large conjunctions of similar hypotheses.

Nevertheless, so long as we do not attribute to the hypothesis a Humean probability of one, the hypothesis is still affected by Humean uncertainty. The question now arises: what is the cumulative effect of these uncertainties on the conjunction of *all* the hypotheses to which we assign a very high Humean probability? Maybe the Humean uncertainty of the conjunction is too great to make it rational to believe the conjunction? This is probably the rationale behind the following argument of Kyburg for rejecting the conjunction principle:

> Although I claim to have good reasons for believing every statement I believe, I also claim to have good reasons for believing that some of these statements are false. [1970a: 77.][30]

I am not sure whether we have *good* reasons for believing that some of the hypotheses that have a very high degree of Humean probability are false, such as the hypotheses 'This heavy stone will fall when dropped', 'That chicken will die when his heart is removed', 'The Eiffel Tower will not become a raven in AD 1985', etc. Still, it seems reasonable to admit that theoretical reasons suggest (but do not prove) the conclusion that if we form the conjunction of all these hypotheses, the cumulative effect of the Humean uncertainties is indeed too high to make it rational to believe the conjunction. But this theoretical conclusion has no practical effects whatsoever since, when making our decisions, we never have to take into account the whole conjunction. We often do consider very large conjunctions, but then we act as if they have a Humean probability of one. Consider a person who offers price X for a house. When determining the price, he takes into account the evidential probability of several hypotheses.[31] But he does not consider the possibility that the conjunction of the relevant hypotheses that have a very high degree of Humean probability (and are not affected by evidential uncertainty) may be false, such as of the hypotheses 'The first brick will not become a raven', 'The second brick will not become a raven', 'The third brick will not become a raven', etc. The Humean uncertainty that affects the conjunction of these hypotheses does not influence the person's decision to pay price X rather than some other price.

Three meanings of 'to believe'. This suggests that one must distinguish between a theoretical and a practical notion of belief. The theoretical notion is used mostly in philosophical discourse, while the practical notion is related to concrete human behaviour, such as betting behaviour. From now on, I will use the term 'to believe' or 'to believe to be true' for the theoretical notion, and the term 'to practically accept' for the practical notion.

Our discussion suggests the following conclusions. The revised version of Kyburg's principle KYB′ holds only for practical acceptance. We practically accept the hypotheses that have a very high Humean probability and an evidential probability of one, and we also practically accept their conjunction. But KYB′ does not hold for (theoretical) belief. Not only do we not believe that the conjunction of these hypotheses is true, we do not even believe that any of these hypotheses is true. For if we use such a philosophical notion, then of course we must take into account Humean uncertainty not only with respect to the conjunction of the hypotheses, but also with respect to each of them. This is precisely Hume's point. Whatever our evidence, it does not imply 'This stone will fall when dropped'.

Expressing our conclusions more formally, we obtain the following principles for practical acceptance and theoretical belief:

> **PRA** It is rational to practically accept a hypothesis which, relative to what is already practically accepted, has

an evidential probability of one and a very high degree
of Humean probability.

PRB   It is rational to believe a hypothesis which, relative
to what is already believed, has a Humean (and
evidential) probability of one.

Since the conjunction principle CONJ deals only with rational
belief, we replace it by the following principle:

CONJ′   If it is rational to believe (to practically accept) *p*
and also *q*, then it is rational to believe (to practically
accept) *p* and *q*.

It now follows from our discussion that PRA, PRB, and CONJ′
are compatible.

PRB is a trivial principle. But this is unavoidable since, by
definition, the philosophical notion of rational belief is sensitive to
Humean uncertainty.

There still remains a problem. There are cases where the
evidential probability of a hypothesis is less than one and yet,
relative to what can happen to a real person, it seems rational to
practically accept the hypothesis. For instance, let the term 'stonrav'
denote the class which contains all the heavy stones on the earth
and one living raven. Then the general hypothesis

(8)   All stonravs fall when being dropped

is false. But the evidential probability of the particular hypothesis

(9)   This stonrav will fall when dropped

is so high that, for all practical matters, we can accept it as true.
Notice, moreover, that although (9) is affected by evidential
uncertainty—our evidence tells us that there exists at least one
negative instance of (8)—we are not able to specify a definite
rational number which expresses the evidential probability of (9),
since we do not know how many heavy stones there are on the
earth. Hence, we cannot propose a concrete bet that would show
the irrationality of practically accepting (9).

There is therefore almost no doubt that it is rational to
practically accept 'This second stonrav will fall when dropped',
'This third stonrav will fall when dropped', etc. Ultimately, the
conjunction principle will bring us to contradictory results.

Now there is a clear difference between

(10)   This heavy stone will fall when dropped

and (9). Our evidence tells us that the general hypothesis which stands behind (10), namely,

(11)   All heavy stones fall when dropped

is affected only by Humean uncertainty.[32] On the other hand, our evidence tells us that the general hypothesis (8) which stands behind (9) is actually false.

This shows that a further distinction has to be made. One must distinguish between the practical acceptance of a hypothesis that is affected only by Humean uncertainty and the practical acceptance of a hypothesis that is (also) affected by an evidential uncertainty which is too small to influence the decisions of a (real) person. With respect to the former, the conjunction principle CONJ' is valid. With respect to the latter, however, the principle does not hold. And I believe that this agrees with our intuitions. The cumulative effect of the evidential uncertainties that affect a number of hypotheses, even if they are minimal, may be too great to ignore the effect in the case of a conjunction of these hypotheses. Since such conjunctions may be relevant to the practical decisions of a person, it would no longer be rational to practically accept them.

In order to avoid counterintuitive results, I therefore confine CONJ' to hypotheses whose rational practical acceptance agrees with the conditions of PRA.

In a paper on the lottery paradox, Derksen states the following conclusion

> There is thus a *probability gap*, which may, and often does, increase when the conjunction of more beliefs gets involved. In fact, the gap may, and often does, increase to such an extent that the (not specified, and not precisely specifiable) justification-limit (of the probability that *p*) for the belief that *p*, will be transgressed. [1978: 72.]

Our analysis suggests that this conclusion holds for the notion of belief—in our terminology, for the notion of practical acceptance—which is applied to hypotheses that are affected by a very small evidential uncertainty. With respect to the decisions in which only one of these hypotheses has to be considered, the uncertainty is too small to be taken into account. But when a conjunction of such hypotheses becomes relevant to a decision, it may no longer be rational to ignore the cumulative effect of the evidential uncertainties.

The solution to the paradox. The lottery paradox calls our attention to the need to distinguish between three different concepts that are expressed in ordinary language by the terms 'to believe' or 'to accept'. One is the philosophical concept which takes into account the Humean uncertainty of a hypothesis even if it is very small. With respect to this concept, the conjunction principle can be accepted without any qualm, since here we deny the rationality of believing (true) even a single hypothesis (if it is affected by the uncertainty).

According to the second concept, it is rational to practically accept a hypothesis provided it has a very high Humean probability and is not affected by evidential uncertainty. When using this concept, the conjunction principle can also be accepted. For, with respect to the conjunction of hypotheses that practically influence the decisions of a person, the cumulative effect of the Humean uncertainties is too small to make it irrational to practically accept these conjunctions.

Finally, the third concept corresponds to the practical acceptance of hypotheses which are affected by evidential uncertainties that are too small to be taken into account in the decisions of a person. When using this concept, however, the conjunction principle cannot be accepted, since the cumulative effect of the evidential uncertainties may be too great for making it rational to ignore this effect in the case of certain conjunctions of these hypotheses.

These conclusions can be considered as a satisfactory solution to the lottery paradox. They enable us to distinguish between three meanings of the terms 'to believe' or 'to accept', and they state the validity of the conjunction principle with respect to these meanings. To be sure, the conclusions have been formulated only with respect to simple hypotheses: hypotheses of the form 'All C are P' and their positive instances. It is likely, however, that the conclusions can be naturally extended to also cover more complex hypotheses. But even if the correct account of the belief or acceptance of more complex hypotheses requires a different treatment, there is no doubt that by solving the lottery paradox for simple hypotheses, an important step has been made towards the formulation of a general theory of rational belief or rational acceptance.

In our solution, a fundamental role is played by the distinction between Humean and evidential uncertainty and the parallel distinction between Humean and evidential probability. It is with the help of these distinctions that the three meanings of 'to believe' and 'to accept' have been characterized. But why didn't Kyburg consider these differences? The reason is probably the following. The examples which he studies concern predicates—classes and properties—that are intuitively projectible, such as coins, balls, dice, American males, etc. Since such predicates usually conferred a very high degree of Humean probability on the corresponding hypotheses, the need for considering Humean uncertainty did not arise. The only uncertainty that seemed relevant was evidential uncertainty. But if Kyburg had also discussed hypotheses with predicates that are not intuitively projectible, such as 'The next randomly drawn non-raven is grue', he might have noticed that these hypotheses are affected by two different kinds of uncertainty: Humean and evidential.

47   A Summary of Part II

The expanded generalization theory GT. In Part I, I investigated the most basic learning processes that enable an organism to acquire knowledge and beliefs about the world. A conceptual framework was developed that made it possible to describe these processes and to account for their effects in a simple and intuitive manner. The conclusions that were obtained constitute the generalization theory GT.

In Part II, I studied more advanced learning processes. The most important among them were the processes leading to the inference of hypotheses about restricted, criterial, and feature classes, of disjunctive hypotheses, and of hypotheses about frequencies. The conclusions obtained in Part II are to be added to GT.

Although the learning processes studied in Part II are more advanced than those of Part I, they are still of an elementary nature. But in this essay I will not investigate processes that are more advanced, apart from those that form the basis for language acquisition. This will be the topic of Part III.

Solutions for various problems. In addition to the investigation of learning processes, I was concerned with another topic in Part II, namely, with the justification of the inductive inferences that reflect the effects of processes. Several interesting results were obtained with the help of conclusions from evolutionary theory. The most important are expressed in the regularity theses T1 and T2 (**20, 30**), which describe those qualities possessed by the generalizing dispositions of well-developed species that gave them survival value; they enabled the members of the species to draw inductive inferences that were highly reliable. Since theses T1 and T2 are supported by a large and varied body of data, they allow us to justify the inductive inferences that originate in the well-adapted generalizing dispositions. These inferences are described in the schemata S3 and S5 (**23, 30**).

If one also assumes the validity of the continuity postulate CP (**26**), one can justify an additional class of inductive inferences: inferences about the future. They are described in schemata S3f and S4 (**28**). But we recall that the support for CP is affected by two weaknesses.

Some of the other inductive inferences that were examined in Part II also receive significant justification from evolutionary theory. But I didn't introduce formal schemata for describing them. Regarding the remaining inductive inferences studied in Part II, evolutionary theory gives us little ground for justification; additional devices are required.

We have seen that theses T1 and T2 describe the features of generalizing dispositions that gave them survival value in our terrestrial environment. Therefore the theses implicitly describe part of the structure or uniformity of the world—the part to which the dispositions were well adapted. This gives the theses the status of an ontological theory (**20**).

The conclusions that were received in Part II enabled us to solve various problems with which philosophers have been concerned. The most important are the Hempel and Goodman paradoxes and the lottery paradox. Regarding Hume's problem, we obtained only a partial solution, which is as it should be. Our conclusions also allowed us to clarify a number of problematic issues. These include the notion of rationality, the "principle of induction", and the role of trial and error in scientific inquiry. Finally, the discussion in **41** and **42** shows that one can eliminate the notion of a feature, and replace it by the notion of a generalization class.

A foundation for a general theory of human knowledge. In Parts I and II, I have investigated several types of process that enable us to acquire knowledge and beliefs about the world. Some of these processes are of an elementary type, while others are more advanced. Still, even the advanced processes are much simpler than the learning processes which occur in sophisticated scientific inquiry, the processes that enable people to acquire beliefs or hypotheses about gravitation, atoms, phlogiston, evolution, the Oedipus complex, etc. As said above, I will not study such sophisticated learning processes in this essay. But this does not diminish the value of what has been achieved here. For the basic learning processes which were examined in Part I and II have played and continue to play a crucial role in scientific inquiry. History or prehistory tells us that human knowledge started with beliefs acquired in these learning processes. And psychology tells us that it is with the help of these processes that the child—i.e. the future scientist—begins with the acquisition of his empirical knowledge. Since GT gives an adequate account of the basic learning processes, and since theses T1 and T2 explain why the beliefs acquired in these processes were highly reliable, we have obtained a theoretical framework that can serve as a fruitful basis for a general theory of human knowledge.

PART III

The Generalization Theory of Language Acquisition GTLA

48 The Acquisition of Language

Among the sorts of knowledge which children acquire, a central position is occupied by linguistic knowledge. Most normal children learn at a very early age a great number of the rules that govern the language of their community. Moreover, language plays a crucial role in the development of advanced scientific knowledge, since scientific theories are complex linguistic structures containing different types of theoretical terms. Therefore, a study of the roots of human knowledge would be incomplete, if it did not consider language acquisition. However, I will not engage here in an exhaustive study of the learning processes that are involved in language acquisition, since I have dealt with many of these processes in previous publications (see especially Stemmer 1973b, 1978, 1979a, 1981b). I will therefore confine myself to the investigation of certain fundamental aspects of the learning processes.

In spite of this limitation, we will arrive at various interesting conclusions which clarify several problematic points that affect existing theories or views on language acquisition. In particular, since a central part of our study is concerned with the notion of (linguistic) meaning, it will give us sound foundations for the development of a methodologically correct theory of semantics.

We will see that the generalization processes studied in Parts I and II play a central role in language acquisition. I will therefore take as our basic framework the generalization theory, GT. The theory comprising GT and the conclusions that will be obtained here will be called the *generalization theory of language acquisition*, or *GTLA* for short.

49 Verbal Pairing Situations

Children begin to learn the language of their community by being exposed to certain kinds of pairing situation.[1] In these experiences, they hear one or more utterances of a verbal expression while paying attention to a salient aspect of the environment. As a consequence, they often become able to apply the expression to a class of entities. For example, a two-year-old child hears his parents saying 'dog' (or 'doggy' or 'wow-wow') while he is looking at a dog. Such an experience often gives the child the capacity to apply the term 'dog' to the elements of a particular class, usually a class containing certain medium-sized quadrupeds such as dogs, cats, foxes, sometimes even horses and cows. Let us use the letter 'M' to refer to this class of medium-sized quadrupeds.

I have spoken of the child acquiring the ability to *apply* an expression to a class C. In order to clarify this notion, let us consider how one might confirm a hypothesis which states that a child has acquired such an ability. Suppose we want to test whether the child in our example has indeed acquired the ability to apply 'dog' to the class M. One way is to present different types of entities to the child while asking him, e.g. 'Show me the dog!'. By noting that the child selects medium-sized quadrupeds, we have found supporting evidence for our hypothesis. Or we may ask questions such as 'What is this?', while showing him different kinds of entities. If he answers 'dog' only when the entity is an element of M, then again we found supporting evidence for the hypothesis. Another method is Quine's procedure of query and assent (Quine 1960: 29ff, 1973: 45ff) where we ask the child questions such as 'Is this a dog?' while showing him different types of entity. On the basis of the child's assent, dissent or abstention, we will be able to determine (probabilistically) whether or not the child applies 'dog' to the elements of M.[2]

The pairing situations that enable a child to learn to apply a verbal expression to the elements of a class C will be called *verbal* pairing situations, and the processes by which he learns this will be called *linguistic* learning processes; for short, linguistic processes. Instead of *learning by exposure to verbal pairing situations*, I will also say *learning by exposure to ostensive (pairing) situations*; for short, *learning by ostension*.

If a person has learned to apply an expression E to a class C by going through a number of ostensive situations, I will say that E is an *ostensive expression* for the person.[3]

One aspect of ostensive learning processes immediately strikes us as familiar, namely, the generalizations that occur in the processes. The child becomes able to apply the expression not only to the original entity (or entities) but to other entities as well.

Hence, the processes are generalization processes. Moreover, the generalization classes used by the child in these linguistic generalization processes are very similar to, probably identical with, the classes used in non-linguistic generalization processes. In particular, he does not use "strange" generalization classes such as the class of non-ravens or the class containing a few dogs and all emeralds.

Another familiar aspect is the salience condition. The entity that is paired with the verbal stimulus must be a salient aspect of the child's environment. Moreover, the conditions that determine the salience are again very similar to, probably even identical with, those that determine this factor in non-linguistic generalizing processes.

The similarity between linguistic and non-linguistic generalizing processes is not surprising, because at this stage there are no essential differences between the learning processes. To make this clear, suppose a young child hears the barking of a dog for the first time. He looks in the direction of the sound and he sees a dog, also for the first time. Such an exposure to a (non-linguistic) pairing situation will often bring the child to acquire the expectation

(1) All W signal the appearance of an M

where W is the child's generalization class with respect to the barking sounds—say, all instances of a canine 'wow-wow'—and M contains certain medium-sized quadrupeds. This learning process is an instance of the elementary generalization processes we have investigated in Part I (see especially the last part of **9**).

But now suppose that everything was equal except that the dog was silent and one of the child's parents said quite loudly 'wow-wow' (or 'doggy', etc.), just before the child looked at the dog. Further, let us assume for the sake of argument that this is the first time the child hears a human voice. Then there is no reason why the process should be different from the one in which the child hears the canine 'wow-wow'. The child is exposed to a pairing situation in which he hears a sound and sees a dog for the first time. It is therefore likely that in this case, too, the child will acquire an expectation, probably the expectation

(2) All W' signal the appearance of an M

where W' is the child's generalization class with respect to the human 'wow-wow'. The process is again an instance of the learning processes of Part I.

In general, if the only difference between the exposure to a verbal and a non-verbal pairing situation is that in one case the first stimulus is a verbal expression while in the other it is another kind of stimulus, there is no reason to expect different results. It is not surprising, therefore, that in such cases the child uses the same generalization classes and is subjected to the same salience conditions.

(Although I have assumed that the generalization class of (1) is W while that of (2) is W', the classes need not be different, even if the child perceives a difference between the human and the canine 'wow-wow'. If the distinction does not play the role of a discriminating feature, the generalization classes may still be identical.)

So far, I have assumed that the verbal expression is the first stimulus of the pairing situation to which the child is exposed. But it can also play the role of the second stimulus if, for instance, the child sees first the dog and then his parents utter 'doggy' or 'wow-wow'. This can of course also occur in non-verbal generalizing processes as when the child first looks at the dog and the dog begins to bark only later. The two stimuli may even be perceived simultaneously as when the child sees the dog and at the same time he hears his parents saying 'doggy'.

In most cases, the order of presentation of the stimuli will not be maintained in subsequent occasions. Even if a child has learned to apply 'doggy' to the elements of M by first seeing a dog and then hearing 'doggy', he will later have the occasion to first hear 'doggy' while seeing the dog afterwards.

It is important to recall that by saying that a child has acquired an expectation 'All C are P' or 'All C signal a P', I am merely individuating a neural or mental trace that was left in certain experiences while hinting at the behaviour that may derive from the trace (see **9** and **10**). And the expressions 'All C are P' or 'All C signal a P' do not intend to express the content of the neurological or mental trace.

50   Complexes of Expectations

Before continuing with linguistic learning processes, let us consider again the generalization processes by which an organism acquires non-linguistic expectations. Suppose a child is burnt by a fire. Then his later behaviour will usually suggest that he has acquired the expectation:

(1) Fires are (always) hot.

Similarly, the child who for the first time sees a dog and simultaneously hears him barking will usually acquire the expectation:

(2) Dogs are always barking.[4]

But whereas the former expectation is relatively reliable, the latter is not. Dogs bark only sometimes. The child will therefore very soon observe falsifying instances of (2) in which he sees dogs which are not barking. If he notices features that distinguish between the situations where dogs bark and where they do not, then he may restrict (2). Now it is likely that he will indeed discover some of such features. He may notice, for instance, that when somebody runs very quickly towards a dog, the dog will usually bark. Still, not even these features are always reliable indicators of barking dogs. Moreover, in many cases he will notice no difference between the situations where dogs bark and where they do not. As a consequence of all these experiences, the child will normally replace (2) by a complex of expectations that correspond to the different observations made by the child about the barking of dogs. These expectations will mainly be disjunctive expectations such as 'All dogs are silent or bark (but e.g. do not sing, or bite)', and restricted expectations such as 'All angry dogs (e.g. dogs that are violently attacked) do bark'.

In some cases we may be able to formulate plausible hypotheses about the complex of expectations that replaces (2). Usually, however, we either cannot give a detailed specification of the complex or we are not interested in such a specification. In theses cases, we generally use a terminology that expresses the central core of the complex without going into details. In the present case, for example, we might describe the complex of expectations that replaces expectation (2) as a single expectation having the form:

(3) All dogs *can* bark.

Formulations such as (3) will be called *simplified* formulations of complexes of expectations; for short, *simplified expectations*.

In (3), the term 'dogs' and 'bark' have the same function as in other descriptions of expectations. They intend to individuate the two parts of the neurological trace that is produced by the child's perceptions of the two stimuli. In accordance with the conclusions and conventions of **9**, the terms are normally supposed to describe correctly the theoretical generalization classes that originate in these perceptions. The term 'can', on the other hand, has a different function. It indicates that we are dealing with the neurological trace corresponding to the child's complex of expectations about these generalization classes.

By describing with the help of a simplified expectation the outcome of a generalization process that originates in a series of experiences centred around two stimuli, we thus intend to describe only the basic aspects of the neurological trace left by the experiences. But we leave open the possibility of adding details in case we are able and also interested in doing so.

51   Linguistic Expectations and the Notion of Meaning

Simplified linguistic expectations. Let us consider again the case of the child who sees a dog for the first time while hearing his parents shouting 'doggy'. Such an experience may enable him to acquire the expectation:

(1)   Appearances of dogs are always accompanied by the sound 'doggy'.

But very soon the child will note that (1) is too wide. When he sees a dog he hears an utterance of 'doggy' only sometimes. If he notices features that distinguish between the cases where people say and do not say 'doggy', he will be able to replace (1) by a restricted expectation. For example, he may observe that when his brother points to a dog while asking his parents 'What is this?', his parents indeed say 'doggy'. Still, even though some of these features may be good indicators of utterances of 'doggy' (in the presence of dogs), they are not fully reliable. Moreover, in many cases where he hears an utterance of 'doggy' while seeing a dog, he will notice no special feature at all that distinguishes these cases from those where he does not hear such utterances. The consequence of all these experiences will be that the child replaces (1) by a complex of expectations, mainly restricted and disjunctive expectations, that correspond to the different observations made by the child regarding dogs and utterances of 'doggy'. Now, in general we are not able to give a detailed specification of this complex, or we are not interested in doing so. In these cases, we will take recourse to formulations that express the central core of the complex of expectations, just as in **50** we used (3) to express the core of the child's expectations regarding dogs and their barking.

There are several formulations that lend themselves to this purpose, and I will introduce some of them on the basis of our example. Thus any of the following formulations will be used for describing the central core of the complex of expectations acquired by the child who has observed the different usages of 'doggy':

(2) All dogs are *called* 'doggy'.
(3) All utterances of 'doggy' *name* or *refer to* dogs.
(4) The term 'doggy' *is associated with*, *names*, or *refers to* dogs.

Complexes of expectations about verbal expressions that are expressed in such simplified forms will be called *linguistic* expectations, and we test the acquisition of such expectations by methods such as those described in the beginning of **49**. If a person associates the elements of the class C with an expression E, then C will often be called the *extension* of E for the person.

By describing the results of a series of experiences with the help of a linguistic expectation, we thus ignore a great number of details that are part of the complex of expectations acquired in these experiences. But we leave open the possibility of adding further details.

Suppose we attribute to a person the linguistic expectation:

(5) All utterances of the ostensive expression E name elements of the class C.

It then follows from our discussion that (5) describes the basic aspects of the neurological (or mental) trace left by a series of experiences about utterances of an expression and instances of some salient aspect of the environment. 'E' and 'C' are supposed to describe correctly the theoretical generalization classes that originate in the utterances and instances.

In order to avoid too many complications, I will generally assume that E contains only utterances of the "same" verbal expression that were pronounced during these experiences.[5] Suppose that a child has heard only utterances of 'sheep', but his generalization class also includes utterances of 'ship'. In this case, I will usually assume that the child has already undergone appropriate experiences which enable him to distinguish between these utterances (see **53**), and that *E* therefore contains only utterances of 'sheep'.

Meanings, understanding, and application traces. We are now in a position to introduce a notion of linguistic meaning that is relatively close to one of the central ways in which the notion is used. Suppose we have reasons to believe that a child has acquired the linguistic expectation (5) in an ostensive learning process. Then I will say that the child has learned *to associate a meaning* with *E* and that the meaning is [C] (cf. **7**). If most normal members have acquired a similar expectation regarding *E*, I will say that the child has learned to associate with *E the* (correct) meaning of *E*, or that he knows or has learned *the* (correct) meaning of *E*. Instead of the latter formulation, I will sometimes say simply that the person *knows*, or *has learned*, or *understands E*.

If we express the meaning of an ostensive expression as [C] than '[C]' intends to individuate the part of the neurological trace that is produced by the child's perception of the non-linguistic stimulus. On the other hand, '*C*' is supposed to describe correctly the theoretical generalization class that originates in the stimulus. Hence, we identify the meanings of ostensive expressions with neurological (or mental) traces, and we individuate them with the help of the corresponding theoretical generalization classes: the extensions which the expressions acquire for the person.

It is important to realize that since we identify the meaning of an ostensive expression *E* with a neurological (or mental) trace, we cannot identify the meaning of *E* with its extension. The former is a neurological (or mental) entity while the latter is a generalization class containing all kinds of entities.

The use of generalization classes for individuating the meanings of ostensive expressions confers *explanatory* and *predictive* power on these meanings (cf. **9**). We expect, for example, that if a child has learned to associate the meaning [C] with an ostensive expression *E*, then utterances of 'Show me an *E*' will frequently induce the child to point to an element of *C* (if the child sees one), or that seeing an element of *C* while being asked 'What is this?' will often elicit an utterance of *E* from the child. Notice that such predictions need not be based on linguistic data. Since meanings are individuated with the help of generalization classes, we can use the means described in Parts I and II for determining the elements of the extension of an expression. In particular, we can use introspection for this purpose, as explained in **15**.

By individuating the meaning of an ostensive term, i.e. the neurological trace, with the help of its extension we apparently do not use all of our resources. The extension reflects the effects of the trace: the class of entities to which the person learns to apply the ostensive term. But the nature of the trace is of course principally determined by the factors that give origin to the trace: the non-linguistic stimulus perceived by the child during the ostensive experience. By taking into account the origin of the trace, we therefore increase the precision of the individuation. However, our conclusions in the second part of **7** suggest that the extension of an ostensive term—the generalization class that originates in the non-linguistic stimulus—normally reflects not only the effects of the trace but also the psychologically relevant features of its origin. Hence, when dealing with an ostensive term we obtain a satisfactory individuation of the trace that is formed—i.e. of its meaning—by using only the extension of the term.

The factors that give origin to the meaning [C] of an expression E will be called the *meaning origin* of [C].

I have introduced the notion of meaning with the help of (simplified) linguistic expectations. Since these expectations only give a simplified account of the complex of expectations that are acquired by a person, the notion of meaning is also affected by the simplification. A meaning [C] does not give us all the details of the child's expectations regarding the relation between the expression E and the elements of the class C. Consequently, meanings are not only theoretical entities, but also idealizations. They express in a condensed way certain basic information about the neurological (or mental) trace left by a series of experiences concerning utterances of E and elements of C.

Learning the meaning of an expression E produces a neurological (or mental) trace that gives the person the capacity to *apply* E to a class of entities C. For this reason, I will often call such traces *application* traces.

52 Neutral Stimuli

In **4**, I used Baege's experiment to illustrate various characteristics of the generalizing behaviour produced by exposure to the pairing of two stimuli. The stimuli, we recall, were a cigarette and the smell of this cigarette; the effect of the exposure was the formation of a neurological (or mental) generalization trace; and the effect of the trace was the generalization behaviour, which consisted in avoiding the elements of class K and sneezing in their presence. Class K contained other cigarettes, rolled pieces of white paper, and probably other "similar" entities.

It was, of course, very convenient for Baege that perceptions of this smell usually elicit typical reactions from puppies, such as avoidance behaviour and sneezing. It made it easy for him to obtain clear evidence indicating that the exposure indeed left a neurological generalization trace. The elements of the corresponding observational generalization class—the concrete objects shown to the puppies—elicited typical reactions, even though the puppies perceived no instance of the smell.

In general, for experimental purposes it is handy to use, as the second stimulus of a generalization process, a stimulus that usually elicits typical reactions from the normal members of the species to which the generalizing organism belongs. It facilitates the reception of observational evidence indicating that the exposure to a pairing situation did leave a neurological generalization trace. But experiments on so-called sensory preconditioning show that this is not a necessary condition for the formation of such traces. The traces are also formed if the organism is exposed to the pairing of two *neutral* stimuli—i.e. stimuli that do not usually elicit typical reactions from the normal members of the species— provided the stimuli are relatively salient for him. In these experiments (see e.g. Mackintosh 1974: 19ff), an organism is exposed in a first stage to a few pairings of two neutral stimuli S_1 and S_2, e.g. a light and a sound. In the second stage, it is exposed to the pairing of S_2 with an *active* stimulus S_3, e.g. an electric shock. Going through these experiences has two consequences. The first is the usual effect produced by the exposure to the pairing of a neutral stimulus with an active one (which is the experience of the second stage). Stimulus S_2, more exactly, the elements of the corresponding generalization class C_2, now elicit reactions that are very similar to the organism's reactions to S_3. Hence, S_2 has now become an active stimulus for the organism.

The second consequence is that the elements of the generalization class corresponding to S_1, say, of the class C_1, now also elicit such reactions, even though none of its instances was paired with S_3. This shows that the experiences of the first stage—the exposure to the two neutral stimuli S_1 and S_2—had *latent* generalization effects, which became manifest once S_2 started to elicit typical reactions from the organism. In neurological terms, the experience of the first stage left a neurological generalization trace, which gave rise to generalizing behaviour after the neutral stimulus S_2 began to elicit observable reactions.

Most generalizing behaviour which derives from the exposure to verbal pairing situations derives from latent generalization traces, i.e. neurological traces that produce latent generalization effects. This is because most of the entities that play the role of second stimuli in ostensive learning processes are neutral stimuli. The entities to which a child learns to apply ostensive terms such as 'table', 'tree', 'song', 'sweet', 'big', or 'nice', do not usually elicit typical reactions from normal children. Still, the latent generalization traces will normally show their hidden potential, once the child learns to react to these entities in certain circumstances. In particular, the circumstances described in the beginning of **49** for testing a child's ability to apply an expression to certain entities, can be used for eliciting typical reactions from stimuli that are generally neutral. For example, we ask a child 'Show me a table!'. If the child points to a table (rather than, say, to his dog or to a window), he is making a reaction which is, in these circumstances, a typical reaction to the presence of a table.

Notice that performing such a reaction is an instance of *generalizing* behaviour, because the sound 'table' which occurs in the verbal order is merely similar to (not identical with) the utterance of 'table' which the child heard when he ostensively learnt the meaning of the term. Likewise, the table need not be identical with the original table which the child saw on this occasion. It is sufficient that it belongs to the class which the child uses to generalize from the original table, i.e. to the generalization class that derives from this table.

One of the conditions for sensory preconditioning to occur is that the two stimuli be salient for the organism. This condition is normally satisfied in ostensive learning. Not only are relatively loud sounds salient for children, but they also learn to pay attention to finer phonetic distinctions, once they have observed that such distinctions are important.[6] And data about the early language of children show that the non-linguistic stimuli are also salient for children. It is almost impossible to teach young children the meanings of terms that refer to aspects of their environment that are non-salient for them, such as the meaning of 'rectangle' or of 'lobed (leaf)'.

In **51** we concluded that linguistic expectations are normally simplified descriptions of complexes of expectations. In the present section, we saw that the extensions of many ostensive terms contain relatively neutral stimuli. Together, these results explain why it is not always easy to detect and to predict the generalizing reactions that originate in the exposure to verbal pairing situations. (In this connection, see also Quine's answer (1973: 15) to Chomsky's claim (1969: 57) that the notion "probability of a sentence" is a useless one.)

53   Different Types of Linguistic Generalization Process

In **51**, I examined certain experiences that may induce a child to replace an expectation about the relation between a verbal expression E and a class of entities C by a complex of expectations, usually of restricted or disjunctive expectations. These changes are normally not reflected in the descriptions one gives of the results of these experiences. By saying, for example, that a child has learned to associate 'dog' with certain quadrupeds, we do not mention the fact that he does not expect utterances of 'dog' to be followed *always* by the appearance of such quadrupeds. The simplified linguistic expectations that express the effects of the different experiences mention only the basic aspects of the complex of expectations acquired in the experiences. (See also the discussion of (2) and (3) in **50**.)

In this section, I investigate changes in expectations which we normally take into account when describing the effects of the relevant experiences. In addition, I discuss certain ostensive learning processes that are based on some of the other generalization processes dealt with in Parts I and II.

Consider a child who has learned by ostension that 'ship' applies to ships, and who then notices that some of the elements of his generalization class that originates in the sound 'ship' do not apply to ships but rather to sheep. The child might first conjecture the disjunctive expectation that these sounds apply sometimes to ships and sometimes to sheep. But further experiences of this kind, together with the child's tendency to engage in hypothesis behaviour (see **32**), will probably induce the child to pay attention to the acoustic difference between 'ship' and 'sheep'. This will then allow him to replace the disjunctive linguistic expectation by two restricted linguistic expectations: one connecting 'ship' with ships and the other 'sheep' with sheep.

Now when describing the child's linguistic expectations regarding ships and sheep, one usually acknowledges the effects of these experiences by writing 'ship' in one case and 'sheep' in the other. With this, one indicates that the child does distinguish between these types of utterances.

Another type of restricting process, and one that plays a very important role in language learning, concerns the non-verbal stimulus rather than the verbal one. Consider, for example, the word 'dog'. Children who begin to learn the meaning of this term, by seeing dogs while hearing utterances of 'dog' (or 'doggy' or 'wow-wow', etc.), usually "overgeneralize". Their generalization class M, which originates in the observed dogs, is normally wider than the class to which most speakers of English apply the word 'dog'; it normally contains all kinds of medium-sized quadrupeds (see e.g. Clark 1973). But undergoing appropriate falsifying experiences generally enables children to replace the linguistic expectation that all M are called 'dog', by the restricted linguistic expectation that only the M which have some discriminating feature F are called 'dog'. F may be the typical shape of a dog's head, the property (to be able) to bark, or any other feature which children use in order to distinguish between the M that are called 'dog' and those that are not named with this term (see also **29** and **32**).

If we have reason to assume that a child has made such a restriction, then we will try to express it in the linguistic expectation we attribute to the child. Instead of saying that the child has the expectation 'All M are called 'dog'', we will say that he has replaced this expectation by the restricted one 'All M that are F are called 'dog''.

Learning the meaning of 'poodle' requires additional falsifying experiences and the observation of additional discriminating features. Such experiences may enable the child to learn to apply 'poodle' only to those dogs that have additional discriminating features. Finally, learning to apply 'Fido' to the appearances of a particular dog only (and perhaps of his twin brother) requires further experiences of this type (cf. Part II, n. 15).

The generalization classes used by the child can also be expanded (criterial) generalization classes. Consider the process by which a child learns the meaning of 'toy'. Suppose he hears an utterance of the term while seeing a ball and also while seeing a train. Such experiences may induce him to acquire the linguistic expectation:

(1)   Balls as well as trains are called 'toy'.

But will the child now also generalize from the balls and the trains to, say, little blocks? Will he also be able to apply 'toy' to such blocks, even if he has not heard utterances of the term while seeing little blocks? The answer is that once the class containing balls, trains, and little blocks becomes a generalization class for the child, he can make the generalization. Our analysis in **38** shows that the union of the three classes can become an expanded generalization class if the child undergoes experiences that enable him to acquire the expectation that the elements of the classes share an expected property P. And, indeed, it is very likely that the child will have such experiences. He observes elements of each of the classes and he notes that they share the property of being objects with which one can play. Once the child has acquired the corresponding expectation

(2)   One can play with balls, trains, and little blocks

the union of the three classes is likely to become an expanded generalization class for the child. Hence, he is now able to use the union as a generalization class with respect to other expected properties, including the property "to be called 'toy'". Consequently, he may now have the capacity to apply 'toy' to little blocks even though he has heard utterances of the term only in the presence of balls and trains.

By undergoing more experiences of this kind, the child acquires the capacity to apply the term 'toy' to additional classes with respect to which he acquires the expectation that one can play with their elements. Eventually, he learns to apply the term to most of the objects adults call 'toy' (see also Stemmer 1978).

Psycholinguists usually describe such learning processes by using the notion of a function. Thus they might describe the process of learning the meaning of 'toy' as learning to associate this term with the function "to be something with which one can play" (cf. Nelson 1974). Our analysis makes it clear that the psychological processes by which one learns to associate a function with a verbal expression are actually generalization processes. They are processes in which an organism's generalization class agrees with an expanded generalization class.

Children can also learn to apply terms to feature generalization classes. They learn this by undergoing the experiences described in **41**. For example, a child may learn in this way that 'red' applies to the elements of the feature class U which contains only red elements.[7] Psycholinguists may speak in these cases of learning to associate an expression with a property or a feature.

The child, then, by going through appropriate experiences and by using many of his innate and acquired capacities—e.g. his generalizing capacities, his perceptions of salience, his restricting dispositions, etc.—learns to associate meanings with ostensive terms. These meanings become gradually more similar to the meanings which adults associate with the terms. In these learning processes a crucial role is played by the very strong species-uniformity of the capacities the child is applying. Because of this uniformity, children, who undergo similar experiences, learn to apply the terms they hear in these experiences to generalization classes that are significantly similar. Were there no such uniformity, then even going through exactly the same experiences would not produce the acquisition of similar linguistic knowledge. For suppose that some children born in an English-speaking community had the disposition to generalize from poodles to the class of dogs while others to the class of non-ravens. Then the meanings which these children would learn to associate with 'doggy' would be different. The behavioural effects of the neurological traces formed in the experiences would be radically different.

It is important to notice, however, that the uniformity between the capacities is not sufficient to ensure a uniform use of ostensive terms. The children must also have learning experiences that are significantly similar. Yet, most data show that the ostensive pairing situations to which children of the same linguistic community are exposed are indeed very similar (cf. Ninio 1980).

54 Contextual Ostensive Processes

In the processes examined so far, the child could learn the meaning of a term without having to know the meanings of other terms. Very soon, however, the learning processes become more sophisticated, and although they may still be ostensive—the learning occurs as a consequence of an exposure to a pairing situation—they require the knowledge of other terms. Consider, for example, the difference between learning to apply 'dog' to a class of entities and learning to apply 'holds' to a class of aspects. A child can learn to associate 'dog' with the elements of class M by hearing an utterance of the term while a dog is nearby. Since dogs are frequently salient for children, the dog will often attract the child's attention. It is therefore likely that the child will pay attention to the "correct" aspect of the stimulus situation. But a holding aspect is normally not sufficiently salient to attract his attention. Therefore, hearing an utterance of 'holds' while a holding aspect is present, e.g. while the child's father is holding a ball, will generally be insufficient for enabling the child to acquire an expectation that is even partially correct. But suppose the child already associates 'Daddy' and 'the ball' with the appropriate entities, i.e. with his father and with balls. Then, hearing an utterance of 'Daddy holds the ball', while the child sees his father holding a ball, may be sufficient to draw the child's attention to the relevant aspect, the aspect that is "related" to the father and the ball. Therefore, such an experience may indeed enable the child to learn to associate utterances of 'holds' with a class of aspects (perhaps only when 'holds' occurs within a suitable context, e.g. together with 'Uncle John . . . the book').

These processes will be called *contextual* ostensive processes. The learning is by exposure to verbal pairing situations, but it requires knowing the meanings of at least part of the context terms. In our example, the child has to know the meanings of 'Daddy' and 'the ball'. (For more details on such learning processes, see Stemmer 1971b, 1973b, 1978.)

Contextual ostensive processes play an important role in language acquisition. It is very likely that many children learn the first meanings of terms such as 'heavier', 'is longer than', 'under', 'that is' (as 'house that is red'), or 'with' in these processes.[8]

The terms which a person has learned in contextual ostensive processes will also be called *ostensive terms*. But in order to distinguish between the ostensive terms that were learned without the help of context terms and those that were learned with their help, I will sometimes call the former *isolated* ostensive terms and the latter *contextual* ostensive terms.

The experiences by which a person learns to apply a contextual ostensive term to a class of entities (aspects, relations, actions, etc.) leave, as usual, a trace in the person's neurological (or mental) system. Again, we identify the trace with the meaning which the term has acquired for the person. Moreover, in order to individuate the meaning—i.e. the trace—we again use principally the extension which the term has acquired for the person, that is, the corresponding theoretical generalization class. In the present case, however, it is often not easy to determine the extension. Nevertheless, with some ingenuity, it may be possible to arrive at relatively satisfactory conclusions. For instance, we can ask a child 'Does Uncle John hold the ball?', while his uncle is throwing a ball. On the basis of his answers to such questions we may be able to determine (probabilistically, of course) the class of aspects to which the child has learned to apply the term 'holds', or the class of situations to which he has learned to apply expressions of the form '. . . holds . . .'. Once we have determined the extension of a contextual ostensive term for a person, we can then use it for individuating the meaning which the term has acquired for him.

55   Non-ostensive Compounds and Creativity

A creative capacity. Contextual ostensive processes give rise to very wide generalization classes. The child acquires what has been called a *creative* capacity (see e.g. Chomsky 1968: 10). He is now able to understand and produce new combinations of terms, provided the terms themselves are old terms, terms whose meanings he already knows. For example, if he has learned 'holds' by hearing 'Daddy holds the ball' (while observing a corresponding situation), he now understands not only further utterances of 'Daddy holds the ball' but also of other expressions, e.g. of 'Uncle John holds the book', provided he already knows the meaning of 'Uncle John' and 'the book'. Similarly, the child who has learned the meaning of 'with' by hearing 'bread with cheese' (while seeing bread with cheese) is able to understand new compounds such as 'toast with jam' if the already knows the meaning of 'toast' and 'jam'. He acquires the capacity to apply this new compound to the class of slices of toast with jam.

New compounds (of old terms) are usually non-ostensive expressions for the child, even if each of their components is ostensive. The child in our example did not acquire the capacity to apply 'toast with jam' because he heard an utterance of this compound while paying attention to toast with jam. He has the capacity because he has previously learned the meanings of 'toast', 'with', and 'jam'.[9]

Expressing this in neurological (or mental) terms, we attribute the child's capacity to apply the compound 'toast with jam' to toast with jam to the previous formation of application traces corresponding to 'toast', 'with', and 'jam'. Because of the existence of these traces, an utterance of 'toast with jam' produces in the child a particular neurological state. And it is this state which then allows him to apply 'toast with jam' to toast with jam.

So far, I have always spoken of neurological (or mental) *traces*. Here I am using the expression neurological *state*. This terminological difference does not intend to express an essential difference. It only hints at a difference in origin. If a person is learning the meaning of a new expression by undergoing an appropriate experience, then I generally speak of the *trace* that is left by the experience. But if he hears the utterance of an old expression or of a combination of old expressions, then I usually speak of the *state* that is formed by the activation of the traces that were left when the old expressions were learned.

Activation processes. We have seen that a child who has learned the meanings of contextual ostensive terms usually acquires the creative capacity to apply new compounds to the elements of certain classes, such as the compounds 'toast with jam' or 'Uncle John holds the book'. We attribute this capacity to a neurological (or mental) state which comes into existence when the child hears an utterance of the compound. The utterance activates the neurological traces corresponding to the old terms of the compound, and this activation produces the state.

If we wish to use these neurological states for explanatory or predictive purposes, we need a method for individuating them. I will now consider the individuation of such states by considering first the neurological state corresponding to the compound 'toast with jam', say the state tj. I assume that the terms 'toast' 'with' and 'jam' are ostensive, whereas the compound is non-ostensive; it is a new combination of old terms. Moreover, I assume that the neurological traces corresponding to 'toast', 'with', and 'jam'— whose activation gives rise to the state tj—are the traces t, j, and w.

As usual, there are two main instruments for individuating the neurological state tj: its effects and its origin. Beginning with the former, we note that just as with ostensive terms, the most specific effect of tj is reflected in the extension which the compound 'toast with jam' has for the child. Therefore, if we observe that the child applies the compound to the elements of the class TJ, we can use TJ for individuating tj. TJ distinguishes tj from states that give rise to different extensions, and it hints at the behaviour that is elicited by utterances of the compound.

But as will be seen in the sequel, there are reasons to believe that the extension TJ may be insufficient for giving a satisfactory individuation to tj (see the discussion of 'animals with a heart' and 'animals with kidneys' in **59**). This therefore confers great importance on the second individuating instrument of tj: the origin of this state.

The origin of state tj is, as said earlier, the activation of the traces t, w, and j, as a consequence of an utterance of 'toast with jam'. This activation process is, of course, non-observational. We therefore need a method for individuating the process, in order to use it for scientific purposes. Such a method has been discussed in **7**. We concluded there that the generalization class which originates in the exposure to a pairing situation gives a good individuation to the activation of the trace that is left in the exposure. For the class contains those entities that activate the trace (thus inducing the organism to give the typical reaction R).

Let us now apply this method to our problem. Suppose that the child's extension for the ostensive term 'toast' is the class T. Consequently, T is the generalization class which derives from the non-linguistic stimulus of the ostensive experience that left trace t in the child's neurological (or mental) system, and its elements are the entities that activate this trace. (Perceiving an element of T may induce the child to give a typical reaction. For example, he may say 'toast' rather than keeping silent.) The extension T gives us therefore a good individuation of the activation of trace t, and it distinguishes it from the activation of other traces.

Trace t is also activated by other entities: utterances of the term 'toast'. This activation will also often elicit typical reactions from the child. In particular, the activation of t by utterances of 'Show me some toast' or even of the single term 'toast' will often induce the child to point to an element of T rather than to elements of other classes.[10] Here, the extension T is the (theoretical) generalization class which derives from the second stimulus of the ostensive experience in which the child hears first an utterance of 'toast' and then sees some toast. Now, our discussion in **8** shows that this class reflects again the specific nature of trace t. We can therefore use T for individuating not only the activation of t by elements of T but also the activation of this trace by utterances of 'toast'. T allows us to distinguish between the activation of t by an utterance of 'toast' and the activation of other traces by utterances of other terms.

Now, the neurological (or mental) state tj is formed when an utterance of 'toast with jam' activates the traces t, w, and j. Since T gives a good individuation to the activation of t by an utterance of 'toast', it allows us to individuate the contribution of this activation to state tj.

Similar conclusions hold for the other contributors to the state tj—the activation of the traces w and j by the utterance of 'with' and 'jam'. The extensions of these expressions also individuate the corresponding activation processes, and therefore the corresponding contributions to state tj. Consequently, we can use for the individuation of state tj not only the extension of 'toast with jam'—the effects of tj—but also the extensions of the components of 'toast with jam'. The latter reflect the psychologically relevant features of the origin of tj: the activation processes of the traces t, w, and j.

The individuation of the neurological (or mental) traces and states that have been discussed in this essay is always indirect, since we have no direct access to the traces and states. It is therefore very important to take into account all the relevant evidence we possess in order to individuate such neurological entities. An individuation that considers only part of the evidence may be insufficient.[11] Therefore, our analysis of the individuation of tj suggests the following conclusion regarding the individuation of the neurological state s, which corresponds to a person's understanding of a non-ostensive compound c of ostensive terms. Suppose the extension of c is C and the extensions of the ostensive terms that make up c are E_1, E_2, .., E_n. Then, we should use not only C but also the extensions E_1, E_2, .., E_n for individuating state s. Since the latter extensions reflect the activation processes of the corresponding ostensive traces, they reflect the psychologically relevant features of the origin of s.

Consider, for example, the compounds 'toast with jam' and 'jar with jam', and let us assume that we have no data at all concerning the extensions which these compounds have for a child. Then we still have tools that might allow us to distinguish between the neurological states that correspond to the compounds, say the states tj and jj. If we observe that the child applies 'toast' to toast and 'jar' to jars, then the difference between the two extensions shows that the traces corresponding to these terms are different. This therefore suggests that the activation of these traces by utterances of the compounds produces differences in the states tj and jj.

I have concluded only that the evidence *suggests* that the states are different. The reason for avoiding a stronger conclusion is that we have no exact knowledge about the effects of the activation of the traces corresponding to the other terms of the compounds. Perhaps the activation of the trace which corresponds to 'with' eliminates completely the difference between the activation of the traces which correspond to 'toast' and 'jar'. Still, this is unlikely. For the extensions of most compounds of the form 'X with Y' suggest that the activation of the trace of 'with' does not have such effects. Take the compounds 'toast with jam' and 'toast with cheese'. The only difference between them is the one between 'jam' and 'cheese'. Yet, this difference is sufficient to produce different neurological states. For the difference between the extensions of the compounds shows that the states have different effects. Consequently, the activation of the trace of 'with' does not cancel the difference between the activation of the traces of 'jam' and 'cheese'. And similar results obtain for most compounds of the form 'X with Y'.

A highly interesting conclusion follows from our discussion. Let s be the neurological state corresponding to a non-ostensive compound of ostensive terms. The origin of s consists of the activation of the neurological traces of the ostensive terms. Hence, the origin of s is clearly non-observational. Nevertheless, we often possess very good information about the psychologically relevant features of this origin. The extensions of the ostensive terms give a very good individuation to the processes produced by activations of their traces, i.e. to the contribution of these activations to the state s. They therefore reflect strongly the psychologically relevant features of the origin of s.

This conclusion presumes the validity of the assumption that the exposure to pairing situations, including verbal pairing situations, leaves specific neurological or mental traces which are activated by the elements of the corresponding generalization classes. This assumption is, of course, not supported by direct evidence. It is the conclusion of an inference to a good explanation and it has, like many other conclusions of such inferences, a hypothetical character (see **7** and **10**). This is no reason, however, for rejecting it so long as no alternative explanation is available that is less hypothetical. But so far as I know, there exists no explanation which is hypothetical to a lower degree, and which accounts for generalizing behaviour, including the generalizing behaviour that occurs in language acquisition.

Let me also point out that, although I assume the existence of non-observable traces and activation processes, the individuation of these entities is based on behavioural evidence, mainly on the appropriate generalization classes. This is important when one compares our account with alternative approaches. For the behavioural individuation diminishes considerably the degree to which our account is hypothetical.

The individuation of meanings of non-ostensive compounds. What consequences do our conclusions have for the notion of meaning? We decided above to identify the meanings of ostensive terms with corresponding neurological (or mental) traces, and to individuate the meanings—i.e. the traces—with the help of their extensions. Now, the meanings of non-ostensive compounds of ostensive terms such as 'toast with jam' or 'Uncle John holds the book' can also be identified with the appropriate neurological states. But the extensions of the compounds do not always completely individuate the meanings, i.e. the states. We receive a more complete individuation if we also consider their origins. The origins are the activation processes of the neurological traces that correspond to the ostensive terms which make up the compounds—the traces that are activated by utterances of the compounds. Since these processes receive a very complete individuation from the extensions of the ostensive terms, we can therefore also use these extensions for individuating the meanings of the (non-ostensive) compounds. Although it is sometimes not easy to determine these extensions, very often there are no special problems involved. In these cases, we can give a relatively satisfactory individuation to the meanings of the compounds by using these extensions, in addition to the extensions of the compounds themselves.

These conclusions can be summarized in the form of a thesis. But since we will obtain similar conclusions with respect to non-ostensive terms, I will later (58) formulate a general thesis that covers both the individuation of non-ostensive compounds and of non-ostensive terms.

In 51 we decided to represent the meaning of an ostensive term by [C], where *C* is the extension of the term. We see that it would be a mistake to adopt this method for non-ostensive compounds, since the extension may be insufficient to give a satisfactory individuation to the meaning of the compound.

56   Non-ostensive Learning Processes; Conclusion CN

Further developments take place. The child learns so-called semantic and syntactic formation rules including transformation rules, again with the help of his generalizing capacities. (See Stemmer 1973b, 1981b.) But I will not enter into this here. What I want to discuss is another kind of processes that enable children to learn the meanings of new terms. These processes, too, are generalizing processes, but they are not based on exposure to pairing situations. They will be called *non-ostensive* learning processes.

Consider the English terms 'therefore', 'idea', 'abstract', 'to deduce', 'evolution' or 'meaning'. It is clear that no one has learned to apply these terms to classes of entities—aspects, relations, objects, etc.—by hearing utterances of the terms while perceiving the entities that were being named, i.e. by exposure to ostensive pairing situations. Rather, these terms were learned by hearing them within an appropriate verbal context, and the paired situation was normally irrelevant. Such learning processes are therefore non-ostensive. (There is actually a gradual transition from learning processes where the paired situation is relevant, and those where they play no role at all (see e.g. Stemmer 1973b: 87ff). But I will not study these processes in this book.)

Non-ostensive learning processes have many important characteristics, and some of them I have already investigated (1973b, 1979a). I will examine here two characteristics that bear directly upon the notion of meaning. The first will be discussed here and in **57-9**, and the second in **60**.

The first characteristic concerns the crucial role performed by the context terms in non-ostensive learning processes. A person can learn the meaning of a new term in a non-ostensive process only if he knows the meanings of at least a minimal number of the terms that make up the verbal context. Suppose a six-year-old child does not associate a meaning with the terms 'ardillas', 'pardas' and 'polars'. Then hearing an utterance of

(1)   Polars are ardillas pardas

will usually not enable the child to acquire a (correct or incorrect) linguistic expectation. On the other hand, if he hears an utterance of

(2)   Polars are white bears

and if he already knows the meaning of 'are' and of 'white bears', then he will normally acquire a linguistic expectation. He will acquire the capacity to apply the term 'polar' to a class that is close to the class of white bears.

What is the difference between hearing (1) and (2)? Why does the child learn something in the latter case but not in the former? The most plausible answer—the inference to the best explanation (cf. **22**)—is to attribute this to the fact that in the latter case the child already knows the meanings of the relevant context terms while in the former he does not. Hence, only in the latter case has the child's neurological (or mental) system application traces that correspond to the context terms 'white' and 'bear'.[12] Hearing an utterance of (2) activates these traces which brings into existence the state corresponding to the meaning of the compound 'white bear'. And this state, or a very similar state, becomes now the application trace of the new term 'polar' which appeared in (2).

This explains why the new trace gives the child the capacity to apply the term 'polar' to a class that is close to, perhaps even identical with, the class he associates with 'white bear'.

On the other hand, the child has no application traces corresponding to 'ardillas' and 'pardas'. Therefore, hearing an utterance of (1) produces no neurological state that may give rise to an application trace for the term 'polars'.

Our discussion suggests the validity of the following conclusion about non-ostensive learning processes:

> CN   If a person learns the meaning of a new expression *E* in a non-ostensive process, then the application trace that is formed in the person's neurological (or mental) system is very similar to, probably even identical with, the trace or state corresponding to the particular combination of the (old) context terms.

Let me also formulate CN by using more extensively the notion of meaning:

> CN′   If a person learns the meaning of a new term *E* in a non-ostensive process, then the meaning which *E* acquires for the person is very similar to, probably even identical with, the meaning he has learned to associate with the particular combination of the (old) context terms.

CN is an inference to the best explanation. It is only supported, not verified, by the phenomena it explains. Moreover, CN expresses only some very general features of non-ostensive learning. It must be refined considerably. But for the purposes of this essay, this rough formulation is sufficient.

CN is of course not new. Similar ideas have been formulated by other people such as Osgood (1953), Carnap (1956), Quine (1960, 1975), and Staats (1968). Moreover, Osgood suggests that non-ostensive learning processes are some kind of second-order conditioning processes. This position is also adopted in Stemmer (1973b).[13]

One of the reasons why CN is a plausible conclusion is that it expresses our casual intuitions. Whatever a person learns in a non-ostensive process, it can derive only from what he has learned about the context terms. There are no other sources, since we assume that the paired situation is irrelevant. The only factor that can help the child to learn something about 'polar' when hearing an utterance of (2) is the meaning he has learned to associate with 'white bears', i.e. the neurological state corresponding to this compound. Since we are assuming that the situation is non-ostensive, the child has no other elements available to him.

This intuition is confirmed by the results of non-ostensive learning processes. A child who hears an utterance of (2) and who is aware of the irrelevance of the paired situation, normally learns to apply 'polars' to white bears and not to (say) white eggs. According to *CN*, the reason is that (2) contains the term 'bear', and the meaning of this term is related to bears and not to eggs. And even if the child has already learned to associate the meaning [eggs] with some term, say, with 'egg'—that is, the child's neurological system already has a trace that is related to eggs— this meaning will not suddenly make its appearance in the meaning of the new term 'polar', since the term 'egg' does not occur in (2). To be sure, it is possible that, perhaps by mistake, the child has learned to associate 'bear' with a class that contains eggs. But in this case, of course, the result of the learning process—the child applies 'polar' to white eggs—is again a supporting instance of *CN*.

One can also learn the meanings of new terms in non-ostensive processes in which some or all of the context terms are themselves *non-ostensive terms*, i.e. terms that the person has learned in non-ostensive processes. According to *CN*, the meanings that are learned in these processes are also very similar to the meaning of the combination of the old context terms. Suppose the child in our example hears an utterance of:

(3)   Bipolars are big polars.

Such an experience will usually give the child the capacity to apply 'bipolar' to a class that is very similar to the class of big white bears and clearly different from (say) the class of small brown eggs.[14]

The process can continue of course. For instance, the same child may learn the meanings of new non-ostensive terms with the help of the non-ostensive term 'bipolar'.

This suggests that terms can be ordered in a hierarchy. Ostensive terms belong to the zero order, a non-ostensive term that is learned with the help of only ostensive terms belongs to the first order, etc. In general, if a term V is learned with the help of a combination of context terms in a non-ostensive learning process, and if the highest order of the terms of the combination is n, then V belongs to the order $n + 1$.

Applying this hierarchy to our example, we note that 'polar' belongs to the first order. Its meaning derives from the meanings of the zero order ostensive terms 'white' and 'bear'. The non-ostensive term 'bipolar' belongs to the second order. Its meaning derives from the first order non-ostensive term 'polar' and from the zero order ostensive term 'big'.

57   The Ostensive Basis of Non-ostensive Meanings

In the examples of non-ostensive processes given in the previous section, the meanings of the old context terms had a relatively clear character. But the child can also learn the meanings of non-ostensive terms with the help of less definite meanings. Suppose that instead of hearing sentence (2) of **56**, the child hears an utterance of:

(1)   Polars are friends of bears.

It is likely that the child will often not be sure whether a particular entity does or does not belong to the extension of 'polar'. But the degree of indeterminacy will usually be identical with the one that affects the extension of the context terms 'friends of bears'. Moreover, whatever (indefinite) extension the child learns to associate with 'polar', it will be very similar to the one he has learned to associate with 'friends of bears', and therefore clearly different from the one he associates with (say) 'legs of bears'.[15]

This shows that conclusion CN (**56**) also applies to such non-ostensive learning processes. The meanings of the new terms are very similar to those of the old context terms.

But what about non-ostensive processes in which a person learns the meanings of terms such as 'therefore', 'besides', or 'abstract'? Does CN also hold for these processes? In order to answer this question, it is necessary to examine such learning processes more closely. Consider the term 'therefore'. There is no doubt that children do not learn the meaning of this term ostensively. Rather, they learn it by hearing some kind of discourse in which 'therefore' occurs. What this discourse consists of is almost impossible to determine. But whatever it is, the meaning which 'therefore' acquires for the child who hears such a discourse derives exclusively from the meanings of the terms that appear in the discourse. There are no other sources. The same holds for, say, 'besides'. Whatever the discourse that teaches the child the meaning of 'besides', the meaning derives exclusively from the meanings of the terms occurring in the discourse. And if the meanings he learns to associate with 'therefore' and 'besides' are indeed different, then the discourses must have been different. Only this can explain the difference between the meanings.

Moreover, whatever the meanings the terms acquire, they derive from the known terms of the discourse. The unknown terms contribute nothing. Suppose a child has already learned the meaning of 'concept' but not of 'idea' and 'abstract'. Then, whatever the child learns to associate with 'idea' when hearing an utterance of

(2)   An idea is an abstract concept

it derives from the known term 'concept'. The term 'abstract' contributes nothing. There is also no "mutual support" between the unknown terms 'idea' and 'abstract'. Example (2) gives the child the same information as we receive from:

(3)   An X is a Y-concept.

And clearly we can neither learn something about 'X' from 'Y' nor about 'Y' from 'X'.

Our discussion suggests that conclusion CN also applies to the meanings which a person learns to associate in non-ostensive processes with terms such as 'therefore', 'besides', 'abstract', or 'idea'. The meanings which these terms acquire—the neurological traces—derive exclusively from the meanings of the known context terms. There are no sudden intrusions of meanings corresponding to terms that do not occur in the contextual discourse.

An important conclusion can be derived from our analysis. The meaning of a non-ostensive term derives from the meanings of the relevant context terms. These meanings fall into two categories, depending on whether the context terms are ostensive or non-ostensive. The meanings of the ostensive context terms derive directly from the relevant stimulus of the paired situation (see **51**). The meanings of the non-ostensive context terms derive again from the meanings of the relevant context terms, and the process repeats itself. But since there are no extraneous intrusions, there is a point where the process finishes. All the context terms are ostensive, i.e. they belong to the zero order. It follows that the meaning of a non-ostensive term derives ultimately from the meanings of the ostensive terms with which it is *directly or indirectly connected.*

The totality of the meanings of the ostensive terms from which the meaning of a non-ostensive expression E derives will be called the *ultimate* or the *ostensive* meaning origin of E.

58   The Individuation of Non-ostensive Meanings: Thesis T3

The meanings of non-ostensive expressions will be called *non-ostensive* meanings. As usual, we identify these meanings with the corresponding neurological traces or states. Now, in order to give a scientific status to the notion of non-ostensive meanings, we need criteria for individuating the meanings. Again, our main individuating tools are the effects of the meanings and their origin. The effects we determine principally on the basis of the extensions which the terms acquire for the person who has learned their meanings.[16] But just as with non-ostensive compounds (see **55**), the extensions of non-ostensive terms do not always give us the best information about the neurological traces or states that give origin to the meanings (see the discussion of the non-ostensive terms 'centaur' and 'unicorn' in **59**).

In order to obtain more information about non-ostensive meanings, we must pay more attention to their origin. Now, we have seen that the meaning origin of a non-ostensive expression E is the combined meaning of the relevant context terms, i.e. the neurological trace or state which is activated by an utterance of the context terms. This points to two possibilities, depending on whether the context terms are ostensive or whether some or all of them are non-ostensive. In the former case, the individuation of the meanings of the context terms is achieved with the help of their extensions (see **51**), and we can therefore use this individuation in order to individuate the meaning of E. In the latter case, we examine these alternatives with respect to the non-ostensive context terms until we arrive at the non-ostensive context terms of the first level. The context terms of these terms are ostensive, and we can therefore individuate the meanings of these ostensive terms with the help of their extensions. These meanings constitute the ultimate meaning origin of the non-ostensive expression E. By then working upwards, we can individuate the meanings of the non-ostensive context terms of each level with the help of the extensions that individuate the ultimate meaning origin of E, until we obtain an individuation of the meaning of E that is based on these extensions.

Our analysis suggests the validity of the following thesis which will be called the *modest thesis of extensionalism for non-ostensive meanings*:

T3   The meaning of a non-ostensive expression E can be individuated on the basis of its extension and of the extensions of the ostensive terms with which E is directly or indirectly connected.

Thesis T3 is modest in several senses. First, with respect to many terms, including ostensive terms such as 'is-greater-than', 'holds', or 'with' it is very difficult to determine their extension. When applications of T3 require the use of such extensions, the practical value of T3 is thus greatly reduced. Second, with respect to many, perhaps even most non-ostensive terms it is very difficult to reconstruct the verbal context that gives them their meanings. Even in those cases where we can formulate plausible hypotheses about the context, we usually still have problems in finding out the ostensive terms with which these context terms are directly or indirectly connected. Thus let us make the plausible assumption that speakers of English normally learn the meaning of 'bachelor' by hearing something like 'A bachelor is an unmarried male'. We then still have the problem of finding out the ostensive terms from which the meaning of 'unmarried' and perhaps even of 'male' is derived.

Finally, and this is perhaps the most important reason for qualifying the extensionalist thesis T3 as modest, we do not individuate the meaning of a non-ostensive expression on the basis of its own extension only. We also need the extensions of the other terms mentioned in the thesis.

We can thus individuate the meanings of verbal expressions, at least in principle, with the help of the extensions of ostensive terms. These extensions are the theoretical generalization classes used by the child to generalize from the non-linguistic stimulus of the relevant ostensive pairing situation. We must recall, however, the crucial role played by conscious or unconscious introspection in the determination of theoretical generalization classes (see **15**). It follows that although we can individuate meanings with the help of certain classes, our knowledge of the nature of these classes is essentially based on introspective knowledge.

We see that the extensionality of T3 is strongly dependent on introspection. Is this a further reason for qualifying it as a modest thesis? At first blush, we might tend to give an affirmative answer. But a moment of reflexion shows that this would be a mistake. The need for using introspection in determining theoretical generalization classes does not derive from linguistic considerations. It is implicit in our notion of generalization class which belongs to the general learning theory GT. And the role of introspection in determining the extensions of verbal expressions— i.e. ultimately in the individuation of their meanings—is merely a consequence of the fact that extensions are generalization classes. Consequently, the dependence of the notion of extension on introspection holds not only for non-ostensive but also for ostensive terms.

59   Two Applications of T3

In the literature, various examples have been given illustrating the fact that the extension of an expression is often insufficient for individuating its meaning. I will examine two of them in the light of our thesis T3. Our conclusions will give direct support to this thesis.

Consider the compound expressions 'animals with a heart' and 'animals with kidneys'. These compounds have the same extension. Nevertheless, we would intuitively say that they have different meanings.

This result does not have to surprise us. Since people do not normally learn the correct meanings of the compounds by having ostensive experiences, the compounds are non-ostensive. It is therefore possible that their extensions do not completely individuate their meanings.

Since this seems to be the case, T3 suggests basing the individuation of these meanings not only on the extensions of the compounds but also on the extensions of the ostensive terms with which the compounds are directly or indirectly connected. Let us assume that the constituents of the compounds, namely 'animals', 'with', 'a heart', and 'kidneys' are ostensive. The non-ostensive compounds are then directly connected with the ostensive constituents, and their meanings derive from the combined meanings of the constituents (i.e. the neurological states which correspond to the meanings of the compounds derive from the activation of the traces of the constituents). Now, the extensions of 'a heart' and 'kidneys' are different. Consequently, T3 suggests (but does not prove) that the meanings of the compound expressions are indeed different. Some of the terms with which the compounds are directly connected have different extensions.

We cannot prove that the meanings are different, because of the reasons given in the last part of **55**. It is possible that the activation of the trace corresponding to 'with'—the meaning of this term—cancels the difference between the traces of 'a heart' and 'kidneys' in the compounds 'animal with a heart' and 'animal with kidneys'. It follows that although we use different elements when individuating the meanings of the compounds—the different extensions of 'a heart' and 'kidneys'—it is possible that this difference is not reflected in these meanings.

Still, this is unlikely. For we have seen that the extensions of most compounds of the form '*X* with *Y*' support the conclusion that the meaning of 'with' does not cancel a difference between the meanings of the other terms. It is therefore reasonable to conclude that the individuation method suggested by T3 indeed enables us to distinguish between the meanings of the compounds 'animals with a heart' and 'animals with kidneys'.

I have been assuming that the constituents of the compounds are ostensive. This assumption is unnecessary, however. Suppose that 'a heart' and 'kidneys' are non-ostensive. Since they have different extensions, their meanings are different, which means that the origins of these meanings are different. Consequently, some of the extensions of the ostensive terms with which 'a heart' is directly or indirectly connected are different from those of the ostensive terms that have such connection with 'kidneys'. Hence, in this case, too, T3 strongly suggests that the meanings of the compounds 'animals with a heart' and 'animals with kidneys' are indeed different; their ultimate (ostensive) meaning origins are different.

The second example concerns the terms 'centaur' and 'unicorn'. Both have the same extension—the empty class—yet our intuitions tell us that their meanings are different for normal speakers of English. Now, these terms are non-ostensive.[17] Hence, it is possible that their extensions do not individuate their meanings (see **58**). T3 therefore suggests basing the individuation of the meanings not only on the extensions of these non-ostensive terms but also on the extensions of the ostensive terms with which they are directly or indirectly connected. To be sure, it is not easy to determine which are these ostensive terms. It is likely, however, that many people have learned the meanings of the two terms by hearing sentences such as 'A centaur is (like) a horse with human body, arms, and head' and 'A unicorn is a (fabulous) animal with horse's body and single straight horn'. Hence, among the ostensive terms with which 'centaur' and 'unicorn' are connected for these persons are terms that have different extensions such as 'human body' and 'horse's body'. T3 therefore suggests (but again does not prove) that for many people the meanings of 'centaur' and 'unicorn' indeed are different.

I proposed thesis T3 on the basis of our analysis of the origin of non-ostensive meanings (**58**). This gives indirect support for T3. The capacity of T3 to account for our intuitions in the cases studied here and in similar cases gives direct support for this thesis. It shows its explanatory power.

Many proposals have been advanced to account for the fact that certain expressions have identical extensions but apparently different meanings, a point raised by Frege (1892). But I will examine only Goodman's proposal (1949) which is one of the few that are expressed in relatively unproblematic terms. Goodman introduces the notions of *primary* and *secondary* extension of an expression E. The former is the extension of E and the latter is the extension of any of its compounds. He then proposes to individuate the meaning of E on the basis of its primary and secondary extension. This allows him to distinguish between the meanings of, for example, 'centaur' and 'unicorn', since the compounds 'picture of a centaur' and 'picture of a unicorn' have different extensions. But this method of individuation has the counter-intuitive consequence that if 'P' and 'Q' are different expressions, then their meanings will always be different. For inscriptions of the phrase 'a P that is not a Q' are elements of the extension of the compound 'P-description' but not of the extension of the compound 'Q-description'.

It is clear that the method of individuation based on T3 has no such consequences. If two different expressions have the same origin and effects, then the method assigns to them identical meanings.

In a later paper (1953), Goodman suggests a device which avoids the counterintuitive results. He proposes to exclude from the individuation process those compounds for which the corresponding compounds of every two terms have different extensions. However, the revised method has a strong *ad hoc* character. Why should 'centaur picture' but not 'centaur description' be used for individuating the meaning of 'centaur'? Our method, on the other hand, is not based on *ad hoc* devices. It derives from a plausible analysis of the psychological origin and effects of the relevant neurological or mental entities. This suggests that the method of individuation based on T3 is superior to Goodman's original and revised method.

60   The Extensions of Non-ostensive Terms

The second aspect of non-ostensive learning processes (see **56**) which I want to discuss concerns the extensions of non-ostensive terms. It is not difficult to specify the extensions of certain types of non-ostensive term. For instance, the extension which 'polar' has for the child who learned its meaning by hearing 'Polars are white bears' is probably the class of white bears. It becomes already more difficult to specify the extension which a person, who already knows the meaning of 'abstract' and 'concept', learns to associate with 'idea' by hearing 'Ideas are abstract concepts'. But specifying the extensions of terms such as 'therefore' and 'besides' is almost impossible. Nevertheless, it is important to realize that the *existence* of such extensions follows, almost by definition, from the fact that people can learn to use these terms quite correctly. For what does it mean to have learned to use the terms 'therefore' and 'besides'? It means that in certain circumstances, for example when telling a story, the person is able to use in certain places 'therefore' and in other places 'besides'. More exactly, in all those places— hence, in a *class* of places—where a discourse possesses a "therefore-quality", i.e. it possesses something that makes it appropriate to use 'therefore' rather than (e.g.) 'besides', the person is able to say 'therefore' or to understand it correctly when somebody else uses it in such places. On the other hand, in the class of discourse places that possess a "besides-quality", he is able to correctly use the term 'besides'.

This shows that even such terms acquire an extension for the person who learns their meaning. But since one can hardly give an intelligible description of the extensions, I make no specific use of them. In particular, I do not use the extensions for individuating the meanings of the terms. My purpose in bringing up the topic is to stress the fact that the non-ostensive learning processes in which such terms are learned are also generalizing processes. The person hears an utterance of the term in a particular verbal context and he becomes able to apply it in "similar" verbal contexts, i.e. in a class of contexts—the contexts that belong to the generalization class which derives from the particular verbal context. And this explains why the class he uses for generalizing

from the original context in which he learned 'therefore' is usually
different from the class he uses for generalizing from the context
in which he learned 'besides'. Because the original contexts were
different for him, they gave origin to different generalization classes.

Clearly, I do not maintain that we have direct evidence telling
us that the extensions of terms such as 'therefore' or 'besides'
contain entities—usually discourse locations—which have features
like therefore-features or besides-features. It is again an inference
to the best explanation. It intends to explain why children are
able to learn to apply terms such as 'therefore' and 'besides' on
different occasions—more exactly, on different classes of
occasions—as a consequence of hearing utterances of the terms on
particular occasions.

61   Terms and Sentences

So far I have spoken only of terms and expressions but not
of sentences. In this section, I want to examine some aspects of
the notion of a sentence. But I will limit myself to certain very
elementary points.

Suppose a child observes at t_1 a fire, notices that it is hot, and
consequently becomes afraid of "similar" fires. Assuming that 'fires'
and 'hot' correctly describe the corresponding generalization
classes, we can then express the effects of the experience as the
acquisition of the expectation:

(1)   All fires are hot.

Instead of the acquisition of an *expectation*, let me speak in
this section of the acquisition of *information*. We can then say
that as a consequence of the experience, the child has acquired
the information that all fires are hot, i.e. the information described
in (1).

This information has a general character; it says something
about the elements of a class of entities. Therefore, once the
child has acquired the information, he possesses a tool for
acquiring more specific information. Suppose that at t_2 the child
sees a fire. This experience may then give him the information
that may be described as:

(2)   There exists now and nearby an instance of heat.

The information received at t_2 has a very limited character. It only tells the child that now and in his neighbourhood something is happening.

In order to distinguish between the type of information received by the child at t_1 and t_2, I will say that the former is *general*, while the latter is *spatially and temporally limited*; for short, it is *limited* information. (We note that the ability to acquire such limited information depends on the prior acquisition of appropriate general information.)

Let us now suppose that a second child has a somewhat different experience at t_1. He also perceives an instance of heat, but he does not see its source. Instead of this, he hears an utterance of 'hot'. In other words, he undergoes an ostensive pairing experience in which he hears 'hot' while feeling a sensation of heat. As a consequence he may now perform typical avoidance reactions when hearing further utterances of 'hot'. Ignoring many finer points (see e.g. **51**), we can describe the information acquired by this child at t_1 as:

(3)   All utterances of 'hot' signal an instance of heat.

This information is general and, like the information described in (1), may serve as a basis for the acquisition of (spatially and temporally) limited information. For example, if at t_2 the child hears an utterance of 'hot', he may acquire the limited information described in (2).

Once the child has acquired the general information (3), language has become a useful tool for him. He can acquire limited information by hearing utterances of a verbal expression. Notice that this limited information is conveyed to the child with the help of a single term. In our example, the term is 'hot'. If a child receives such limited information with the help of a verbal expression, then I will say that the expression is a *single-term expression*. This will be extended also to other cases where as a matter of fact more terms occur, but the information is of the limited type. For instance, if an utterance of 'dog' gives the child the limited information that there is a dog in his vicinity, then 'black dog' may convey to him the limited information that there is a black dog in his vicinity. In this case 'black dog' will be called a single-term expression, standing, so to speak, for 'black-dog' or perhaps 'blackie'.

The information described in (3) is general; yet, its usefulness is rather restricted. The child can receive a warning of the presence of heat only if a person is present who is able and willing to produce an utterance of 'hot'. It would normally be more useful for the child, if he acquired the general information described in (1). In this case, he could learn about the presence of heat from a naturally occurring indicator, namely, from the sight of a fire. Now, we know that a child can usually acquire such knowledge with the help of verbal communication, for example, by hearing 'All fires are hot', or 'Fires are hot', or perhaps the still shorter 'Fire burns'. If he has already learned the meanings of the relevant terms, such utterances will normally give him the general information described in (1). This brings us to the question: how does he learn to acquire such knowledge by verbal communication? What are the psychological processes that give the child the capacity to acquire general information by hearing sentences such as 'All C are P'?

It is difficult to give a definite answer to this question. But it seems that the following hypothesis, which harmonizes with the different conclusions we have obtained so far, gives a plausible description of this learning process.

> H1   If a child has learned to associate two expressions V and W with two generalization class C and P, then the neurological trace left by an utterance of $V + W$ is behaviourally very similar to the trace left by the pairing of an element of C with an element of P.

For example, if the child already associates 'fire' with fires and 'burns' with burning sensations, then hearing 'fire burns' produces a neurological trace that is, according to H1, behaviourally very similar to the trace produced when the child sees a fire while feeling a burning sensation.

I do not want to enter into the question of whether the learning process described in H1 is directly based on innate capacities—which might perhaps point to a significant difference in the learning capacities of humans and animals—or whether it derives from the child's usual learning capacities, especially his generalizing abilities including abilities like those manifested in sensory preconditioning (see **52**) and second-order conditioning (see note 13 in **56**). The point I want to stress is that the child indeed acquires the ability to obtain, through verbal communication, the information he receives by observing the pairing of an element of a class C with an element of a class P. He receives it by hearing utterances that basically contain the two terms V and W which he has learned to associate with C and P.

The child who has acquired the general information 'All C are P' by hearing an utterance of V and W (which he associates with C and P) can now also receive limited information, either by observing an instance of C or by hearing an utterance of V. Suppose, for example, that a child has learned that all fires are hot by hearing an utterance of 'Fire (is) hot'. Then seeing a fire or hearing an utterance of 'fire' informs him of the presence of an instance of heat.

According to H1, the expressions that give the child the general information which he receives from an exposure to the pairing of an element of C and of P have the form $V + W$, such as the expression 'Fires hot'. But as a matter of fact the child notices that (at least in English) there are usually a number of different expressions that give the same information, such as 'Fire is hot', 'Fires are hot', or 'All fires are hot'. The common feature of these formulations is the essential occurrence of two terms V and W which refer to two generalization classes. In order to agree on a standard formulation, I will say that these expressions have the form 'All C are P', where it is assumed that the child applies 'C' and 'P' to the generalization classes C and P.

Sentences of the form 'All C are P' give thus the child the general information he receives in the most basic generalization processes, the processes in which he is exposed to the pairing of two stimuli. But he also acquires the capacity to receive through verbal communication the general information which is obtained in more advanced generalization processes. I will examine here only one of these cases, namely, the verbal transmittal of the general information obtained by an organism who is first exposed to a pairing situation and who subsequently undergoes the falsifying experiences that induce him to replace the expectation he acquired in the first experience by a disjunctive expectation (see **37**).

Suppose a child acquires at t_1 the expectation 'All grapes are sweet' by eating a sweet grape. At t_2 he eats a sour grape, and he does not notice any discriminating feature that distinguishes the sweet from the sour grape. His behaviour will then frequently suggest that he has replaced the former expectation by the disjunctive expectation:

(4)   All grapes are either sweet or sour (but not e.g. bitter, tasteless, etc.).

Using again the notion of information, we can say that as a consequence of going through the two types of experiences, the child has received the disjunctive information described in (4). But for reasons that will soon become clear, let me express this information in the following form:

(5)   Some (but not all) grapes are sweet and some (but not all) grapes are sour, and the two classes together make up the whole class of grapes.

Children can learn to receive disjunctive information through verbal communication. To this effect, they have to learn the meanings of expressions such as 'some', 'not all', 'not every', 'some (but not all)'. But I will not deal here with the processes by which children learn such meanings.[18]

An (English-speaking) child can receive disjunctive information by hearing sentences such as (4) or (5). Usually, however, he will hear shorter formulations such as 'Some grapes are not sweet', 'Not all grapes are sweet', or 'Some (but not all) grapes are sweet', and the missing information is provided by the general context. I will use the formulation 'Some C are P' (supplemented sometimes by 'and some C are Q') as our model for representing the different ways which enable a child to acquire such information.

It is important to realize that disjunctive information is general information. The child who has acquired the information described in (4) or (5) believes that the class of grapes has two subclasses such that *all* the elements of one are sweet and *all* the elements of the other are sour. This also holds for the partial information he receives when hearing 'Some C are P'. The sentence tells him that there is a subclass S of C such that *all* its elements have property P.

Since 'Some C are P' gives the child general information, he can use the information given by such sentences for acquiring limited information in a later stage. If he has been told at t_1 'Some grapes are sweet', then seeing a grape at t_2 gives him the information that it is possible (perhaps even likely) that the grape is sweet. And if he has also been told 'and some grapes are sour', then when seeing a grape at t_2 he may perform the disjunctive behaviour described in **37**.

We see that both 'All C are P' and 'Some C are P' gives the child general information. On the other hand, single-term expressions give him only spatially and temporally limited information. Hence, there is an essential difference between the information given by the former expressions and single-term expressions, at least in the first phases of language acquisition. And this difference is often externally marked. In order to give general information, one needs at least two different expressions

V and *W*, each applying to a different generalization class. But in order to give limited information, one term, applying to one generalization class, is sufficient.

Many scholars have argued that the single terms which the child produces in the first stage of his language acquisition have the status of a sentence for him. When he says 'hot', he means by this what we would express with the sentence 'There exists now and nearby an instance of heat'. And when his parents use single words, then the words have again a sentential status for him. The single terms are "holophrastic" sentences (see e.g. McNeill 1970).

There is nothing in our analysis that speaks against this view. Still, it suggests that if one indeed maintains that these single-term expressions are sentences, then one should make a fundamental distinction between two types of sentence. One type contains expressions of the form 'All *C* are *P*' and 'Some *C* are *P*' which give general information, and in which at least two different terms *V* and *W* must occur, each referring to a different generalization class. The other type contains single-term expressions, which give limited information, and in which only one term, referring to one generalization class, must occur.

In usual logical notation, the sentences of the form 'Some *C* are *P*' (which we have seen give general information) are represented as having the form '$(Ez)(Cz.Pz)$', which means approximately 'There exists (at least) a *z*, and *z* is *C* and *z* is *P*'. If one were to represent a single-term expression in such logical notation, one would probably use something like '$(Ez)(Pz,s,t)$' meaning approximately 'There exists a *z*, and *z* is *P*, and *z* is at location *s* at time *t*'. If one uses this kind of notation, one might receive the impression that a sentence of the form 'Some *C* are *P*' has the same character as a single-term expression. Both begin with the so called quantifier '$(E..)$' meaning 'There exists . . .'. But we see that this impression is mistaken. The former gives general information, and therefore requires at least two terms *V* and *W*. In our example, the terms are '*C*' and '*P*'. The latter gives spatially and temporally limited information and therefore needs (at least in principle) only one term. In our example, the term is '*P*'.

Linguists distinguish between terms (or words) and sentences. For the purposes of the present essay, there is no need to enter into this distinction. But the conclusions of the present section suggest that the distinction between terms and sentences probably has its origin in the distinction between single-term expressions, which give limited information, and the sentences of the form 'All *C* are *P*' and 'Some *C* are *P*', which give general information.

62   GTLA

Normal people are able to learn many things. Geniuses, so we are told, are able to learn still more things. But when it comes to the learning of language, every child is a genius. For language embodies an enormous number of highly sophisticated and complex skills, beginning from the learning of the (ostensive and non-ostensive) lexicon, passing through the learning of grammatical rules (see e.g. Chomsky 1965) and finally learning that language may be used for various purposes (see e.g. Austin 1962). Therefore, the development of an adequate and comprehensive theory of language acquisition is perhaps one of the most difficult tasks, and no significant shortcuts should be expected.

Some of these difficulties we have seen here. I have dealt only with a very limited aspect of language learning; yet, many important details, pertaining to this limited aspect, had to be left out.

As mentioned in **48**, I assume that the conclusions that have been obtained here are added to our generalization theory GT, giving rise to the expanded theory GTLA: the generalization theory of language acquisition.

According to GTLA, the linguistic knowledge which children acquire derives from two sources which are equally important: innate predispositions and specific experiences. This approach is usually identified with empiricist views. We can therefore conclude that GTLA is basically an empiricist theory of language acquisition (cf. **18**).

GTLA deals only with the most elementary processes that occur in language acquisition. It constitutes, however, an adequate foundation for treating more advanced and more complicated phenomena of language acquisition, such as the creative aspect of language use and the structure dependence of the semantic and syntactic rules learned by the child (see e.g. Chomsky 1965, 1975; Katz 1966; Aitchison 1976). These phenomena can be explained by assuming only general learning capacities like those examined in GTLA. But I will not enter into this here, since I have already dealt with them in other places. See Stemmer (1971b, 1973b: 61ff, 1978) on the creative aspect of language use and Stemmer (1981b) on structure dependence.

Many theories of language acquisition have been proposed, and they differ in essence or detail. But most of them can be classified as following either the cognitivist or the behaviourist approach. We will see that GTLA appears to have important advantages over both types of theories.

In the next section, I will analyse some basic aspects of the usual cognitive theories of language acquisition. Our analysis will show that these theories face very serious problems. Yet none of these problems affects GTLA. This points to a clear superiority of GTLA.

Behaviourist theories of language acquisition also confront various problems. Chomsky's criticism (1959) of Skinner's theory (1957) is well known. And I have discussed some of the short-comings of the theories proposed by Mowrer (1960) and Staats (1968) (Stemmer 1973b; see also Fodor 1965.)

From the behaviourist theories, I will discuss in this essay only Quine's theory which is probably the most sophisticated and adequate behaviourist theory of language acquisition (especially Quine 1960, 1973). The discussion (in **65**) will be confined to Quine's notion of perceptual similarity, which he uses for explaining the generalizations that occur in learning in general, and in language learning in particular. We will see that there are serious problems with Quine's notion. Now, generalizing behaviour is one of the most basic phenomena that occur in language acquisition. It plays a crucial role in every aspect of this learning process. Since GTLA gives an unproblematic account of generalizing behaviour, the fact that Quine's treatment of this behaviour faces grave problems suggests that GTLA has significant advantages over Quine's theory.

63   Cognitive Theories and GTLA

Linking labels with concepts. There are many types of cognitive theories of language acquisition. However, those that are being considered nowadays seem to share the following central assumption. When the child begins to learn the language of his community, he already possesses a number of concepts (or other kinds of mental entities). Then, by undergoing appropriate experiences—in the beginning, ostensive experiences—he learns to connect the terms he hears in the experiences with some of the concepts. The concepts then become the meanings of the terms, or to use Quine's expression (e.g. 1969: 80), the terms become the labels of the pre-existing concepts.

It is possible that some theories of language acquisition that are considered as cognitive do not make such an assumption. In order to avoid misunderstandings, I will restrict the term *cognitive theory* (*of language acquisition*) to those theories that include such an assumption.

GTLA does not explicitly assume the notion of a concept. However, I have left open the possibility of speaking of mental entities that correspond to neurological traces and states (cf. **10**). If we now use the term 'concept' for these mental entities, then GTLA may be considered a cognitive theory. But GTLA is not a cognitive theory in the sense just defined. According to GTLA, the neurological traces that are formed in the ostensive experiences of the first phases of language acquisition do not have to exist before the experience. Rather, they are produced in the experiences themselves. Hence, the mental entities that correspond to these traces—if we want to speak of mental entities—do not have to exist before the ostensive experiences. It follows that GTLA is not a cognitive theory (in the restricted sense). The terms do not become labels of pre-existing mental entities.

To be sure, GTLA assumes that when the child has reached the stage in which he begins to learn his language (by going through ostensive experiences), he already possesses a great number of innate and acquired capacities, such as the capacity to generalize, to perceive certain aspects of an experience as being more salient than others, to acquire neurological traces when going through pairing experiences, etc. Whether to call these capacities cognitive is a matter of definition. But it is clear that these capacities are not the specific traces that are formed in ostensive experiences, such as the trace formed when children learn the meaning of 'aeroplane' by hearing an utterance of the term while seeing an aeroplane.

Thus, according to cognitive theories (in the defined sense) the child learns to link verbal expressions with concepts that he already possesses. There are different opinions about how the child comes to posses the concepts, but the most frequent view is that he acquires them through his interactions with his environment. For example, Bowerman (1976), summarizing the opinions of several representative authors, states that

> ... the child is now commonly viewed as coming to the language learning task well equipped with a stock of basic concepts that he has built up through his interactions with the world. His problem is to discover how these concepts can be mapped into language. [p. 112.]

Here and in the next part of this section I investigate this type of cognitive theory, and then I discuss cognitive theories which assume that part of the child's concepts are innate. Our analysis will show that cognitive theories have not only several disadvantages in comparison with GTLA (at least with respect to the early stages of language acquisition), but it is very likely that many of them are close to being devoid of any scientific value.

Let us examine how a cognitivist theory (of the first type) explains the process by which a child learns his first terms. Consider, for instance, a child who learns ostensively to apply the term 'dog' to the elements of a particular class. According to the theory, the child has previously acquired a concept in relation with these elements. Then, by observing one or more instances of the concept and noting that they are called 'dog'—i.e. by going through verbal pairing experiences—the child learns to link the concept with the word. Normally, this concept is assumed to be different from the concept that adult speakers of English associate with 'dog', since children who have such experiences usually learn to apply 'dog' not only to dogs but also to other animals such as cats, foxes, and sometimes even to cows and horses. If we use 'M' for denoting the class of objects to which the child first learns to apply the term 'dog'—the extension which it acquires for him—we can then describe the process in the following way. Before the ostensive experience the child has already acquired the concept corresponding to M, say, the concept a. The child then observes certain elements of M and he notes that people refer to them with the term 'dog'. This has the effect that he now links the concept a with the term 'dog'. Since the instances of a are the elements of M, the link formed between 'dog' and a gives the child the ability to apply 'dog' to the elements of M.

Problems. But there are several difficulties that affect this view. The first derives from the following consideration. According to the cognitivist (of the first type), the child has acquired the concept a through his experiences with instances of a, i.e. with the elements of M. But how are these experiences supposed to produce a? Consider the following typical experiences which at least some children have gone through before they learned to apply 'dog' to the elements of M. The child has seen the dogs and cats in his neighbourhood—say, two black poodles, one collie, and two black cats—while they were eating, he has been scratched by one of the cats, he has observed the collie and the other cat while they were running, a cow and a dog who were sleeping, a horse pulling a cart, and the collie while he was barking. Now these experiences are assumed to give rise to the concept a whose instances are the elements of M. But in order to become able to evaluate this assumption we must be given the laws that are supposed to govern the formation of such concepts and that enable us to predict, at least in principle, that in the described experiences the child acquires the concept *a* rather than (say) a concept that also includes birds, or one that contains only dogs and horses but no cats and foxes, or only sleeping dogs. However, there are no cognitive theories which have formulated in a clear manner such laws. Notice that Piagetian theories can give us no help with this, since they deal with the acquisition of very general concepts such as conservation or those that correspond to certain relations between classes. But we need a theory that governs the acquisition of concepts that are much more specific, concepts such as *a* which corresponds to the elements of *M*, as *b* which corresponds to the elements of the class containing the entities to which children learn to apply 'milk', or as *c* which corresponds to the extension which 'shoe' acquires for children, etc. Hence, the first problem of cognitive theories is the absence of an adequate theory—i.e. a theory having a minimal degree of explanatory or predictive power—covering the acquisition of the specific concepts which, according to the theory, are supposed to get linked with particular verbal expressions.

The second problem derives from the fact that, whatever the laws the cognitivist will formulate, it is clear that he will have to admit that in the series of experiences described earlier the child acquires not only the concept *a* but also many other concepts. These concepts will correspond not only to those entities and aspects of the experiences that I have explicitly mentioned such as cats and horses or sleeping and running aspects, but also to those that are implicit in these descriptions. The latter include, e.g. the child's observation that some of the animals have horns while the others not, that all of them have legs but only some have long tails, that some bark while others miaow, that all have eyes, that some walk in a peculiar way, that some animals are bigger than others, and so forth. We must therefore conclude that besides the concept *a*, the child also acquires in the experiences a series of concepts $b_1, .., b_n$, all of them related to the elements of *M*. The instances of these concepts will be, for example, sleeping instances, barking instances, peculiar walking instances, horns, tails, heads, legs, black dogs, black running dogs, black running and barking dogs, non-black horses, instances of being black, instances of being bigger than, and so forth. Therefore, the cognitivist must not only state the laws that govern the acquisition of all these concepts but he must also deal with the following problem, which I will call the *superabundance problem*.

According to the cognitivist theory, when the child hears an utterance of 'dog' while seeing one or more elements of M, he learns to link 'dog' with the concept a. The question is, why does this experience produce a link between 'dog' and the concept a rather than with some of the concepts $b_1, .., b_n$? Since the latter concepts are also related to the elements of M, reasons must be given why, from all the concepts $a, b_1, .., b_n$ that are available to the child, he selects a for linking it with the (at this stage still meaningless) sound 'dog'.

I am not sure whether cognitivist theories are able to solve the superabundance problem. But there is no doubt that it is not an easy problem for them. In any case, and so far as I know, there are no adequate cognitive theories that have solved this problem.

The third problem is first-time learning. This is probably the most difficult to solve.

According to the cognitivist theories we are considering here, the child first acquires a number of concepts by interacting with the world. Then, by having certain linguistic experiences—in the beginning, ostensive experiences—he learns to link some of the acquired concepts with certain expressions. This implies that the specific concept a, which gets linked to a particular expression E, is acquired by the child *before* the linguistic experience. But children can ostensively learn to apply an expression E to the elements of a particular class C before they have observed any instance of the concept a corresponding to C.

Consider, for example, a seven-year-old child who has never seen a giraffe, nor a picture of a giraffe, nor any other representation of a giraffe. He goes with his parents to the zoo, and when coming to the cage of the giraffes he sees a giraffe. At this moment, one of his parents says 'This is a giraffe'. There is abundant evidence showing that very often such experiences confer to the child the capacity to apply the term 'giraffe' to the elements of a class G which contains almost exclusively giraffes. According to the cognitivist, this implies that when seeing the giraffe while hearing 'giraffe' the child selects one of the concepts he has acquired earlier, say the concept c, and this concept corresponds to the class G, that is, the instances of c are the elements of G. He then links 'giraffe' with c which gives him the ability to apply this term to the elements of G. But the first time the child saw an instance of c was when he went through the ostensive experience. Hence, concept c could not have been acquired before the experience. It is therefore impossible that, as claimed by the cognitivist, the child learned to link the word with the concept c

in the ostensive experience. The concept was not yet acquired by the child.

A possible answer is that although the child has not yet acquired the concept c by observing giraffes, he has already acquired a set of "related" concepts $d_1, .., d_m$, such as of horses, sleeping horses, legs, necks, heads, etc. On the basis of these concepts, the child forms a set of "derived" concepts $c_1, .., c_n$ such as of horses with a long neck and two legs, horses with a short neck and six legs, sleeping donkeys with two heads, etc. And one of these concepts is the concept c corresponding to (big, or perhaps small) giraffes. But for this view the superabundance problem becomes even more critical. For now the child must select the particular concept c not only from those concepts that correspond to perceived stimuli, but also from those corresponding to "possible" stimuli. Although this solution may get us out of the first-time learning problem, it would make the superabundance problem much more difficult to solve.

Another possible solution is to assume that in some cases a child can learn to link an expression E with a concept a even though the concept was not acquired previously. In these cases, the concept is acquired during the ostensive experience itself. This would imply that the child possesses two different learning capacities. One is very weak—it enables the child to learn to link an expression E with a concept a, only if he has previously undergone experiences that enabled him to acquire a. The other is much stronger—the child can learn to link E with a, even though he has not undergone such experiences. According to this solution, the child sometimes uses the weak capacity, e.g. when learning to apply 'dog' to certain animals, while on other occasions he uses the strong capacity, e.g. when learning to apply 'giraffe' to certain animals. But since there are no significant differences between these occasions, the assumption that the child applies two different capacities in such ostensive learning processes would be unwarranted. It would not be founded on objective data.

If we now look at GTLA we see that it is not affected by any of these problems. Hence, it is clearly superior to the cognitive theories we are considering here. But GTLA has a further, very important advantage. According to GTLA, the learning processes that enable the child to ostensively learn the meanings of verbal expressions are *general* learning processes. They are the same processes that enable him to acquire non-linguistic expectations. According to cognitivist theories, on the other hand, there are two types of process involved. One type enables the child to acquire non-linguistic expectations such as the expectation that fires are hot or that dogs can bark. The other enables him to link previously acquired concepts with verbal expressions. Consequently, GTLA attributes fewer capacities to the child than do cognitivist theories. Therefore, considerations of parsimony also confer a clear advantage to the former theory over the latter.

Innate concepts. There are authors who assume the existence of innate concepts that play a role in the learning of meanings. Katz, for example, states that 'innate semantic principles include a finite set of primitive senses which provide the stock of elementary concepts' (1979: 362). It is unlikely, however, that they want to maintain that these innate concepts are the *specific* concepts which children supposedly learn to link with verbal expressions. Since young children can learn ostensively the meanings of terms such as 'car', 'piano', and 'aeroplane', they would have to admit that the child is born with the specific concepts that correspond to these terms. Yet the entities to which these terms refer are known to the human race for a very short time, which makes it extremely implausible that the corresponding concepts actually exist in the child's innate cognitive structure.

We may thus conclude that "semantic nativists" do not assume that children are born with specific concepts that get linked to terms such as 'dog', 'fire', or 'aeroplane'. They probably hold the view that such specific concepts are the product of the interaction between certain basic innate concepts and certain types of experiences. But if this is their position, then the three problems that affect the cognitive theories studied above also affect this cognitive theory. First, we need an adequate theory (with sufficient predictive or explanatory power) that covers the formation of specific concepts on the basis of innate concepts and certain experiences. Then, we must again solve the superabundance problem, since there will always be a plurality of concepts that are "related" to the stimulus perceived in the ostensive experiences. Finally, we must solve the first-time learning problem. Moreover, this cognitive theory again assumes the intervention of more learning processes than does GTLA. Hence, GTLA also has clear advantages over the cognitive theory which assumes the existence of certain types of innate concepts.

Generalization classes as concepts. There still exists another position. One can maintain that the concepts which persons learn to link with verbal expressions are our generalization classes: the classes which, according to GTLA, intervene in the learning processes.[19] But if this view is adopted, concepts would no longer be mental entities. They would be classes containing all kinds of entities such as black poodles, songs, or sensations of heat. Moreover, we would have to admit that not only humans, but also all those animals who show generalizing behaviour use concepts in this behaviour. Finally, concepts would become *relative* to original entities. They would no longer have an independent status. Thus, we would not be able to speak of *the* concept "black poodles". Rather, we would have to speak of a concept "black poodle" that originates in poodle *a*, of another concept "black poodle" originating in poodle *b*, of a third concept whose origin is the sleeping poodle *a*, of a fourth one originating in the same poodle but who is now eating, etc.

Of course, one can arbitrarily assign to the term 'concept' a meaning that conforms with such features. But since the usual connotations of the term 'concept' are very different, this would probably be more misleading than helpful. On the other hand, the intuitive connotations of the term 'generalization class' harmonize perfectly with what is attributed to these classes by GTLA. In particular, since one generalizes *from* certain entities *to* other entities, the relative character of a generalization class with respect to original entities—sleeping dogs, eating poodles, etc.—is implicit in the term 'generalization class'. This suggests that if one wishes to identify concepts with generalization classes, it is preferable to forget the term 'concept' and use instead the term 'generalization class' itself.

Our discussion shows that if a theory indeed intends to identify concepts with generalization classes, it is misleading to speak of a *cognitive* theory. The label *empiricist* theory is in this case much more appropriate, provided we do not really identify generalization classes with mental entities (or concepts) but only use the former for individuating the latter.

PART IV

Analyticity, Similarity, and Universals

In the final part of this book, I apply the conclusions that have been obtained to clarify three topics with which philosophers have been concerned. The first and the second topic are also of interest for psychologists.

64 Meanings, Beliefs, and Analyticity

Semantic effects of beliefs. Suppose that at t_1 a child learns to associate the term 'dog' with (approximately) the class of dogs by having a number of ostensive experiences (and perhaps some appropriate falsifying experiences). We can then describe the neurological trace left by these experiences as the acquisition by the child of the belief:

(1)   All utterances of 'dog' name dogs.

Moreover, we can individuate (or describe) the meaning which the child associates with 'dog'—i.e. the relevant part of the neurological (or mental) trace—as [dogs], where 'dogs' is supposed to be the English term that correctly describes the relevant theoretical generalization class: the extension which 'dog' has acquired for the child (see **51**).

Further, suppose that at t_2 the child is bitten by a dog. If we note that after t_2 the child becomes afraid of dogs, we can individuate (or describe) the neurological trace left by the second experience as the acquisition of the belief:

(2)   All dogs can bite.

But the second experience may also have consequences relating not only to dogs but also to the term 'dog'. After t_2, the child may perform typical fear reactions when hearing utterances of the term 'dog' and not only when seeing (real) dogs. The question now arises: should we attribute the new reactions to 'dog' to a change in the meaning which the child associates with 'dog' or rather to the combination of the belief acquired in the second experience and the unaltered original meaning? Expressing these alternatives in neurological terms we obtain the following positions. According to one view, we assume that the second experience not only produces the neurological trace described in (2) but also modifies in a particular manner the meaning part of the trace described in (1). And because of this change in the meaning part, utterances of 'dog' now produce new effects. According to the other view, we assume that the second experience does not alter the original meaning part of the trace formed at t_1. Rather, the new trace, the one formed at t_2, combines in some manner with the former part to elicit the new reactions.

The situation becomes still more complex once we consider further experiences. For example, besides noting that dogs can bite, the child may undergo experiences that give him the beliefs that dogs can bark, eat, run, swim, have a heart, have kidneys, that some eat sandwiches, that none can climb trees, etc. Some of these experiences may have the effect of eliciting new reactions to utterances of the term 'dog'. For instance, the child may hide his sandwich when hearing an utterance of 'dog'. (He is, so to speak, afraid the dog may steal his sandwich.) We can therefore ask again the question whether these effects are caused by changes in the meaning which the child associates with 'dog' or whether they derive from the combination of the beliefs acquired in the experiences and the original unchanged meaning.

The child's behaviour is insufficient for deciding between the two alternative views. Each of them is compatible with the child's behaviour.

Notice that our problem is not that the behaviour does not tell us where to draw the line between meaning and belief. The problem is that, once we consider further experiences, the behaviour does not tell us whether such a demarcation exists.

This result will be called the *indeterminacy of the meaning–belief distinction*. It is not difficult to see that it is closely related to Quine's thesis of the indeterminacy of translation (see e.g. Quine 1960, 1969).

Is there another type of evidence that might decide the issue? In the literature, frequent mention has been made of a phenomenon that seems to be relevant here. It has been observed that the answers people give to questions such as

(3) Would you apply '. . .' to something that is (or has, or does, or is not, etc.) . . .?

depend on how the blank spaces are filled out. For example, many speakers of English will give a negative answer to the question 'Would you apply the term 'dog' to something that is similar to a dog but cannot bark (or has no heart)?'. On the other hand, they might give a positive answer if instead of 'cannot bark' (or 'has no heart') the question has 'cannot swim' (or 'has no kidneys').

Similar results are also observed if in the questions one uses modal terms such as 'necessary' or 'possible'. Many persons, for example, will agree that it is necessary for dogs to have a heart, while they may admit that even if an animal has no kidneys, it nevertheless can be a dog.

Now, it has been suggested that by using the answers to such questions we might be able to decide whether some feature is or is not part of the meaning which a person associates with an expression. For example, Carnap (1955) proposes to ask a person the question 'Are you willing to apply 'horse' to a thing similar to a horse, but having one horn in the middle of the forehead?' His answer may allow us to decide whether having a horn in the middle of the forehead is or is not part of the meaning which the person associates with 'horse'.

The answers to such questions apparently allow us to arrive at a decision about the meaning–belief dichotomy. Suppose that the child, who at t_2 acquires by direct observation the belief that dogs can bark and have a heart, gives a negative answer to the question 'Would you apply 'dog' to something that is similar to a dog but cannot bark or has no heart?' Then this answer seems to support the conclusion that the belief has become part of the new (modified) meaning which the child now associates with 'dog'. This would indicate that the acquisition of these beliefs did indeed modify the original meaning he learned to associate with 'dog' at t_1. But now suppose that the child, who at t_2 acquires by direct observation the beliefs that dogs can swim and have kidneys, gives a positive answer to 'Would you apply 'dog' to something that is similar to a dog but cannot swim or has no kidneys?' Then the answer suggests that the acquisition of these beliefs did not alter the original meaning.

Such answers, however, do not determine a meaning–belief distinction. For one can maintain that the difference between the answers merely points to a difference in the strength which the beliefs have acquired for the person (see **11**), or in the degree of centrality which the beliefs have with respect to the person's "view of the world", i.e. with respect to the network formed by all his beliefs.[1]

In our example, the answers given by the child might merely indicate that he believes more strongly that dogs can bark than that they can swim, or that the belief that dogs have a heart has for him a higher degree of centrality than the belief that they have kidneys. Hence, when the answers are interpreted in this way—and there are apparently no reasons why one should not give them this interpretation—one can insist that none of the experiences changes the original meanings.

Even the explicit use of the term 'meaning' in questions given to speakers of English (or of "analogous" terms such as '*significado*' if the speaker is Spanish), does not decide the issue. For suppose a person gives a positive answer to the question 'Is the barking capacity part of the meaning of 'dog'?' Then, when evaluating this answer we are faced with two uncertainties. First, it is almost impossible to determine the exact meaning which the person has learned to associate with the term 'meaning' since it is a non-ostensive term. Is it a meaning that covers only "pure" meanings, or does it also include central and important beliefs? Second, we are not sure whether the person correctly interprets his own feelings about the issue. Whatever the feelings he has learned to associate with the term 'meaning' (when he heard utterances of the term within a non-ostensive discourse) they probably do not give him very clear sense data. Because of these uncertainties, one cannot justify basing a meaning–belief distinction on the answers to such questions.

Our analysis suggests that there probably is no behavioural evidence that might enable us to establish a meaning–belief dichotomy. But this result does not contradict the conclusions of our theory of language acquisition GTLA. For this theory only states that the behaviour elicited by a verbal expression is produced by the neurological traces left by certain experiences. However, it does not limit these experiences to linguistic ones. GTLA is therefore not committed to a specific view regarding the question whether or not the traces left by the experiences can be separated into a meaning part and a belief part.

In **51**, I proposed to individuate the meaning of an ostensive term E with the help of the extension which E has acquired for the relevant person. If C is the extension, then we individuate the meaning by using '[C]'. Now, 'C' is supposed to give a correct description of all and only the elements of *C*. But our conclusions show that we usually cannot determine whether the entities a person includes in *C* are there because of the (original or modified) meaning he associates with *E* or because of beliefs he has acquired about these entities.

For this reason I did not claim that the notion of meaning introduced in **51** is identical with the intuitive notion of meaning. Since the intuitive notion seems to demand a relatively strict distinction between meanings and beliefs (but see Stemmer 1979a), I only stated that the introduced notion is close to the intuitive one. The present analysis suggests that if the intuitive notion indeed presupposes a strict distinction between meanings and beliefs, then it is likely that the intuitive notion has a rather restricted range of application. It applies only to cases where there are no acquired beliefs or where these beliefs are clearly irrelevant.

We see that our technical term 'meaning' has the status of an *explicatum* in Carnap's sense (see Carnap 1950). It is a well-defined term that allows us to deal in a methodologically correct way with a great number of the phenomena that have been described by using the term 'meaning' of our everyday language, the *explicandum*. Since the explicandum is highly vague and ambiguous, the introduction of a clear explicatum, which has explanatory and predictive power, enables us to deal in an adequate way with these phenomena.

Non-ostensive terms. The examples I have given so far suggesting the validity of the indeterminacy conclusion concerned only ostensive terms. There is still more indeterminacy when one considers non-ostensive terms. Suppose we ask a person 'Would you apply the term 'concept' to something that is not an idea?' or 'Is it possible for concepts to be possessed by animals?'. Whatever the answer given by the person, it seems equally possible to attribute it to the meaning he has learned to associate with 'concept' (and also with 'idea' and 'animal') or to the beliefs he has acquired about concepts (as well as about ideas and animals).

Notice that here the indeterminacy arises much earlier. A person learns the meaning of a non-ostensive term by hearing a verbal context in which the term appears. But generally one cannot distinguish between linguistic and non-linguistic information which the person receives from the context. Suppose a person hears the term 'concept' for the first time by being told 'All animals that can acquire concepts have a well-developed neurological system'. Then there is no way, or at least I see no way, for deciding which part of this context gives rise to a meaning trace for the term 'concept' and which part to a belief trace.[2] Hence, with respect to non-ostensive terms there is usually no behavioural evidence (including verbal behaviour) that might enable us to separate meanings from beliefs, not even in the first stages of the processes in which the person learns to use these terms.

Uniformity in semantic judgements. There exists a further phenomenon that one might consider as supporting a meaning–belief distinction, namely, the significant uniformity that is observed in the semantic judgements given by different people. For instance, most adult speakers of English agree that 'car', 'dog', 'to maintain', 'bachelor' and 'concept' have the same or almost the same meanings as 'automobile', 'hound', 'to claim', 'unmarried male', and 'idea' respectively, that 'John throws the ball' has about the same meaning as 'The ball is thrown by John', and that the meaning relation between 'poodle' and 'dog' is very similar to the one between 'horse' and 'mammal', while it is different from the one between 'whale' and 'fish'. Since there are differences in the beliefs which people have acquired about the entities to which the expressions refer, the uniformity suggests the existence of a separate meaning element that is shared by normal speakers of a language.

This argument is different from the one given in the first part of this section, because it concentrates on the uniformity of certain judgements rather than on the explicit use of semantic terms. Nevertheless, the argument does not contradict the indeterminacy thesis, since the uniformity can be attributed to other factors. In certain cases, the judgements refer to effects of the learning processes (of the expression) that are not affected by beliefs acquired later. In these cases, the uniformity derives from the significant similarity between the effects of the learning processes. In the other cases, the uniformity derives from the significant similarity between the beliefs which normal speakers of the language have acquired about the relevant entities (in addition to the similar effects of the learning processes).

Consider, for instance, the terms 'car' and 'automobile'. Normal speakers of English have learned their meanings either by seeing concrete cars (i.e. concrete automobiles) in ostensive experiences, or by hearing sentences in which one term is directly explained in terms of the other (e.g. 'Automobiles are cars'), or indirectly (e.g. 'Automobiles are vehicles having such and such characteristics' and 'Vehicles having such and such characteristics are cars'). By undergoing such experiences, they learn to apply both terms to the same entities (see especially **56**, conclusion CN). Therefore, the beliefs they acquire about the entities named by 'car' are the same as those acquired about the entities named by 'automobile'. Hence, the uniformity of their judgements about the identity between the meanings of 'car' and 'automobile' can be attributed to the similar effects of the learning processes, and with respect to these judgements, the acquired beliefs are irrelevant. Since the beliefs are about the same entities, they are identical.

Similar conclusions hold for the other pairs mentioned above, although it may be more difficult to show this. For instance, it is likely that different speakers of English have learned the meaning of 'bachelor' by hearing different types of contexts. Nevertheless, if their judgements about the meaning relation between 'bachelor' and 'unmarried male' agree with those of the majority, then they will apply both terms to the same entities (probably because most of them have learned the meaning of 'bachelor' by hearing sentences that can be "reduced" to sentences like 'A bachelor is a man who is not married'). Therefore, the beliefs they acquire about the entities named by 'bachelor' are identical with those acquired about the entities named by 'unmarried male'. Hence, here, too, we explain the uniformity of the judgements as a consequence of the similar effects of the processes by which speakers of English learn the meanings of the terms.

Regarding the judgements about the similar meaning relation between pairs such as ⟨'poodle', 'dog'⟩ and ⟨'horse', 'mammal'⟩, we can attribute the uniformity between these judgements to the similarity between the relevant acquired beliefs (besides the similar effects of the learning processes). Consider the third pair ⟨'whale', 'fish'⟩. I said earlier that people agree that the meaning relation between this pair is different from the one between the other two pairs. Actually, this is true only if we consider well-educated speakers of English. Many children and uneducated persons will disagree; they will maintain that the three pairs stand in the same meaning relation. Now there is no doubt that this difference in opinion derives from a difference in beliefs. Educated adults have acquired the belief that the mammalian characteristics of whales are biologically more important than, e.g. their swimming capacity or their fish-like shape, whereas children and uneducated people have not acquired such belief. This suggests that in those cases where there is indeed a uniformity in semantic judgements, it derives from a similarity in relevant beliefs. In our example, it suggests that normal speakers of English agree about the degree of importance of the canine features of poodles, and of the mammalian features of horses.

Finally, the uniformity of our semantic judgements about sentences in active and in passive forms can be attributed to the process by which one learns the active–passive transformation. The person learns that two corresponding sentences—e.g. 'John throws the ball' and 'The ball is thrown by John'—refer to the same situations (see Stemmer 1973b: 82ff). Consequently, there are no differences in the beliefs which one acquires about the relevant entities. Since the situations are identical, the beliefs are also identical.

We see that the uniformity of these types of semantic judgement can be attributed either to the fact that beliefs acquired later are irrelevant or that they are similar. Hence, the uniformity does not prove that one can separate meaning elements from belief elements. It follows that it does not rebute the thesis of the indeterminacy of a meaning–belief dichotomy.

To be sure, I have examined here only a limited number of semantic judgements. But since these are typical semantic judgements, it is likely that our conclusions also hold for other types of such judgement.

The analytic–synthetic dichotomy. Our indeterminacy conclusion bears upon the distinction proposed by several scholars between sentences that are *analytic* for a person, i.e. true in virtue of the meanings of their terms,[3] and those that are *synthetic* for him, i.e. true or false because of factual beliefs (in addition to the meanings of their terms). It suggests that with respect to most sentences it is generally an indeterminate issue whether the sentence is analytic or synthetic for an adult speaker of a language. In all those cases where we cannot separate a meaning component from a belief component with respect to an expression E, one cannot make the distinction if E has a significant role in the sentence.

This will occur in particular in those cases where E is a non-ostensive expression, since here the indeterminacy is very strong. For example, there are no data that might enable us to determine whether the sentences 'Animals do not have concepts' or 'Concepts are ideas' are analytic or synthetic for a speaker of English. But it will also occur when E is an ostensive expression. Consider 'Dogs can bark' or 'Dogs have a heart'. Since we usually cannot decide whether the beliefs expressed by these sentences have or have not become part of the meanings which a person associates with 'dog' (and also with 'bark' and 'heart'), we cannot decide whether these sentences are analytic for him or, rather, synthetic.

There is a further difficulty with the analytic–synthetic dichotomy. The usual notions about this dichotomy seem to oppose certain intuitive notions about meaning. Consider the term 'scissors'. We would like to maintain that the cutting capacity of scissors is part of the meaning which most normal speakers of English associate with 'scissors'. This would make the sentence 'Scissors can cut' analytic for them. But at least a significant part of these speakers have acquired by direct observation the belief that scissors can cut, some of them even before they had heard any utterance of the term 'scissors'. Hence, for these persons the sentence would be synthetic.

In Part III we decided to use the extension T of an expression E as one of the main individuating tools for the meaning of E, i.e. for the neurological (or mental) application trace or state a that is formed when a person learns to use E. T reflects the nature of a. In particular, it reflects the part of a that determines the person's reactions to the tests which give us E's extension (see the beginning of **49**). Now the conclusions of this section suggest that among the experiences that determine the nature of a, there may be experiences that are not strictly linguistic. While giving the person factual knowledge about certain entities, the experiences may also influence the way he uses E. In particular, they may play a role in determining which objects he includes in T. This shows that the extension T is indeed a very efficient individuating tool for a. For T reflects not only the effects of linguistic experiences, but frequently also the linguistic effects of experiences that have a factual character.

65 Similarity

Explanatory and predictive power. The second topic I want to examine is that of similarity. It can be seen that I have made little use of the notion of similarity in this essay. This may seem surprising, since many people have used this notion in order to account for the phenomena that have been investigated here. For instance, in **28** we have seen that Hume describes inductive inferences as inferences in which we expect that 'similar powers will be conjoined with similar sensible qualities'. And Quine uses the comparative notion of a being perceptually more similar to $b_1, .., b_m$ than to $c_1, .., c_n$ to characterize the generalizations that occur in basic learning processes, including linguistic learning processes. However, I have tried to avoid using the notion of similarity because it is affected by many problems, some of which are very difficult to solve. For this reason I have preferred to introduce the theoretical frameworks GT and GTLA, which are based on the notion of generalization class rather than of similarity.

In Stemmer (1981a), I have discussed extensively the difficulties of the notion of similarity. I will therefore examine here only the most fundamental problem, namely, the incapacity of the usual notions of similarity to explain and to predict the generalizing behaviour of organisms including humans.

Suppose we observe that a child generalizes from the black poodle *a* to the elements of the class *M* which contains medium-sized quadrupeds. If we were to explain this generalization in terms of similarity, we would attribute it to the similarity which holds between *a* and the elements of *M*. But poodle *a* is not only similar to these elements; *a* is similar to other black poodles, to poodles in general, to black dogs, to dogs, to quadrupeds, etc. It follows that *the* similarity between *a* and other entities explains not only the generalization that indeed occurred but also other generalizations that did not take place.

The same problem arises with prediction. We want to predict how a child will generalize from the black poodle *a* to other entities. If we base our prediction on the similarity between *a* and other entities, then we arrive at many different predictions. Each different similarity suggests a different prediction.

Replacing the absolute notion of *a* being similar to *b* by the comparative notion of *a* being more similar to *b* than to *c* does not help us much, since in its usual version, the comparative notion, too, lacks the power to explain and predict the generalizations of organisms. Suppose we again want to predict the child's generalization from the black poodle *a*. The poodle *a* is not only more similar to his twin brother *b* than to other black poodles, but also more similar to *b* than to poodles in general, than to dogs, than to black quadrupeds, also more similar to other black poodles than to other animals, more similar to black dogs than to three-dimensional black objects, etc. In view of all these similarities, which is the generalization that the child will make? Will he generalize to the class of poodles which are more similar to *a* than are dogs in general, or rather to the class of black dogs which are more similar to *a* than are quadrupeds in general? The comparative notion of similarity does not allow us to decide between such alternatives. And it is easy to see that identical problems arise when this notion is used for explanatory purposes.

Speaking of degrees of similarity is no great improvement. When using this notion we would attribute to the similarity between poodle a and his twin brother b (say) the degree n_1, between a and other black poodles the degree n_2, between a and black dogs the degree n_3, etc. But now suppose we want to predict the generalizations a child will perform when learning ostensively the meanings of 'dog' and of 'poodle'. Will it be according to the similarity of degree n_1, of degree n_2, or perhaps of degree n_7? Clearly, we need something else, some additional notions, to give predictive power to this notion. And it is not difficult to see that this notion is also unable to explain why the child's generalization agreed with a similarity of degree x rather than with one of degree y.

Hence, the usual notions of similarity lack the power to explain and predict the generalizations that occur in elementary learning processes. Now, we have seen that our theoretical framework GT (including GTLA), which is based on the notion of a generalization class, indeed has this capacity. This justifies the position I have adopted in this essay to replace the usual notion of similarity by the notion of a generalization class.

Quine's notion of similarity. Quine, in his book *The Roots of Reference* (1973), introduces the comparative notion of a being perceptually more similar to $b_1, .., b_m$ than to $c_1, .., c_n$. He assumes the similarity notion to be disconnected, which means that in many cases it makes no evident or useful sense to say that a is perceptually more similar to $b_1, .., b_m$ than to $c_1, .., c_n$ (p. 18). This notion has the capacity to explain and to predict those generalizations that occur when an organism is exposed to (positive) pairing situations and appropriate negative instances. However, as I made clear in Stemmer (1981a), Quine's notion has a number of characteristics that constitute serious disadvantages in comparison with the notions of GT. The most important are the following.

Quine's notion differs significantly from the familiar notion of similarity, especially because it is disconnected in spite of being comparative. Therefore, the advantage of using a familiar notion (instead of the relatively unfamiliar notions of GT) becomes a disadvantage, since people will not always be aware of the fact that Quine's notion is different from the usual notion of similarity.

The second disadvantage is that one cannot apply the notion in those cases where a generalization derives from the observation of positive instances only, as in the case of Baege's pupies (see **4**), or when children learn the meanings of very "wide" terms such as of 'animal' or 'thing'. This weakness derives from the comparative nature of Quine's notion (see the discussion of comparative similarities above). It is not clear how Quine intends to account for such generalizations.

Finally, the framework based on Quine's notion is less economical than GT (and GTLA). For besides the notion of similarity it also needs our notion of a generalization class (or something equivalent) in order to describe the results of generalizations, as when one speaks of the extension—the class—which a term has acquired for a child. Moreover, it will also need such a notion in order to account for those generalizations that derive from the observation of positive instances only.

The problems of Quine's notion of similarity affect seriously his account of language acquisition. Because of the comparative and multi-relational character of the notion, his treatment of all those aspects that are based on the application of our generalizing dispositions—and there is almost no part of language acquisition that is not based on such an application—is extremely complex. And because of the limitations of the notion, those generalizations that do not require negative instances cannot be accounted for by Quine.

The theory described in Quine (1973), which largely agrees with empiricist views, is probably one of the most adequate theories of language acquisition that satisfy behaviourist constraints. However, it has made little impact on psycholinguists. It is likely that at least part of this can be attributed to the difficulties deriving from Quine's similarity notion, especially from its comparative and multi-relational nature.

Our theory of language acquisition GTLA also satisfies behaviourist constraints. But Quine's problems do not affect GTLA, since it makes no use of a similarity notion. Its basic notion is the simple, intuitive, and unproblematic notion of a generalization class. Moreover, GTLA can easily explain those generalizations in which no negative experiences occur. For the generalizations that agree with innate generalization classes (12) and a number of those that agree with criterial generalization classes (38) derive from the observation of positive instances only.

Our analysis shows that GTLA has several important advantages over Quine's theory of language acquisition. This suggests the convenience of replacing the latter theory by GTLA. And one of the consequences of such a step may be to encourage psycholinguists not to abandon behaviourist principles when trying to account for language acquisition.

Modified notions of similarity. We have seen that the usual notions of similarity lack the power to explain and predict the generalizations which take place in elementary learning processes, and that Quine's notion also has several disadvantages. But we can introduce a qualified similarity notion that directly reflects the different generalization classes of our framework GT. Such a notion might have the necessary explanatory and predictive power. For example, in those cases where *a* and *b* are elements of an innate generalization class *C* (for an organism) we can say that *a* is *innately similar* to *b*. Thus if we assume that the class of dogs is an innate generalization class for a child, then dogs would be said to be innately similar for this child. Or in those cases where *a* and *b* belong to a restricted subclass *D* of *C*—e.g. when *D* is the class of poodles, or the class of black dogs, or the class of black poodles, etc.—we might say that *a* is *restrictedly similar* to *b*. Or if *a* and *b* are elements of a criterial class *F*—e.g. when *F* is the class of mammals, or animals, or black animals, of bodies, etc.—*a* and *b* would be *criterially similar*.

But this qualified notion of similarity is still insufficient. Suppose we have observed that a child applies the term *u* to dogs, *v* to poodles, and *w* to black dogs. Assuming that the class of dogs is an innate generalization class for the child, we would attribute the child's use of *u* to the generalization based on the innate similarity between dogs, his use of *v* to the generalization based on the restricted similarity between poodles, and his use of *w* to the one based on the restricted similarity between black dogs. But *v* and *w* have different extensions for the child. Hence, we must further qualify the two restricted similarities, in order to account for the difference in extensions. It is not clear, however, whether concepts exist, or whether one can invent concepts, that harmonize with the notion of similarity and which can correctly qualify the different types of restricted similarities that are needed to account for such generalizing behaviour.

Note that in GT it is very easy to account for the difference between the two extensions. Both the class of poodles and the class of black dogs are restricted subclasses of the innate generalization class of dogs. Yet each is determined by different discriminating features. The former by the features that distinguish between dogs in general and poodles, and the latter by the features that distinguish between dogs in general and black dogs. And the fact that the child applies *v* and *w* to different restricted classes would be attributed to a difference in the falsifying experiences. In one case, the negative instances lacked the former features, while in the other case they lacked the latter features (see **29**).

Instead of introducing the previously described similarity notions, we might again think of using the gradual notion of similarity mentioned in the first part of this section. Suppose we establish a scale from 1 to 10. The highest degree of similarity, say, the one holding between a black poodle and his twin brother would be assigned the value 10, and the lowest, say, the one holding between a black poodle and all kinds of three-dimensional objects the value 1. The degree of innate similarity between dogs might then be about 5, the stronger (restricted) similarity between poodles might have degree 7, and this would perhaps also be the degree of the similarity between black dogs, while the degree of similarity between black poodles might obtain the value 8.

But this is again insufficient. Suppose that two restricted classes, say the class of poodles and the class of black dogs, have the same degree of restricted similarity, and that a child applies v to one class and w to the other class. Then besides stating that both classes have a particular degree of similarity for the child, we must affirm something more about the similarity in order to account for the child's (different) generalizations.

These conclusions suggest that so long as no adequate framework based on modified concepts of similarity has been proposed, it is better to avoid the notion of similarity for dealing with generalization processes. But even when such frameworks will be available, it is still possible, and I believe, it is likely, that GT will turn out to be a simpler, more intuitive, and more efficient framework.

The informal notion of similarity. Our analysis suggests that although it is possible that modified notions of similarity do have the power to explain and predict elementary generalizing behaviour, this is not the case for the usual notions. Nevertheless, as a matter of fact people often use very sensibly the notion of similarity, even in explanations and predictions. For example, when being told that a young child, who has been bitten by a dog, has become afraid of *similar* things we will usually expect the similar things to be dogs or other kinds of medium-sized quadrupeds. Nobody will assume, for example, that he has become afraid of apples, in spite of the fact that apples are similar to dogs by being bodies, by being non-ravens, by weighing less than 1000 kg, less than 1001 kg, etc. And I myself have used the term 'similarity' on some occasions.

What stands behind such informal uses of the notion of

similarity? How do we manage to apply the notion meaningfully, in spite of the many problems that affect it? The answer seems to be the following. When we say that *x* is similar to *y* we implicitly assume that there exists a generalization class *C* which is operative in the circumstances, and *x* and *y* belong to *C*. Moreover, we assume that the context, together with a projection of our intro-spections (see **15**), give us relatively clear indications regarding the nature of *C*.

To come back to the young child who was bitten by a dog, we usually expect the similar things he now avoids to be the elements of the child's innate generalization class which originates in the particular dog, and we rely strongly on introspection for determining the nature of the class. But if from the context we infer that the child has already acquired the belief that dogs with a muzzle cannot bite, then we expect the class to be a properly restricted subclass of the innate generalization class.

A bridge between behaviourist and cognitivist theories. One of the characteristics of behaviourist learning theories is their explicit or implicit use of the notion of similarity. But our analysis here has shown that this notion is affected by serious difficulties.

One of the characteristics of many, perhaps even of most cognitivist learning theories is the use of the notion of a concept or of related notions. But in **63** we have seen that this notion, too, is affected by serious problems, at least when it is used for dealing with language acquisition.

Both notions are related to generalization classes. Informal talk of similarities is mostly a context-dependent way of speaking about certain generalization classes (see above). And when the cognitivist states that a person links concept *a* with a term *V*, then we can usually express this by saying that he associates *V* with a particular generalization class *C* (see **51** and **63**). Now, the notion of generalization class is not affected by the problems of the other two notions. This suggests that a theory which uses this notion may become an adequate bridge between behaviourist and cognitivist theories of learning.

This conclusion is of great importance for determining the status of our generalization theory GT. If the conclusion is correct, then it is possible (perhaps even likely) that GT constitutes an adequate basis for developing a *unified theory*, a theory that covers the phenomena dealt with by both behaviourist and cognitivist theories of learning.

Finally, a word on the behaviourist's notion of generalization gradients. It is clear that generalization gradients are closely related to our generalization classes (see e.g. **5**). But there is no direct connection between generalization gradients and concepts. The reason is that whereas concepts are usually interpreted as classes or as determining certain classes, generalization gradients are normally not interpreted in this way. Therefore, the notion of generalization *classes* also establishes a connection between the generalization gradients of the behaviourist and the concepts of the cognitivist.

66   Universals

What are universals? Do they actually exist? What role do they play in the acquisition of knowledge? These are some of the elements that constitute the problem of universals. It is obvious that GT, including GTLA, is insufficient to solve all aspects of the problem. But it does enable us to clarify and perhaps to solve some of them. This will be the topic of our last section.

Universals and particulars. One aspect of the problem of universals concerns the distinction between particulars and universals (see e.g. Loux 1970). Regarding this distinction, GT shows that the processes by which organisms (including humans) acquire knowledge and beliefs about the world begin with *particular* perceptions of stimuli. Feeling a sensation of heat, seeing a dog, hearing an instance of the sound *do*, are all individual, particular perceptions. However, the perceptions become part of the organisms' cognitive system—of their network of beliefs—only after the active intervention of their *generalizing* capacities.

Consider a dog which at t_1 is burnt by a fire. Such a particular experience usually leaves traces in the dog's neurological system. But these traces become significant parts of its cognitive system only after it has generalized from the experience, e.g. after it has acquired the disposition to avoid "similar" fires. Note that among the similar fires—more exactly, among the elements of the corresponding generalization class—are not only other fires, but probably also the same fire after, say, thirty seconds. If the dog avoids the same fire after 30 seconds (in spite of no longer perceiving its heat) then it is using its generalizing capacities. It has generalized from the perception of the fire at t_1, at which time it also felt the burning sensation, to the new perception of the fire, the one 30 seconds later.

We thus notice a clear distinction between a particular perception (of a stimulus) and the cognitive product of this perception. The former is something particular, while the latter is essentially dependent on the application of an organism's disposition to generalize from certain stimulations to other stimulations.

It is possible that some types of perceptions leave "neutral" traces. They are stored just as they are perceived. And one might say, perhaps just by definition, that such traces have also become part of the organism's cognitive system. I am not sure whether one can justify considering such traces as cognitive entities. But it is clear that if the traces are not processed with the help of generalizing capacities, then their cognitive effects in terms of the acquisition of specific knowledge or specific beliefs is minimal.

The generalization from a stimulation to *similar* stimulations, i.e. to the elements of the corresponding generalization class, has been considered as one of the main phenomena showing the cognitive role of universals in the acquisition of knowledge. This suggests that the generalization classes, which are the results of these generalizations, correspond to at least part of the universals that have been discussed by philosophers. Therefore, in so far as the notion of universals matches our notion of generalization classes, the conclusions of this essay point to a sharp distinction between certain particulars and certain universals: the particular perceptions perceived by an organism and the generalization classes to which the perceptions give rise.

Epistemic reality of universals. In addition to emphasizing the distinction between certain particulars and certain universals, GT also points to the fundamental cognitive role—the epistemic reality—of these universals. Every significant part of our basic cognitive system is expressed in terms of generalization classes: innate, restricted, criterial, feature classes, classes corresponding to different kinds of expected properties, etc. Hence, the universals that correspond to these generalization classes are the basis of all our knowledge and beliefs.

Of special importance here is the result obtained in **42** which shows that the cognitive role of features can be expressed in terms of certain generalization classes. This spares us the need to postulate an additional type of universal, the type containing features. Features, in so far as they are cognitive entities, are merely generalization classes. One consequence of this conclusion is that the distinction between a particular perception and the generalization class to which the perception gives rise also applies to features. We distinguish between certain particular perceptions (see e.g. the experiences described in the beginning of **41**), and the feature generalization classes which originate in these perceptions.[4]

Bodies as particulars. I examined above the distinction between particular perceptions and generalization classes, which reflects a difference between particulars and universals. But many philosophers who discussed the distinction between particulars and universals had in mind another distinction. They meant by 'particulars' what Quine calls 'bodies': three-dimensional entities such as this stone, the man Socrates, or the dog Fido. If one uses the term 'particular' in the sense of body, then we obtain a different relation between (such) particulars and universals.

First we note that the original distinction also applies here. We must distinguish between a body and a particular perception of this body, between Fido and seeing Fido at a specific time point.

Regarding the status of bodies themselves, our analysis in **32** suggests that they are highly restricted generalization classes. Consider, for instance, the child who acquires the expectation 'All dogs emit the peculiar barking sound Z' after seeing Fido while hearing his unusual barking. After going through several falsifying experiences, in which the child observed other dogs who do not bark in this manner, the child finally arrives at the highly restricted expectation 'All elements of F emit the barking sound Z', where F contains only appearances of (the body) Fido, and perhaps of his twin brother.

A child may thus acquire beliefs about the elements of a generalization class C that contains as its only element a particular body. But he may also acquire beliefs about bodies in general. He may note that the elements of certain generalization classes $C_1, .., C_n$, such as of the classes containing stones, apples, or dogs, have certain "body-unifying features". On the other hand, the elements of other generalization classes do not possess such features, e.g. the classes containing sounds, smells, views of the blue sky, or sensations of heat. (What exactly these body-unifying features are is difficult to say, but they probably are features like those mentioned by Quine (1973: 54), e.g. synchronic visible continuity and diachronic continuity of displacement and deformation.) Now, after the child has acquired the belief that the elements of $C_1, .., C_n$ have such features, the union U of these classes may become a criterial generalization class for him (see **38**).

Once the class U has become a generalization class for the child, he can generalize from observations about certain bodies to other bodies, or to other bodies of a particular type, i.e. to the elements of some subclass of *U*. For example, by taking in his hand a number of bodies he may acquire the belief that other bodies, too, can be held in one's hand. Similarly, he may note that the individual dog *a* does not suddenly change its colour (although different dogs may have different colours). This may give him the belief that other individual dogs—i.e. dogs as bodies—do not suddenly change their colour.

Hence, *GT* points to two distinctions corresponding to the classical distinction between particulars and universals. One is the difference between particular perceptions and generalization classes. The other is the difference between generalization classes in general, and certain very restricted generalization classes of a particular type: the classes containing individual bodies.

It should be pointed out, however, that the latter difference is not an essential one, since it is merely a difference between types of generalization class. Similar differences can be found between other types of generalization class, such as the difference between the generalization class containing all sounds of *do* and *re* and the restricted generalization class containing the sounds of *do* and *re* produced by this piano, or between the latter class and the still more restricted class of the sounds of *do* and *re* produced by this piano last Tuesday. On the other hand, the former difference is, at least according to GT, a fundamental one. It is the difference between the perception of a stimulus and the behavioural manifestation of the organism's processing of the perception: the generalization class.

Ontological reality of universals. Philosophers have discussed not only the cognitive role of universals, but also their ontological status. Do universals really exist? GT, and especially theses T1 and T2, make it possible to clarify certain aspects of this problem. They suggest that many of the generalization classes that have been studied in this essay possessed a real existence, in the sense that they reflected certain objective regularities (or uniformities) of our world (see **20** and **30**). Hence, in so far as this kind of objective existence corresponds to the philosophers' claim of the existence of universals, GT supports the objective existence until now of certain universals. And if one accepts the continuity postulate CP (see **26**), then these universals will continue to have objective existence.

But one can also ask another ontological question. This question is about the status of the entities that give rise to our perceptions.

Throughout this essay, I have assumed that organisms can perceive perceptions (or stimulations), and I have assumed that the perceptions are caused by external or internal stimuli: external, as when the child sees a dog or hears the sound of a thunder, and internal, as when he has a headache or feels a sensation of heat. But now the question can be asked: what is the ontological status of these stimuli? Do the dog and the sound waves actually exist? Have the chemical processes which (let us assume) cause the headache a real existence?

To answer this question, we must go far beyond the scope of GT. I will therefore say only that what we accept as real seem to be those entities which are assumed by the simplest, and most coherent network formed by our best theories about the world.

But there is one aspect of this ontological question that does concern GT, since it is related to the acquisition of our knowledge and beliefs. How did we, *qua* scientists, arrive at our beliefs about the existence of stimuli such as dogs, sound waves, chemical processes, electro-magnetic fields, etc.? To this question, GT gives a partial answer, but one that covers the most fundamental point. GT explains how scientists, when they were still children, arrived at their first beliefs. Since these beliefs form the foundations on which people, including scientists, built their most advanced scientific theories, GT covers the first stage of the processes by which we acquire our beliefs about the existence of "real" entities. To be sure, GT does not satisfy the ambitious goal of empiricism which Hart (1976) formulates in the following way:

> What we claim to know should include correct scientific explanations of how we know it. [p. 189.]

But it more than satisfies the modest goal:

> The truth of what we know should not be incompatible with our knowing it. [p. 189.]

For GT contains explanations of how we came to know certain basic things and, at least this is what I have tried to show here, the explanations are correct to a high degree.

The linguistic argument. When discussing the problem of universals, philosophers have often tried to establish the existence of universals from the fact that people can learn the meanings of general terms, of terms that apply to various entities (cf. Armstrong 1978: 12ff).

Regarding this aspect of the problem, GT and GTLA suggest that one should distinguish here between learning the meanings of ostensive terms and learning the meanings of non-ostensive terms. With respect to the former, the learning process is a generalization process, and it is based on the cognitive reality—the psychological validity—of different types of generalization class (see especially **49** and **53**). Moreover, theses T1 and T2 suggest that many of these classes also had a real existence, in the sense that they reflected certain objective regularities of our world. Therefore, in so far as the generalization classes that operate in ostensive learning processes correspond to universals, language acquisition shows the cognitive reality of certain universals. And in so far as the past regularity of these classes corresponds to the objective existence of universals, language acquisition also supports the objective reality of certain universals. (But of course, we have no need of language acquisition to obtain this result. It already follows from our previous conclusions about learning in general.)

Non-ostensive expressions are different. We know the meanings of non-ostensive compounds, and we learn the meanings of non-ostensive terms, because of a generalization that originates in previously formed neurological traces or states (see **55** and **56**), and not because our sense organs are directly stimulated by the non-linguistic element of an ostensive situation. This has two consequences. In the first place, it allows for the possibility that the generalizing processes that occur here are different from those that occur in learning in general, and in ostensive learning in particular. If this is so, then we must acknowledge the cognitive reality of other types of generalization classes. Whether this is indeed the case must be decided by psychology on the basis of relevant evidence.[5] But I do not see in this a philosophical problem. Since living beings are highly complex organisms, it should not surprise us that these beings possess different types of generalizing capacity.

But it also has a second consequence which does have philosophical implications. It makes it possible for a person to understand expressions even if there is nothing in the real world that corresponds to the meanings of the expressions. The terms 'flying' and 'horse' apply to the elements of generalization classes that possessed an objective reality. But the compound 'flying horse' does not refer to elements of such classes. Similarly, for compounds such as 'green sound' or 'circle that is square'. Although they have a meaning for us—utterances of the compounds give origin to neurological application states (see **55**)—the entities to which they refer do not belong to generalization classes having an objective reality. This also holds for non-ostensive terms such as 'centaur' or 'unicorn' which are learned with the help of contexts that are meaningful but which do not refer to existing entities. It follows that there are expressions with which we associate specific meanings but the universals that correspond to the expressions— their extensions—have no objective reality.

Notes

Introduction

[1] In **63** I discuss some of the problems that arise when one uses the notion of a concept, and in **65** the problems of the notion of similarity are analysed.

Part I   The Generalization Theory GT

[1] For example, Black's *rule of induction* is to argue from 'All examined instances of A have been B' to 'All A are B' (1954: 196).

[2] I will frequently ignore the second premiss of the inferences of S1.

[3] See also Zabludowski (1974) and Stemmer (1975, 1979b), for a criticism of Goodman's own solution.

[4] Of course, one selects entities $b_1, .., b_n$ such that one has reason to believe that, were it not for the training processes, the entities would not elicit the reaction from the organism.

[5] Experiments on stimulus generalization frequently give us so called *generalization gradients* which reflect the differences in strength of the elicited reaction.

[6] The experiments on the so-called prototypicality phenomenon are also relevant here (see e.g. Posner 1973: 49ff). They show that generalization classes tend to converge towards certain "focal" elements. But since it is only of marginal interest for our main topic, I will not investigate this phenomenon further.

[7] In certain cases, the second stimulus does not elicit an observable reaction. I will investigate them in **52**.

[8] In Seligman and Hager (1972) several experiments on the preparedness condition are described. The experiments show that some species learn to associate much more easily between certain types of stimuli than between others.

[9] Cf. Quine's remarks on explaining the effects of the psychological processes that occur in language acquisition (1975a: 87):

> In all we may distinguish three levels of purported explanation, three degrees of depth: the mental, the behavioral, and the physiological. The mental is the most superficial of these, scarcely deserving the name of explanation. The psychological is the deepest and most ambitious, and it is the place for causal explanations. The behavioral level, in between, is what we must settle for in our descriptions of language, in our formulations of language rules, and in our explanations of semantical terms,

and on the explanation of dispositions to behaviour (1975a: 94):

> The deepest explanation, the physiological, would analyze these dispositions in explicit terms of nerve impulses and other anatomically and chemically identified organic processes.

187

[10] I will generally omit the qualification 'behavioural'.

[11] We will see later (see especially **10**) that principle PC can also be given a mentalistic interpretation. Under this interpretation, the causes mentioned in PC are mental and not neurological.

[12] Quine speaks of traces being enlivened (1973: 26f).

[13] Experiments like those of Zener (1937) show that the reaction is not always strictly identical with the one elicited by the original element. It may have some "anticipatory" characteristics. See also the discussion in Mackintosh (1974: 100ff).

[14] For simplicity, I will often omit the clause 'were it to play the role of the first stimulus'.

[15] In **11** I suggest some additional devices for improving the individuation.

[16] In **15** we will see that in order to determine the extension of theoretical generalization classes, one normally makes a crucial use of introspection.

[17] Churchland (1981) presents very strong arguments suggesting that the former assumption gives a much better explanation to the behaviour than the latter. See especially his criticism of the functionalist approach to psychology.

[18] Baron (1965) speaks of an "attentional hierarchy".

[19] In **36**, I discuss cases where an organism learns to pay attention to stimuli that are not innately salient for him.

[20] The process is of course much more complicated, since in a fuller account we would have to describe the acquired expectation as one in which the dog expects that, when taking similar walks in similar forests, similar appearances of a man will perform similar actions with similar sticks. That is to say, the dog's generalization class derives from all the aspects of the situation that were salient for the dog. (On the present use of the notion of similarity, see **65**.)

[21] As I already mentioned above, thesis T1 (**20**) will enable us to give a very plausible explanation for the significant interspecific validity of both the generalizing dispositions and the salience conditions of many species, some of them of rather distant evolutionary relationship.

Part II The Justification of Inductive Inferences

[1] We recall that by attributing an expectation to an organism, we are actually individuating a neurological (or mental) trace, while hinting at the behaviour that stems from the trace (see **9** and **10**).

[2] The fact that unrelated species possess very similar generalizing dispositions allows us to disregard the possibility that the dispositions were useless, but were controlled by genes which also controlled useful traits.

[3] I will frequently omit the qualifications 'terrestrial' and 'of well-developed species'.

[4] In **30**, I mention still more supporting evidence for T1.

[5] We recall that by attributing an expectation to an organism, we are actually individuating a neurological (or mental) trace, while hinting at the behaviour which the trace *will* produce (see **9**).

[6] I arrived at this solution for the Hempel paradox during the year 1968–69 when I gave a course in Inductive Logic, and I presented it in my paper 'Induction and Innate Ideas' delivered at the Second Conference of the Israel Society for Logic, Methodology, and Philosophy of Science, Ramat Aviv, April 1970. This paper was then published under the title 'Three Problems

in Induction' in *Synthese* (Stemmer 1971a). At about the same time, Quine arrived at a very similar solution for the Hempel paradox which he published in his essay 'Natural Kinds' (1969).

[7] Cf. n. 5 above.

[8] It has also ensured the frequent reliability of inferences about "theoretical" classes such as mammals or electrons. But the continuation of this aspect of the uniformity of our world does not invalidate CP. On the other hand, if non-intuitive inferences like those about grue continue to be frequently reliable, CP may turn out to be false.

[9] Goodman's observation that 'qualitativeness of predicates is an entirely relative matter and does not by itself establish any dichotomy of predicates' (1965: 80) expresses this point in a different terminology.

[10] Our discussion in **2** shows that Russell's principle is actually inadequate, since it does not restrict the predicates A and B. This was later acknowledged by Russell (see Russell 1960).

[11] Thagard (1978) introduces a comparative notion of consilience in his very illuminating paper on criteria for theory choice.

[12] I will frequently omit the qualification 'for well-developed species' and the reference to the salience (for the species) of the entity.

[13] As usual, I am assuming that the number of experiences are sufficient for producing this kind of behaviour (cf. **6**). In the present case, it may sometimes be necessary for the organism to observe further positive instances after he perceived the falsifying instances, i.e. he must observe additional elements of *CF* that are *P*.

[14] The subclass *S* of *C* is explicitly mentioned in T1′, which is the alternative version of T1. See also figure 1 in **20**.

[15] The fact that, from a psychological point of view, a class containing one object is normally a generalization class has already been noted by Russell, although in a somewhat different context. For example:

> On behaviourist lines, there is no important difference between proper names and what are called 'abstract' or 'generic' terms. A child learns to use the word 'cat', which is general, just as he learns to use the word 'Peter', which is a proper name. But in actual fact 'Peter' really covers a number of different occurrences, and is in a sense general. Peter may be near or far, walking or standing or sitting, laughing or frowning. All these produce different stimuli. [1927: 57.]

[16] This situation is depicted in figure 1 (**20**), if we assume that *P* is P_3.

[17] On several occasions, Popper mentions that animals also learn by trial and error. But so far as I know, he has not investigated the specific characteristics of animal learning dispositions, such as the use of specific generalization classes.

[18] There are, however, exceptions. Thus in **36** I mention experiments showing changes in salience conditions as a consequence of a series of falsifying experiences in which a particular feature *F* plays the role of a discriminating feature.

[19] It is difficult to predict which expectation the child will acquire in these experiences. Had the eating of the sour grape not been preceded by the eating of the sweet grape, then eating the sour grape would probably have induced the child to acquire the expectation 'All grapes are sour'. But since this expectation has already been falsified by the original sweet grape, it is plausible that eating the green sour grape will bring the child to acquire an appropriately restricted expectation such as 'All green grapes are sour'.

[20] I am ignoring here the limiting case in which the innate generalization class C_i contains only red entities.

[21] It is likely that, at least with respect to some of the expectations, the organism will have to continue to observe positive instances, i.e. he must continue observing red elements while receiving an electric shock. But since these experiences are of the same type as those he had earlier, I do not mention them explicitly.

[22] In **14**, I introduced the notion of salient feature and also of determining feature. But one of these notions is actually sufficient, since the latter notion is defined in terms of the former. This explains why we need here only one notion—the notion of a determining feature class—in order to describe these aspects of generalizing behaviour.

[23] I use *predicate* as a general term for classes and properties and also for the expressions that refer to classes and properties.

[24] To be sure, we have not obtained a thesis which is supported by evolutionary theory and which explains the past reliability of certain inferences about criterial and feature classes. With respect to the reliability of these inferences, our solution has therefore no advantage over the others. But the important point is that we did explain the reliability of the most fundamental inferences— the inferences of S3 and S5 with which all our knowledge begins.

[25] As far as I know, the only solution that does not have the defects is the one given by Quine (1969). (See above, n. 6.) Let me also point out that Goodman's solution, besides suffering from shortcoming (3) and probably also from (1) or (2), has a further drawback. Goodman states that entrenchment 'is effected by the use of language and is not attributed to anything inevitable or immutable in the nature of human cognition' (1965: 96–7). But animals do not use language. Hence, Goodman cannot explain why such a large part of the generalizing behaviour of animals is highly similar to the inductive inferences of humans (see e.g. the discussion on the interspecific validity of innate generalization classes in **12**).

[26] Kyburg states the following condition that has to be satisfied by a logic of rational belief:

> . . . we want to be able to show that any statement which is highly probable relative to what is already believed ought also to be believed. [1961: 83.]

Principle KYB intends to express this condition. See also the passages from Kyburg (1970a, 1970b) quoted in the text.

[27] Originally, Kyburg speaks mainly of *believing* a hypothesis (1961), while later he usually speaks of *accepting* a hypothesis (1970a, 1970b). But since in the latter publications he also speaks of believing hypotheses, in the meantime I will use both notions indistinctly. As far as I can discern, Kyburg does not distinguish between them.

[28] So many publications have discussed theory evaluation, that any selection would be arbitrary. But let me mention again Thagard's 1978 article (see **28**) which gives, in my opinion, an excellent characterization of theory evaluation.

[29] Of course, one must be convinced that everything is normal, e.g. that nobody is playing a trick on us. For example, the (heavy) stone has been carefully examined, the room has been searched, etc. These assumptions are legitimate, since we are testing Humean uncertainty, and not our capacity to avoid being deceived.

[30] See also Kyburg (1974: 192): ". . . among the things I am almost completely sure of, is the thesis that at least one of those things is false".

³¹ He probably also takes into account the statistical probability of certain hypotheses. But since it is likely that the notion of evidential probability corresponds closely to at least an elementary notion of statistical probability, I will not deal separately here with statistical probability.

³² See again n. 29 above.

Part III   The Generalization Theory of Language Acquisition GTLA

¹ See Quine (1960, 1973), Stemmer (1971b, 1973a, 1973b: 6ff), Ninio (1980).

² The first and the last method are based mainly on comprehension, while the second on production. There are experiments suggesting that in certain cases there are differences between comprehension and production (see e.g. Thomson and Chapman 1977). But in order to avoid too many problems, I will assume that the class C to which the child applies an expression E is the one formed by the intersection of the classes determined by comprehension and production.

³ Further developments may produce changes in the ostensive status of an expression. But I will ignore this complication here. Some of its aspects are discussed in Stemmer (1973b: 79, 93).

⁴ For simplicity, I am assuming here that the class of fires and the class of dogs are the generalization classes used by the child in the generalizing processes.

⁵ There are many problems connected with the notion of 'same expression'. However, we do not have to consider them here. See also Quine's discussion of the printer's use of spaces (1960: 13f).

⁶ See e.g. Mackintosh's discussion of the transfer effects in discrimination learning (1974: 589ff). But it is also possible that children are innately predisposed to pay attention to subtle phonetic features.

⁷ The feature classes that correspond to colours are very wide generalization classes. This is probably the reason why it is relatively difficult for children to learn the meanings of colour terms (see e.g. Miller and Johnson-Laird 1976: 350ff).

⁸ The process of learning the meaning of 'is longer than' is discussed in Stemmer (1979a).

⁹ When speaking of *new* compounds, I will normally assume that the relevant person has not learned the compound by undergoing ostensive experiences in which he hears utterances of the compound itself (while paying attention to something in his vicinity).

¹⁰ We recall that one of our methods for determining the extension of an ostensive term makes use of the child's reactions to such questions (see **49**).

¹¹ The fact that 'animal with a heart' and 'animal with kidneys' have the same extension suggests that the effects of the neurological states that correspond to these compounds are indeed insufficient for individuating these states (see below, **59**).

¹² I am ignoring here the rather neutral role of 'are'.

¹³ In second-order conditioning, an organism is exposed in a first stage to the pairing of a neutral stimulus B with an active stimulus C. As a consequence, stimulus B—more exactly, the elements of the generalization class corresponding to the perceived element or instance of B—now elicits typical C-reactions from the organism. In a second stage, the organism is exposed to the pairing of another neutral stimulus A with stimulus B. The effect of this experience is that A also starts to elicit typical C-reactions, although A

was never paired with C. In non-ostensive learning, the new term corresponds to A and the old context terms correspond to B. These context terms had previously acquired a meaning [C] for the person when they were paired with certain elements of C. The pairing of A and B occurs when the person hears the new term together with the old terms, e.g. when he hears an utterance of (2). As a consequence, the new term receives a trace—a meaning—that is similar to the trace which the context terms received when they were learned. (Quine speaks in this connection of a 'transitivity of conditioning' 1960: 12.)

[14] In this section, and also in the next sections, the context will often indicate that I am assuming that the extensions which a child has learned to associate with certain terms are very similar to the extensions associated with the terms by normal speakers of English. Moreover, I usually assume that terms which children often learn in ostensive processes, such as 'white', 'bear', and 'big', have indeed been learned in such processes.

[15] Again, I ignore the role of the term 'are'. On the role of this term see the discussion in Stemmer (1973b: 101–10).

[16] In **60** I will deal with the extensions of non-ostensive expressions.

[17] Expressions such as 'picture of a centaur' or 'replica of a unicorn' may be ostensive. But these are other expressions.

[18] They are probably contextual ostensive processes (see **54**).

[19] This has been suggested by some psychologists in informal conversations.

Part IV Analyticity, Similarity, and Universals

[1] See Quine, especially (1953: 42ff) and Quine and Ullian (1970) on the notion of centrality with respect to the network of our beliefs.

[2] Carnap's main reason for attributing only a partial meaning to theoretical terms is related to this point (see Carnap 1956, 1966: 237ff).

[3] In Carnap's terminology (cf. Schilpp 1963: 991), these sentences would be called *analytically true*.

[4] With respect to the status of universals such as colours and shapes, see Quine's very important analysis of the way children learn the meanings of terms such as 'colour' and 'shape' (1973: 70ff).

[5] In **56**, I mentioned the possibility that the generalizing processes are similar to those occurring in second-order conditioning.

References

Ackerman, R., 1969, 'Sortal predicates and confirmation', *Philosophical Studies* **20**, 1–4.

Aitchison, J., 1976, *The Articulate Mammal*, London: Hutchinson.

Armstrong, D. M., 1978, *Universals and Scientific Realism*, Cambridge: Cambridge University Press.

Austin, J. L., 1962, *How to Do Things with Words*, Oxford: Clarendon Press.

Baege, B., 1933, 'Zur Entwicklung der Verhaltensweise junger Hunde', *Zeitschrift für Hundeforschung* **3**, 3–64.

Baron, M. R., 1965, 'The stimulus, stimulus control, and stimulus generalization', in Mostofsky (1965).

Black, M., 1954, *Problems of Analysis*, Ithaca: Cornell University Press.
1958, 'Self-supporting inductive arguments', *Journal of Philosophy* **55**, 718–25.

Blum, A., 1971, 'Sortals and Paradox', *Philosophical Studies* **22**, 33–4.

Bowerman, M. F., 1976, 'Semantic factors in the acquisition of rules for word use and sentence construction', in D. M. Morehead and A. E. Morehead (eds.), *Normal and Deficient Child Language*, Baltimore: University Park Press.

Brown, J. S., 1965, 'Generalization and Discrimination', in Mostofsky (1965).

Carnap, R., 1947, 'On the application of inductive logic', *Philosophy and Phenomenological Research* **8**, 133–47.
1950, *Logical Foundations of Probability*, Chicago: University of Chicago Press.
1955, 'Meaning and synonymy in natural languages', *Philosophical Studies* **7**, 33–47.
1956, 'The methodological character of theoretical terms', in H. Feigl and M. Scriven (eds.), *Minnesota Studies in the Philosophy of Science, vol. i*, Minneapolis: University of Minnesota Press.
1966, *Philosophical Foundations of Physics*, New York: Basic Books.

Cerella, J., 1979, 'Visual classes and natural categories in the pigeon', *Journal of Experimental Psychology: Human Perception and Performance* **5**, 68–77.

Chomsky, N., 1959, 'A review of B. F. Skinner's *Verbal Behaviour*', *Language* **35**, 26–58.
1965, *Aspects of the Theory of Syntax*, Cambridge Mass.: MIT Press.
1968, *Language and Mind*, New York: Harcourt, Brace & World.
1969, 'Quine's empirical assumptions', in D. Davidson and J. Hintikka (eds.), *Words and Objections: Essays on the Work of W. V. Quine*, Dordrecht: Reidel.

193

1975, *Reflections on Language*, New York: Pantheon Books.

Churchland, P. M., 1981, 'Eliminative materialism and propositional attitudes', *Journal of Philosophy* **78**, 67–90.

Clark, E., 1973, 'What's in a word? On the child's acquisition of semantics in his first language', in T. E. Moore (ed.), *Cognitive Development and the Acquisition of Language*, New York: Academic Press.

Derksen, A. A., 1978, 'The lottery paradox resolved', *American Philosophical Quarterly* **15**, 67–74.

Fodor, J. A., 1965, 'Could meaning be an r_m?', *Journal of Verbal Learning and Verbal Behaviour* **4**, 73–81.

Frege, G., 1892, 'Über Sinn und Bedeutung', *Zeitschrift für Philosophie und philosophische Kritik* **100**, 25–50.

Friedman, M., 1973, 'Son of grue: simplicity vs. entrenchment', *Nous* **7**, 366–78.

Goodman, N., 1949, 'On likeness of meaning', *Analysis* **10**, 1–7. (Reprinted in Goodman 1972.)

    1953, 'On some differences about meaning', *Analysis* **13**, 90–6. (Reprinted in Goodman 1972.)

    1965, *Fact, Fiction, and Forecast*, Indianapolis: Bobbs-Merrill.

    1972, *Problems and Projects*, Indianapolis: Bobbs-Merrill.

Harman, G., 1965, 'The inference to the best explanation', *Philosophical Review* **64**, 88–95.

Hart, W. D., 1976, 'Imagination, necessity and abstract objects', in M. Schirn (ed.), *Studies on Frege I: Logic and Philosophy of Mathematics*, Holzboog: Friedrich Frommann Verlag.

Hempel, C. G., 1945, 'Studies in the logic of confirmation', *Mind* **54**, 1–26, 97–121.

Hume, D., 1748, *An Enquiry Concerning Human Understanding*, London.

Katz, J. J., 1966, *The Philosophy of Language*, New York: Harper & Row.

    1979, 'Semantics and conceptual change', *Philosophical Review* **88**, 327–65.

Krechevsky, I., 1932, 'Hypotheses in rats', *Psychological Review* **39**, 516–32.

Kyburg, H. E., Jr., 1961, *Probability and the Logic of Rational Belief*, Middletown, Conn.: Wesleyan University Press.

    1970a, 'Conjunctivitis', in M. Swain (ed.), *Induction, Acceptance, and Rational Belief*, Dordrecht: Reidel.

    1970b, *Probability and Inductive Logic*, New York: Macmillan.

    1974, *The Logical Foundations of Statistical Inference*, Dordrecht: Reidel.

Loux, M. J., 1970, *Universals and Particulars*, New York: Anchor Books.

Mackintosh, N. J., 1969, 'Reversal and probability learning', in R. M. Gilbert and N. S. Sutherland (eds.), *Animal Discrimination Learning*, London: Academic Press.

    1974, *The Psychology of Animal Learning*, London: Academic Press.

McNeill, D., 1970, *The Acquisition of Language*, New York: Harper & Row.

Mill, J. S., 1895, *A System of Logic*, New York: Harper and Brothers.

Miller, G. A. and Johnson-Laird, P. N., 1976, *Language and Perception*, Cambridge, Mass.: Harvard University Press.

Mostofsky, D. I., 1965, *Stimulus Generalization*, Stanford: Stanford University Press.

Mowrer, O. H., 1960, *Learning Theory and Symbolic Processes*, New York: Wiley.

Nelson, K., 1974, 'Concept, word, and sentence: Interrelations in acquisition and development', *Psychological Review* **81**, 267–85.

Nicod, J., 1930, *Foundations of Geometry and Induction*, London: Kegan Paul, Trench, Trubner & Co.

Niiniluoto, I. and Tuomela, R., 1973, *Theoretical Concepts and Hypothetico-Inductive Inference*, Dordrecht: Reidel.

Ninio, Anat, 1980, 'Ostensive teaching in vocabulary teaching', *Journal of Child Language* **7**, 565–73.

Osgood, C. E., 1953, *Method and Theory in Experimental Psychology*, New York: Oxford University Press.

Pavlov, I. P., 1927, *Conditioned Reflexes*, London: Oxford University Press.

Peirce, C. S., 1934, *Collected Papers, vol. 5*, Cambridge Mass.: Harvard University Press.

Popper, K. R., 1968, *Conjectures and Refutations*, New York: Harper & Row.

Posner, M. I., 1973, *Cognition: An Introduction*, Glencoe Ill.: Scott, Foresman, & Co.

Quine, W. V., 1953, *From a Logical Point of View*, Cambridge Mass.: Harvard University Press.

1960, *Word and Object*, Cambridge Mass.: MIT Press.

1969, *Ontological Relativity and other Essays*, New York: Columbia University Press.

1973, *The Roots of Reference*, La Salle Ill.: Open Court.

1975a, 'Mind and verbal dispositions', in S. Guttenplan (ed.), *Mind and Language*, Oxford: Clarendon Press.

1975b, 'The nature of natural knowledge', in S. Guttenplan (ed.), *Mind and Language*, Oxford: Clarendon Press.

Quine, W. V. and Ullian, J. S., 1970, *The Web of Belief*, New York: Random House.

Razran, G. H., 1939, 'A quantitative study of meaning by a conditional salivary technique (semantic conditioning)', *Science* **90**, 89–90.

Russell, B., 1912, *The Problems of Philosophy*, London: Williams & Norgate.

1927, *Philosophy*, New York: W. W. Norton & Co.

1960, 'Non-demonstrative inference and induction', in E. H. Madden (ed.), *The Structure of Scientific Thought*, London: Routledge & Kegan Paul.

Schilpp, P. A., 1963, *The Philosophy of Rudolph Carnap*, La Salle Ill.: Open Court.

Schwartz, B., 1978, *Psychology of Learning and Behaviour*, New York: W. W. Norton & Co.

Seligman, M. E. P. and Hager, J. L., 1972, *Biological Boundaries of Learning*, New York: Appleton-Century-Crofts.

Skinner, B. F., 1957, *Verbal Behaviour*, New York: Appleton-Century-Crofts.

Staats, R. W., 1968, *Learning, Language, and Cognition*, New York: Holt, Rinehart, and Winston.

Stemmer, N., 1971a, 'Three problems in induction', *Synthese* **23**, 287–308.

1971b, 'Some Aspects of Language Acquisition', in Y. Bar-Hillel (ed.), *Pragmatics of Natural Languages*, Dordrecht: Reidel.

1973a, 'Language acquisition and classical conditioning', *Language and Speech* **16**, 279–82.

1973b, *An Empiricist Theory of Language Acquisition*, The Hague: Mouton & Co.

1975, 'The Goodman paradox', *Zeitschrift für allgemeine Wissenschaftstheorie* **6**, 340–54.

1978, 'Similarity, creativity, and empiricism', in F. Peng and W. von Raffler-Engel (eds.), *Language Acquisition and Developmental Kinesics*, Hiroshima: Bunka Hyoron Publishing Co.

1979a, 'On the nature of meaning', *Semiotica* **27**, 307–25.

1979b, 'Projectible Predicates', *Synthese* **41**, 375–95.

1981a, 'Generalization classes as alternatives for similarities and some other concepts', *Erkenntniss* **16**, 73–102.

1981b, 'A note on empiricism and structure-dependence', *Journal of Child Language* **8**, 649–63.

1982, 'A solution to the lottery paradox', *Synthese* **51**, 339–53.

Sutherland, N. S. and Mackintosh, N. J., 1971, *Mechanisms of Animal Discrimination*, New York: Academic Press.

Thagard, P. R., 1978, 'The best explanation: Criteria for theory choice', *Journal of Philosophy* **75**, 76–92.

Thomson, J. R. and Chapman, R. S., 1977, 'Who is 'Daddy' revisited: the status of two-year-olds' over-extended words in use and comprehension', *Journal of Child Language* **4**, 359–75.

Ullian, J. S., 1961a, 'Luck, license, and lingo', *Journal of Philosophy* **58**, 731–8.

1961b, 'More on "Grue" and Grue', *Philosophical Review* **70**, 386–9.

Whewell, W., 1847, *The Philosophy of Inductive Sciences*, London: J. Parkel.

Zabludowski, A., 1974, 'Concerning a fiction about how facts are forecast', *Journal of Philosophy* **71**, 97–112.

Zener, K., 1937, 'The significance of behaviour accompanying salivary secretion for theories of the conditioned response', *American Journal of Psychology* **50**, 384–403.

INDEX

197